S0-AUY-025

"Not everything

that can be

counted counts,

and not everything

that counts can

be counted."

Albert Einstein

(1879–1955)

Heads Count

—AN ANTHOLOGY—

for the Competitive Enterprise

PEOPLESOFT, INC.

PLEASANTON, CA

Reprint permission list in Appendix.

First printed November 2003.

The paper used in this book meets the minimum requirements of the American National Standard for Information Services—Permanence of Paper for Printed Library Materials, ANSI Z39.48-1984

Library of Congress Control Number: 2003097374

Printed and bound in the United States.

PeopleSoft, Inc.
4660 Hacienda Drive
Pleasanton, CA 94588

| CONTENTS |

ACKNOWLEDGMENTS

Special thanks go to the contributing authors in this book: Karen V. Beaman, Naomi Lee Bloom, John Boudreau, Joseph H. Boyett, Jimmie T. Boyett, John Cooper, Jac Fitz-enz, Lynda Gratton, Row Henson, Mark Lange, Jenni Lehman, Edward E. Lawler, Tod Loofbourrow, Alexia (Lexy) Martin, Susan A. Mohrman, Harry Osle, Jeffrey Pfeffer, Peter Ramstad, Libby Sartain, Norm Smallwood, Bob Stambaugh, Robert Sutton, Catherine Truss, and Dave Ulrich. With both passion and wisdom, their insightful words embrace the ongoing and strategic importance of human capital management as a driving competitive advantage to the enterprise.

Accolades to award-winning book designer Bill Stanton who once again showcases his creative excellence and innovation in book layout and design.

Project Direction, Acquisitions and Permissions:
Row Henson, PeopleSoft, Inc.
Mady Gorrell, CoChel Communication Strategies

Book and Jacket Design:
Bill Stanton, BookBlock

Composition:
Bill Brunson, BookBlock

Production Assistants:
Danielle Beeken, PeopleSoft, Inc.
Stephen Thomas, BookBlock

Editorial Assistant:
Windy Johnson, CoChel Communication Strategies

Printer/Binder:
Edwards Brothers, Inc.

| INTRODUCTION |

As we enter the 21st Century heads do count and people matter—maybe more than ever before in our history.

Just over 100 years ago, during the height of the Industrial Age, the value of the enterprise was measured in terms of smokestacks, machinery, and cash. I'm reminded of a quote by Henry Ford, "I hire people *for* their hands, but unfortunately, I have to take their brains with them." Today we hire people for their brains. Our corporate bedrock includes computers, communications, and information—and the acquisition and retention of top talent dominates enterprise value creation.

When I entered the world of human resources in the early 70s (we called it personnel then), most HR functions were focused on "counting heads" and other administrative activities. Today's rapid proliferation of technology and information requires HR be more strategically focused on the knowledge contained in the "heads" of a company's intangible assets—its human capital.

If our profession is to survive this paradigm shift, we must learn to measure the impact of our human capital assets much as our financial counterparts have their fixed assets. Only then can we align individual performance to achieve the overall objectives of each organization. This alignment of individual and groups to overall organizational objectives has the potential to change the face of human capital management (HCM)—and how we define and use information for and about people beyond the HR department, throughout the entire enterprise. This alignment embraces the importance of HCM by providing additional strategic purpose to the discipline—that is, to unleash potential, generate momentum, and realize the vision and value of the collective energy of people.

This anthology is a collection from our industry's most innovative thought leaders on how to achieve this alignment of human capital. In my thirty-two years in the industry (almost a dozen at PeopleSoft), it has been my privilege and pleasure to work directly with many of these human capital influencers. Let me introduce you to them and to our book.

Who best to start Chapter One than Jeffrey Pfeffer from Stanford University? Jeffrey, in his sometimes irreverent, but always thought-provoking style, sets the stage for a strategic discussion of human capital management. In this chapter you will also hear from the elegant and energetic Lynda Gratton from the London Business School and colleague Catherine Truss from Kingston Business School. And finally you will hear from the father of human capital himself, Dr. Jac Fitz-enz.

We have devoted our entire second chapter to the topic of measuring the impact of human capital and have a wealth of knowledge to share with you from some of the top leaders on this topic. My personal hero, Dave Ulrich and his colleague Norm Smallwood, leverage their latest work on *Why the Bottom Line Isn't*, to talk about building intangible value. You will also hear from another champion of this cause—John Boudreau—now on leave from Cornell as a Visiting Professor at USC and his colleague Peter Ramstad. You will also hear from Harry Osle and John Cooper from Answerthink, Inc., as they share HR best practices in performance improvement from research conducted by their organization.

Chapter Three focuses on bridging the technology and people gap and we have four outstanding contributors from the field of HR Technology. Bob Stambaugh has been instrumental in driving the human resources information technology profession. He was one of the founders of IHRIM and continues to stretch us all with his vision for the future. Naomi Bloom needs no introduction—she sets the bar when it comes to human resources technology infrastructure and has been a great friend to both PeopleSoft and myself. Her latest passion around outsourcing HR will be discussed here. Lexy Martin has worked with us over the past five years to research and analyze how great HRIS practices can be measured in terms of ROI. And Tod Loofbourrow, founder of Authoria, Inc., finishes this chapter on the role of content as we bridge our way to the knowledge economy.

Chapter Four brings us into real lessons learned for the HR professional. Joseph and Jimmie Boyett have written numerous human capital thought-provoking books, and have researched best practices from leading entrepreneurs around the world. They will share their findings with you. Libby Sartain was the Chief People Officer at Southwest Airlines when I first met her—now she has that role at Yahoo! Inc. Who better to write on building a talent culture? When I first met Robert Sutton, he had just published *The Knowing-Doing Gap* with Jeffrey Pfeffer and I immediately loved his out-of-the-box style. You will experience it yourself as he talks about corporate "forgiving and remembering." Another tremendous academic with real-world advice is Edward Lawler from USC. He and his colleague, Susan Mohrman, share their thoughts on implementing on the vision for human capital.

Our final chapter focuses on the challenges of going global. I first met Karen Beaman when we were both living and working in this industry in Paris. I was with PeopleSoft and Karen was with ADP. Both of us still enjoy working in those same organizations. While I was struggling to order a meal in French, Karen was working on mastering her fourth language! As editor of the *IHRIM Journal*, Karen has been instrumental in bringing a wealth of information to those trying to better our profession. You will not be disappointed in what she has to share with you in this anthology. And finally two of PeopleSoft's own HCM thought leaders will share their knowledge with you on going global in the networked economy—Jenni Lehman, Vice President, Human Capital Management Global Strategy and Mark Lange, Vice President, Human Capital Management Global Product Marketing.

We start with a vision and work our way into practical strategies. And while each section is varied in scope and focus, each article offers ideas and actions that will no doubt strike a chord with each of you. Without understanding our human capital—without each of our heads counting—there will be no competitive enterprise of the future.

This anthology has been a labor of love for me. Thanks to all who made it happen. Enjoy the pages before you.

Row Henson
PeopleSoft, Inc. Fellow

| CHAPTER ONE |

Embracing Human Capital Management's Strategic Vision

Jeffrey Pfeffer PhD

Jeffrey Pfeffer PhD is the Thomas D. Dee II Professor of Organizational Behavior in the Graduate School of Business at Stanford University where he has taught since 1979. He has served on the faculties of the business schools at the University of Illinois and the University of California at Berkeley. During his noted career Dr. Pfeffer served as the Thomas Henry Carroll-Ford Foundation Visiting Professor at Harvard Business School. He is author and/or co-author of ten books and more than 100 articles and book chapters. A recipient of the Richard D. Irwin Scholarly Contributions to Management Award, Dr. Pfeffer is a member and Fellow of the Academy of Management and a member of the Industrial Relations Research Association. He received his BS in Administration and Management Science and his MS in Industrial Administration from Carnegie Mellon University; his PhD in Business Administration from the Stanford Graduate School of Business. Dr. Pfeffer can be reached at Pfeffer_Jeffrey@gsb.stanford.edu.

one : 1

Why Human Resources Needs Systems Thinking: Avoiding Bad Decisions and Bad Measures

Many human resource professionals are pleased that HR now has more of a place at the senior executive table, increasingly recognized as a business and strategic partner. This does not mean that the professionalization of human resources is complete, that everyone working in and with the human resource function has become a business partner, or that, as a staff function, human resources is immune to the cutbacks and retrenchment that beset all staff functions. But it does mean that the cliché, people are our most important asset, is increasingly taken seriously by organizations that recognize that in a world in which almost every other resource is fungible, talent and culture are truly keys to success—and therefore that people management, one of the responsibilities of human resources, is critical to achieving exceptional performance.[1] It also means that the human resource function and HR activities have come a long way in gaining prominence and legitimacy. For instance, at Stanford business school there is a core course in human resource management, which means that HR is on a par in the curriculum with other subjects such as accounting, finance, and marketing, a fact that is noteworthy in and of itself. Possibly even more significant is that for several years the HR core course has been one of the most popular of the core courses—this in a school where most students are going into general management roles and few see themselves as actually filling an HR job.

Human resources, however, having found its place at the table, now seems to be prone to thinking and acting like the other players from other functional specialties, particularly finance, using the same measures, the same (short) time horizons, and the same business perspectives. Unfortunately, this is a big problem. That is because, in case you hadn't noticed, many organizational decisions are much too narrowly focused and are premised on measures and metrics that are suspect at best and downright misleading at worst. This problem of poor decision making using inappropriate measures occurs in part because as M.I.T. business school professor Nelson Repenning once told me, systems thinking is scarce in organizations—maybe even scarcer than strategic thinking. For example, how would you answer the following questions/dilemmas?

- Your organization is facing rapidly increasing costs for medical insurance, and as an organization that has been around a while, one component of medical costs that is particularly troublesome and growing is retiree medical costs. Should you cut retiree medical benefits and should you measure the amount of money you save by the difference between retiree medical costs prior to the decrease and afterward?
- A company is trying to sell you a product that demonstrably reduces the time to fill an open position requisition, in large measure by automating what had been a manual process and by providing constant reminders to the people involved in the process about deadlines and time elapsed so that the hiring process does not get bogged down. Should you buy the product and should you assess its effectiveness by measuring the reduction, after its implementation, in the average time to hire or to fill a position?

- In an effort to reduce benefits costs, particularly retirement and medical benefits—which are the two largest—you are considering moving to a consumer driven model of benefits delivery, a 401(k) or similar plan for retirement instead of a defined benefit plan and a medical plan that, through its design, causes your employees to be more thoughtful about how they spend and manage their medical care dollars. The people selling you these plans can demonstrate a direct cost reduction in the amount spent on both benefits. Should you adopt this approach, and is the amount saved a valid measure of the effectiveness of this decision?

- In the face of competitive pressures that compel economizing, you and your colleagues are considering altering your organization's tuition benefit program. Whereas in the past you reimbursed any course in any subject an employee completed at an accredited school at 100 percent of the cost incurred, now you are considering reimbursing only, a) courses that are deemed by the company to be job relevant at, b) a somewhat lower percentage of cost, say 80 percent. The rationale for reducing the percentage of cost reimbursed is that because some of the skills acquired are general and can not be necessarily captured by your company, the employee, who will benefit from greater marketability, should contribute more to paying for his or her skill upgrading. Once again, is this a good decision, and is the amount saved measured by the reduction in expenditures in your tuition reimbursement program?

I have witnessed decisions such as these and many other similar choices being made by intelligent, dedicated human resource professionals trying to use quantitative metrics to asses return on investment, efficiency, and all the other things they are called upon to achieve. In almost every case the decisions that were made were at best based upon incomplete or faulty data and logic, and at worst wrong and harmful to the company and its efforts to become more competitive. What I want to do in this article is briefly introduce some ideas from systems thinking and then explore how these ideas can help human resources avoid making the same mistakes as many of the other players at the management table, and instead, add value and insight and provide a different and better perspective to organizational decision making.

Two Basic Ideas

The idea of organizations as systems and systems thinking has at least two components. The first is that decisions and actions have feedback loops—which means that you need to consider not only direct but also indirect effects that emerge sometimes quickly and sometimes with delay. Let's take a classic case of not fully anticipated feedback effects—the death spiral so often observed in retailing—to illustrate the point of how decisions sometimes have unanticipated consequences that extend beyond their direct effects.

Some years ago if you visited Stanford Shopping Center near Stanford University, you would have seen a Saks Fifth Avenue store. Unfortunately, for a number of reasons the store failed to make its budgeted profit targets[2] and the store manager was told to fix the problem. In the short run, of course, there is only one real variable the manager can control—cost—and only one component of cost that is readily decreased in a retail store, the staff. It is hard for the store manager to affect sales in the short run as promotions and merchandise strategy are often set centrally. As to costs, the rent is fixed, as are utilities, property taxes, and in many instances, even the merchandise, which is sourced and allocated by headquarters.

Under pressure to cut costs to meet profit objectives, the store manager did what she had to—she cut staff. In the immediate short run, with fewer staff costs were lower and, therefore, profits were higher. However, there is an interesting phenomenon that, unfortunately, many retailers still have not discovered—customers frequently do not wait on themselves and in an upscale store, such as Saks Fifth Avenue, merchandise is not just bought, it is sold. So, the effect of cutting staff was to produce a lower level of customer service, which over time, led to a lower level of sales and consequently diminished profits. Therefore, there were even more cuts in staffing in a futile effort to achieve the profit targets. I discovered all of this when I went shopping for a present for my wife and discovered, on the second floor of the store during lunchtime, not *one* sales person. The store did have sales staff at the counter at the foot of the escalator, to ensure that people didn't leave the store with merchandise they didn't pay for. The store manager was quite aware of the unfortunate dynamics playing out, but was unable to do anything about the situation.

The eventual outcome was predictable—sales continued to decline and with it, profitability. Saks finally closed the store, and perhaps the logic that guided (or misguided) these decisions is why the company as a whole went through bankruptcy. This example is repeated endlessly in many supposed service businesses, with often equally disastrous results. For instance, most airlines' first response to the diminished passenger traffic after September 11 and the poor economy was to make the flying experience even less enjoyable by reducing telephone reservation staff, customer service staff at the airport, and amenities such as meals. The logic by which making something that is already not very appealing or convenient even less so as a way of increasing profits continues to escape me.

The point is that every cost that you cut almost certainly has some benefit that was associated with the positions or costs that you are cutting. In not every case will those benefits economically justify the cost, and obviously there are instances when reducing staff and service makes good business sense. But simply cutting something without taking into account the subsequent reactions to what is being cut is amazingly shortsighted and will often produce poor business decisions.

So, for instance, to return to one of our examples from the start of the chapter, how do you decide what to do about tuition reimbursement programs? Investing in employees' training has a number of benefits including, obviously, enhancing their skills. There are other benefits as well. Some years ago the British Rover company provided a 100 British pound training budget to all of its staff and the company did not care whether the budget was spent on job relevant classes or cooking classes. That was because senior leadership believed that to turn around what was at the time, a stodgy, inefficient organization, they needed the help and engagement of everyone. They thought that getting people interested in learning and the learning process, regardless of the specific focus of the learning, was probably a useful way of getting people in the habit of expanding their minds and thinking.[3]

But possibly the largest benefit is that investing in employees, in training and education as well as other things, activates the norm of reciprocity. The norm of reciprocity, which has been found in all human societies, simply means that people are conditioned to reciprocate or repay favors done for them by others.[4] So, to the extent that they see the company's investment in them and their skills as a gift or a favor, something that is not necessarily owed to them or expected, people will, in general, be grateful and be motivated to reciprocate in turn, perhaps by being less likely to leave and by engaging in discretionary effort. Cutting education benefits therefore may or may not save money when you consider all of its repercussions—it depends on if, in what way, and how much people respond to the perception that they now owe their employer less.

Possibly the largest benefit is that investing in employees, in training and education as well as other things, activates the norm of reciprocity.

The second thing that systems thinking reminds us is that organizations and their decisions are interrelated, sometimes in complex ways, but often in a very simple and easy to understand fashion. The problem is that we necessarily break big decisions into subcomponents and smaller decisions, and build organizational structures that reify this division of decision-making labcr. In human resources this can be seen in the specialization of roles into compensation, benefits, organizational development, and so forth. Unless we take into account the totality of our actions and their effects on other, related organizational processes and components, suboptimization is almost guaranteed.

Which brings us to the example of retiree medical care. Should you cut your retiree medical benefits to save money? Maybe. But you should certainly never believe you are going to save all the money you think you are. Why? Because in the United States, mandatory retirement is legally proscribed and people are worried, at least until they turn 65 and become eligible for Medicare, about their health care costs. So, it is quite likely that reducing retiree medical benefits, or even the anticipation that you may do so, will decrease the percentage of the work force that chooses voluntary early retirement, thereby increasing wage costs as more senior, and higher paid, people remain in the organization for a longer time. This increase in labor costs from a more senior and higher paid work force can possibly more than offset what is saved by cutting the medical benefit for retirees. I have sat and watched as one HR professional in charge of an organization's early retirement program bemoaned the fact that it was requiring more and more inducement to get high paid senior staff to retire early and fewer people were availing themselves of the option to do so, even while another HR professional, whose job left this person with the responsibility for decreasing health care costs, proposed changes in retiree benefits that would make the likelihood of early retirement even less likely. Two people each doing their job, and working completely at cross purposes because there was little effort to explore the interrelationships among their decisions.

How to Implement Systems Thinking

The formal analysis of systems dynamics can involve building simulation models that illustrate how a set of processes interact over time to produce unexpected or unintended outcomes. For instance, Nelson Repenning and John Sterman wanted to understand why the enormous expenditures on management consulting and training produced such limited results. They described the paradox:

> On the one hand, the number of tools and techniques available to improve performance is growing rapidly.... It is easier than ever to learn about these techniques and to learn who else is using them. On the other hand, there has been little improvement in the ability of organizations to incorporate these innovations in their everyday activities.[5]

Their model shows the trade-off between working harder and working smarter—with a fixed amount of time and effort available, an organization can invest that time and thought into solving immediate problems or in fixing underlying, root causes thereby building the capability of the organization—defined as being able to produce better results with the same or less amount of effort. The problem is that working harder makes things better in the short run as the expenditure of extra effort will almost invariably produce some improvement in performance, while investing in building capabilities can actually make performance suffer in the short term, as investments in solving basic, fundamental problems are both risky and take time to show returns. Repenning and Sterman describe the two basic processes and ideas as, on the one hand, better before worse—working harder provides short term results but in the end results in poor performance as capabilities, machines, and energy declines from the effort—as contrasted with worse before better—investing in addressing basic, fundamental problems, even if it causes some decrement in performance in the short run, eventually results in much higher levels of performance as redesigned work processes and new technologies permit a much greater level of efficiency. Their lesson, and their model, speaks to the insights gained by considering the operation of feedback effects in organizations.

However, one need not be this formal or analytic in order to obtain at least some of the benefits from thinking about things in a more systemic and systematic fashion. My experience has shown that answering the following series of questions, and involving others in the process to get their wisdom and insight, can achieve many advantages by avoiding unexpected and undesirable results:

1. What is the principal benefit expected from the decision you are contemplating (reducing costs, increasing the quality of the staff, etc.)?

2. What are all of the other possible implications of the decision, on people, on costs, on customers and service, on product and process innovation, on suppliers, on the organization's image and brand equity?

3. How likely are each of these implications—what is the probability of their occurring?

4. What are the costs and consequences of each of these decision implications on all of these other affected groups?

5. Considering the anticipated positive effects and the other implications, some of which will be positive and some of which may be negative, does the decision still seem sensible?

All this process asks you to do is to consider the consequences and implications of decisions more broadly and to entertain the possibility that a given decision may set in motion other effects that may outweigh the anticipated positive consequences of the initial decision.

My experience tells me that this is actually not that difficult to do, conceptually. Experienced, knowledgeable people inside companies, and this certainly includes many HR professionals, can readily think of the effect of their decisions on other groups and using a number of outcomes. The problems arise from, a) not doing this analysis comprehensively and in a disciplined, systematic fashion, and specifically not trying to ascertain the costs of these other indirect and interrelated effects—for example, recognizing that a wage freeze may have consequences for morale, discretionary effort, and turnover, but not bothering to try and estimate the costs of this to balance against the direct wage savings; b) overweighting or overemphasizing those elements of the situation that can be more precisely and unambiguously measured at the expense of things that are harder to put a value on—for instance, not really balancing cost savings from reduced benefits or wages with the implications for the organization's reputation as a place to work, an effect that can have impact on the effort required to fill positions and the quality of the people who are attracted to the place as employees; and possibly most importantly, c) being so focused on optimizing some specific cost or dimension of the employment relationship that other effects of the decision are ignored even when they are known or recognized. This latter problem seems to be particularly acute when HR professionals, trying to show that they are as tough and focused as everyone else, deliver what the senior leadership says they want in terms of a decision without providing the information or occasionally the pushback that argues for taking more factors and feedback processes into account.

Some Implications for HR Measures and Decisions

Thinking systemically means that nothing will appear as simple or as clear cut as simple, linear analysis might indicate, and that goes for both measurement issues and the sorts of strategic choices HR professionals are called upon to make on a regular basis. That's the bad news—organizational dynamics are complicated. But in order to make sound decisions, you need to carefully think through *all* of the implications and repercussions of those choices. And the good news is that doing so can help prevent the sorts of variance-amplifying, vicious circle processes that so often create difficulties in and for organizations.

So, for instance, consider what other effects might tell us about employee-driven benefits. Seems like a good idea, until you recognize that the decision to make employees more cost-conscious and more responsible for their own decisions has effects other than possibly reducing direct expenditures on benefits. In most organizations, particularly in times of lean staffing, time is a scarce resource. Time spent making decisions about retirement investments and managing medical care spending accounts is time *not* spent doing something else, like maybe one's job. The question to be asked—and one which I have seen asked all too infrequently—is if employees' time highest and best use is really on becoming cost-conscious benefits consumers or whether it might be more productively spent on producing products and services and organizational innovations that really build competitive advantage.

SAS Institute, the largest privately owned software company in the world, has become justly famous for its generous, family-friendly benefits that include on-site day care, an on-site medical facility and very generous medical benefits, assistance with elder care and adoptions, and exceptional physical recreation and exercise facilities.[6] One obvious saving from these generous benefits is in the reduced turnover that the company enjoys from the loyalty it engenders in its employees. In an industry, software, that typically has turnover of 20 percent or higher, SAS Institute's turnover has invariably been under 5 percent. Another benefit of the company's approach has been becoming known as a great place to work, a reputation that has brought literally thousands of job applicants even when the high technology labor market place was at its tightest.

But there is another important economic advantage from SAS Institute's approach to its employee benefits. People are not distracted while they are at work by all the concerns and worries of finding care for their children, dealing with some managed care plan and its gatekeepers and policies and forms—and therefore, they can be more productively and efficiently focused on their work. After all, what ever happened to the idea of specialization and the division of labor? Isn't it actually less expensive, if you account for all of the costs, to have specialists help employees with their benefits, take good care of the employees, and let people actually do the work for which they were hired and where they actually have knowledge and expertise?

The same logic and advantage from taking a more systemic approach holds as we consider human resource measurements also. Many of the typical human resource measures I encounter are way too simplistic and unidimensional, not capturing the full impact and implications of various policies and practices. Consider, for instance, the measure of time to fill a position. Other things being equal, it would be great to fill positions more efficiently. But other things are seldom equal and what does it mean to be efficient in filling a job vacancy? Let me suggest that it may be less important to fill a job rapidly than to fill a job with someone who will a) perform effectively in the position and b) be more likely to stay in the job because the individual is a good match with the organization and its culture and values. Certainly there are technologies available to help in this sorting and matching process and these technologies can enhance both efficiency and effectiveness, making a good match probably does require more time. But although it may not look efficient for companies such as Southwest Airlines to spend a lot of time and effort carefully screening job applicants, appearances can be deceiving. With reduced turnover and people who buy into the company's mission, values, and culture, Southwest is able to more consistently deliver its particular brand of service and its remarkable cost efficiency is at least somewhat dependent on its skill in getting the right people in the door.

If the people you hire do make the place, and if it is easier and certainly less costly to prevent than to fix hiring mistakes, because getting rid of people once in the job is expensive in many ways, time to fill a position is at best a very imperfect and partial indicator of human resource efficiency.

A similar story could be told for compensation expense. Other things being equal, it would be nice to have lower compensation costs. But why do we believe in efficient markets for everything but labor? Isn't it the case that, for the most part, as an employer you get what you pay for and what you deserve? As George Zimmer, founder and CEO of the Men's Wearhouse, the successful retailer of off-price tailored men's clothing says, the issue isn't what you pay someone, but what they can do and produce. If your objective is simply to minimize salary costs, close down—salary costs can't get any lower than zero.

A company I know, having a bad year because of reduced demand and intensifying competition, decided to save money by compelling all salaried employees to take two weeks unpaid vacation. The company could, and did, calculate quite precisely that this step saved it about $600,000 in direct compensation. It is less clear that the company actually saved any money. This was also an action that sent a lot of messages to the work force: a) the company must be in severe financial distress (it wasn't), so people should think about finding a job at a more stable place with a better long term future; and b) the company felt that people should be willing to sacrifice for a one-time, short-term cost savings, or in other words, there was not much attention to employee well-being in the calculation. What happened was unfortunately, all too predictable—morale suffered. Many of the more talented people began looking for other employment and some left, and a number of people said that they would withhold discretionary effort and not do their best. Recall the idea of reciprocity—it works in reverse, also.

It is ironic that companies facing tough economic times and intense competition often do things that make them less able to successfully meet the competition. After all, when things are going well almost anyone can be successful. It is precisely when times are toughest that an organization needs all of the talent and energy and commitment it can muster. How unfortunate that some companies do not consider the other, systemic implications of what appear to be sensible, short-term cost saving decisions.

What Role Will Human Resources Play?

In seeking to model itself after other, apparently powerful corporate functions such as finance, human resources may not be doing either itself or its clients any favors. Many senior executives, and certainly the finance function, seem excessively obsessed with only one metric or indicator of corporate performance, stock price or total shareholder return. As we recently learned with the blow-up of the internet companies and the wide-spread financial scandals, stock price may not be a reliable indicator of the health of a company, as valuations and companies disappeared in a short time when various business and financial problems came to light. Although much has been written about balanced scorecards[7] and assessing and managing the processes that produce the desired outcomes, in practice, as one senior executive told me, "we use a balanced scorecard but 80 percent of the weight goes to the financials."

Organizations are indeed systems, regardless of how much one would like to simplify decision making and measurement. Feedback processes occur whether or not we want them to, and our decisions often have numerous implications only some of which may have been anticipated or desired. The question facing human resource professionals is whether they will be advocates for systems thinking in company decision making, or whether they will do what all too often they are currently doing—oversimplifying and not considering the many ramifications and implications of choices. There are real competitive advantages to companies that are able to think systemically in a disciplined, comprehensive way about the business situations and challenges they confront. As stewards of the human system of organizations, human resources has much to gain and much value to add by being advocates for and leaders of this approach.

Endnotes

1. There are a number of books and articles that review the extensive evidence on the impact of effective people management on numerous dimensions of organizational performance. See, for instance, Jeffrey Pfeffer, *The Human Equation: Building Profits by Putting People First*, Boston: Harvard Business School Press, 1998; Brian E. Becker, Mark A. Huselid, and Dave Ulrich, *The HR Scorecard: Linking People, Strategy, and Performance*, Boston: Harvard Business School Press, 2001; Brian E. Becker and Mark A. Huselid, "High Performance Work Systems and Firm Performance: A Synthesis of Research and Managerial Implications," in G. R. Ferris (ed.), *Research in Personnel and Human Resource Management*, Vol. 16, 53-101. Greenwich, CT: JAI Press, 1998.
2. The whole problem of managing by budgets in the first place is enormous and is very well described in *Beyond Budgeting: How Managers Can Break Free from the Annual Performance Trap* by Jeremy Hope and Robin Fraser, Boston, MA: Harvard Business School Press, 2003.
3. Pfeffer, *The Human Equation*, op. cit., p. 133.
4. A great discussion of the norm of reciprocity in the context of interpersonal influence is in Robert B. Cialdini, *Influence: Science and Practice*, Glenview, IL: Scott Foresman, 1988. A discussion of the norm of reciprocity itself can be found in A. W. Gouldner, "The Norm of Reciprocity: A Preliminary Statement," *American Sociological Review, 25* (1960), 161–178.

5. Nelson F. Repenning and John D. Sterman, "Nobody Ever Gets Credit for Fixing Problems that Never Happened," *California Management Review, 43* (Summer 2001), p. 65.
6. A description of the company and its strategy and operating philosophy can be found in Charles A. O'Reilly III and Jeffrey Pfeffer, *Hidden Value: How Great Companies Achieve Extraordinary Results with Ordinary People*, Boston: Harvard Business School Press, 2000, Chapter 5.
7. Robert S. Kaplan and David P. Norton, *The Balanced Scorecard: Translating Strategy Into Action*, Boston: Harvard Business School Press, 1996.

Lynda Gratton PhD

Lynda Gratton PhD is Associate Professor of Organizational Behaviour at London Business School. She directs the school's executive Human Resource Strategy program and is Research Director of The Leading Edge Research Consortium. Her main field of interest is human resource strategy where she is acknowledged as one of the world's leading authorities. Her most recent book, *Living Strategy: Putting People at the Heart of Corporate Purpose*, was published by Financial Times Prentice Hall and has been translated into five different languages. Dr. Gratton serves on the Board of the American Human Resource Planning Society and is on the advisory board of Royal Dutch Shell and Exult. Dr. Gratton can be reached at lgratton@london.edu.

Catherine Truss PhD

Catherine (Katie) Truss PhD is Professor of Human Resource Management and Deputy Head of the School of HRM at Kingston Business School. She is also Director of the research unit, SHaPe, which runs a number of research projects and company studies on strategic human resource management. Dr. Truss can be reached at K.Truss@kingston.ac.uk.

one : **2**

Three Dimensional Human Resource Strategy

Why is it that despite their best efforts organizations so often fail to deliver the human resource strategies they design? We have just completed a ten-year study and found that for many of the 4,500 employees we surveyed, the human resource strategy (HRS) had clearly not delivered.

For some employees the HRS had not delivered because, despite the processes being designed, they had not been applied with sufficient rigor. This was particularly the case for appraisal and training processes where we found only:

- 35 percent thought the appraisal system enabled an accurate assessment of their strengths and weaknesses.
- 48 percent thought their work goals were clearly defined.
- 36 percent agreed that they received the training they needed to do their job well.

For other employees the processes may have been applied with rigor, but they failed to be aligned with the key organizational goals. For example, with regard to trust and innovation:

- 34 percent did not have a great deal of trust in management.
- 15 percent believed senior management was well-informed about what people think and do.

Perhaps then it is no surprise that many of the employees we surveyed where unclear about the role and impact of the HR function.

- 20 percent agreed that their HR department had a clear strategy guiding its activities.
- 34 percent felt their HR department was competent at its job.

Our study of the development and implementation of human resource strategies has spanned seven different organizations and lasted the course of an entire decade.[1] During that time, we have been privileged to witness line executives and their HR colleagues grappling with many complex situations. We have seen them deal with mergers and take-overs, corporate crises, large-scale redundancy programs, and significant product and service market changes. We have seen how they have gone about leveraging corporate success, despite the odds, through creative and innovative human resource strategies. We have also borne witness to the many mistakes, frustrations, and traumas inevitably experienced by these executives and their organizations over the same period.

It is clear to us that in many companies the human resource strategy is an unknown quantity. The consequence of this is a significant disconnect between strategy, policy, practices, and behaviors. This disconnect impacts negatively on morale, commitment, motivation, and ultimately on corporate performance.

To avoid this disconnect and make the connection, HR teams need to visualize human resource strategy in three dimensions. The first dimension is vertical alignment between the HR strategy and business goals. The second dimension is horizontal alignment between individual HR policy areas. The third, and perhaps the most important, is the enactment of people strategies through the day-to-day experiences of employees and behavior of line managers. A key message of our study is that the focus in HR strategy needs to be on the third dimension. To put as much energy and resources in making it happen in practice as on developing the right policies and strategies in the first place.

The Three Dimensions of a Human Resource Strategy

What do we mean by "human resource strategy"? Should every company adopt a similar people strategy? Should the aim be to simply establish best practice in each of the aspects? We have long searched for the elusive bundle of HR policies and practices that every company should adopt. But this search has proven to be both difficult and elusive. As one might expect, there appears to be no one single ideal type human resource strategy with its bundle of HR policies and practices that can be adopted off the shelf by organizations seeking to manage their people more strategically.[2]

First Dimension: Vertical Alignment

Instead what constitutes a human resource strategy varies according to the history, environment, and circumstances of the organization. In particular, it varies with the business strategy and the goals of the business. So in order to play a strategic role in the organization, the HR policies and practices that make up an organization's human resource strategy should reflect, reinforce, and support the strategy and goals of the organization. HR interventions can indeed become a creator, and not an inhibitor, of sustained competitive advantage. However, to do so they have to build a strong link between the overall vision of what the organization should look like, and the aims, objectives, and underlying philosophy of the approach to managing people.[3] This link between the human resource strategy and business unit strategy, which we term "vertical alignment," is the first dimension of human resource strategy.

Second Dimension: Horizontal Alignment

Vertical alignment is concerned with the broad link between the corporate and business strategy and the human resource management strategies. Horizontal alignment operates at the level of individual HR policy areas. It occurs when there is a coherent and logically consistent approach to managing people. This consistency permeates the entire domain of activities of the HR function, and we are talking here at the policy level, not the practice level. This distinction is important because we treat the implementation, or enactment, of human resource strategies as the third dimension. Achieving a high degree of horizontal alignment implies that an organization has embraced the value of developing and articulating clear HR policies. It also implies that these policies relate to one another. More fundamentally, it acknowledges the importance of communicating consistent and reinforcing messages to employees.

Although at first sight vertical and horizontal alignment may appear to go hand-in-hand, our research has shown that this is not necessarily the case.[4] Firms that achieve high levels of vertical alignment may not exhibit strong horizontal alignment, and vice versa. This is because they operate at different levels: Vertical alignment is concerned with whether or not the overarching people strategy pursued or implicit in an organization's actions supports the organization's strategic direction. Horizontal alignment, on the other hand, is concerned with the degree of coherence evident in the stated HR policies of the firm.

Third Dimension: Enactment

Many HR teams seem to assume that the mere existence of a HR policy or strategy is sufficient to ensure its enactment. We believe this is absolutely fundamental to the question of whether an organization is delivering in the area of people management. For this reason, we separate enactment as an additional dimension of human resource strategy.[5]

There are two separate, but closely interrelated aspects of enactment. The first aspect concerns the people practices as experienced by

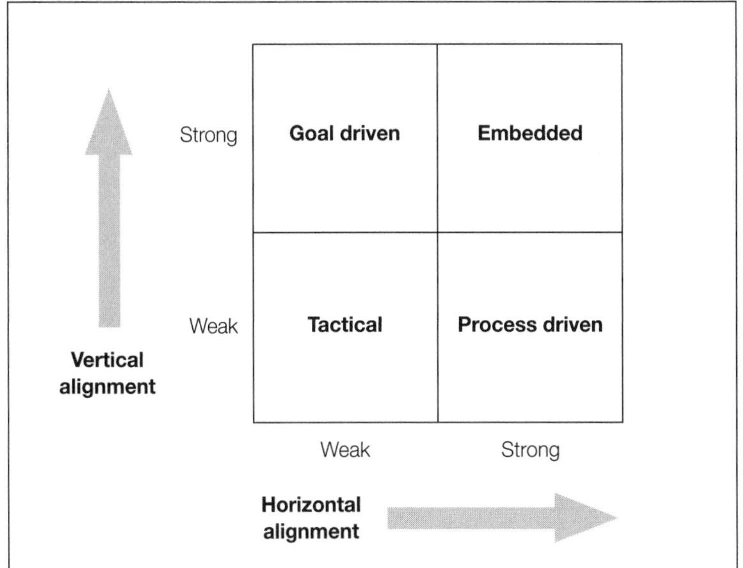

Figure 1.

employees. For example, the policy on appraisal may state that employees have three performance feedbacks with their manager every year and that they are appraised on five different competencies. If this is indeed the experience of employees, then we would describe this policy as enacted. If, on the other hand, employees are rarely party to performance feedback and if, when they are, the manager concentrates on only one competency, then we would describe this policy as not enacted. The second facet of enactment is more subtle. It focuses on the behaviors and values of the managers as they are enacting the policy. It is in their attitudes, conversations, and subtle body language that managers send out very clear messages about their attitude and support of the policy.[6]

If we take the two dimensions of vertical and horizontal alignment, and overlay the third dimension of enactment, we can identify four key potential human resource strategy configurations. Each of these has a continuum of enactment that may exist in an organization, from non-action to action. In our study, we found that companies presented unique combinations of alignment and enactment at any point in time.

Tactical Human Resource Strategy

We found this configuration in the traditional administrative HR function. Here separate HR policies are implemented without a view of their alignment to the business goals, or indeed to each other. Our study revealed some of the real downsides of this approach.

This tactical HR strategy was the case in the Chelsea and Westminster Hospital when we studied it in 1993 and 1994. While the hospital employed over 2,000 staff, there was no statement or shared understanding of the human resource people strategy. At this time there were few formalized HR policies, and no systematic attempts to link the policies to the aspirations of the hospital. Perhaps it was no surprise that only 26 percent of the staff we surveyed agreed that their work goals were clearly defined, and only 36 percent agreed that they received the training they needed to do their job well. As a result, the hospital was failing to recruit and retain the individuals it needed at all levels. Morale and attitudes toward the HR department were negative and, crucially, patient care needs were not being met in some areas. Only 23 percent of staff surveyed agreed that the hospital inspired the very best in job performance from them.

Process Driven Human Resource Strategy

This occurs in instances where the HR function has a strong, integrated set of HR policy goals, but there is little or no attempt to link these with the overall objectives of the business. Sometimes this strong process focus is enacted, other times it is simply espoused, and not actioned. We found the process driven human resource strategy to be a relatively common configuration. In some companies it resulted from a strong disconnect between the senior HR team and the rest of the senior executives of the organization. As a consequence there was limited line support for the HR function. In other companies the senior HR team had strong HR functional skills and knowledge, but weak strategic or business skills. Their expertise failed to be translated into practice because the line managers viewed then as disconnected from the real business drivers.

This strong functional expertise was apparent in the HR team at Citibank when we studied the company in 1997. At this time Citibank was pursuing a strategy of organic growth through building strong relationships with key clients. This represented a move away from its strategy in the early 1990s of a focus on products. The HR function was undergoing a period of transformation. Previously it had a tactical human resource strategy that involved giving administrative support to the line with little strategic involvement. At this time the newly appointed HR Director in the US was keen for the department to play a more strategic role. Our study at the time showed that the focus on one key process had not been enacted.

A key plank in strategic approach adopted by the HR team was to be the Talent Inventory. This was a new process with ten key performance indicators to aid selection, leadership, development, and succession planning. On the face of it, the Talent Inventory represented a significant step toward achieving horizontal alignment within HR. However, we discovered that the processes used in the Talent Inventory were not being enacted. Only 29 percent of employees we surveyed thought that the appraisal system enabled the company to gain an accurate understanding of people's strengths and weaknesses. One person commented, "If people's jobs are dictated by who they know and networking, why does Personnel want this thirty-five tick-box form? The form just gets stuffed in a drawer downstairs and is never looked at again in anyone's life!" By 2000, another manager commented, "The Talent Inventory is dead in the water." The process driven HR strategy had not moved further than the drawing board.

Only 29 percent of employees we surveyed thought that the appraisal system enabled the company to gain an accurate understanding of people's strengths and weaknesses.

Goal Driven Human Resource Strategy

Here the emphasis is on business knowledge and an understanding of the business goals. This can occur when the senior HR team is very close to the business and has high-level strategic skills but lacks the expertise to translate these business objectives into HR policy, or to implement these policies within the organization. In other words, the most common scenario is that the HR Director associates closely with the senior management team, and may be from a non-HR background, but he fails to pull the HR team together to develop a coherent set of HR policies. The challenge for this HR Director is to create a strong team with individuals who possess the HR functional skills that he lacks. Another scenario that is common under this configuration is major organizational change, such as merger, acquisition, or restructuring, where the HR department is called upon to act as change agent. Here the focus is on initially delivering around a single goal focused process.

We saw this clearly at GlaxoSmithKline (GSK). In the mid-1990s, the company went through both a major internal restructuring and a merger with Wellcome. As the company went through the merger process, the human resource strategy was business goal driven. The focus of the HR team was very much on working alongside the senior management team in managing the merger and integrating organizational processes, rather than on building and consolidating a coherent human resource strategy. As this period of turmoil settled down, the HR team could, once again, refocus on achieving horizontal alignment and creating an embedded human resource strategy. But this was not going to be easy. As one member of the HR team described the challenge, "We've come to a situation where we're back on track, and yet none of our standard ways of doing things work any more, because they have rusted due to lack of use or because they don't reflect the new organization."

Embedded Human Resource Strategy

The dream of every HR team is to create strong alignment with the business goals and yet build practices and processes that are coherent and internally consistent. For some this is an aspiration that is never actioned. For others it is a reality.

Some of the HR teams we studied had worked hard to create a strongly articulated human resource strategy that was linked into the business strategy and demonstrated strong internal HR policy linkages. But the strategy remained a dream. It was not enacted in the day-to-day behavior of managers and experiences of employees. We saw this when the HR team was highly skilled in strategy development, but had weak implementation capability, or lacked senior line management support.

In the mid 1990s, this was very much the case at the UK telecoms BT. In the Payphones division we studied, the human resource strategies were geared toward achieving significant cultural change. At that time the company was faced with severe competition and the threat of product substitution through the mass expansion of mobile telephones. To meet this threat, a number of interrelated initiatives were being aggressively pursued. These included a value change program backed up by a Corporate Scorecard for measuring performance; Involving Everyone, an extensive training and development program; a Leadership Program; a Total Quality Management process; an initiative called Breakout to encourage innovation; and a sophisticated performance management system.

Although all this sounds good on paper, a number of problems became apparent. First, the sheer number of initiatives and policies meant that people were overwhelmed by their complexity and the impact of each individual one was lost and people were more confused than motivated. Secondly, and most crucially, the cost containment strategy pursued by the corporate center meant that annual redundancy targets were set between 17 and 20 percent at the managerial level in 1994. Yet another program, Release, had been set up to manage this process. Clearly, however, the ethos of running a large redundancy program was at odds with the spirit and values expressed in the other initiatives being pursued by the company. This did irreparable damage to the psychological contract. As one manager said, "We work at such short-termism that one year is a hell of a long time in BT." The performance management program was clearly not working; 56 percent of those we surveyed at this time said that their reward package was not directly related to their performance at work. Only 10 percent agreed that management cared about the needs and morale of employees.

In other organizations we saw a more actioned approached to HRS. In Kraft Foods, a European subsidiary of Philip Morris, the HR team had moved from the rhetoric to the reality of an embedded human resource strategy. In the early years of the decade the company was going through a period of aggressive growth through acquisition. The HR team supported this by developing an extremely efficient process for taking over the HR systems of the acquired companies. This ensured that the acquisition phase was dealt with rapidly, and the new company quickly became integrated into the parent firm. The firm's second strategic thrust of continuous improvement was supported by a coherent set of HR policies. These were built around recruiting and selecting people against a clear set of criteria, providing targeted training and development, incenting line managers to implement HR policy, and a strong performance management process. By the mid-1990s the company faced changing economic conditions, increased competition in their core brands, and a lack of potential take-over targets. In response to these changes, the strategy focused on growth through innovation. This required a major cultural change that was led by the HR team. A new vision and values statement was introduced and cascaded through the organization. The performance management system was refined to align with the new values of creativity and risk taking. Programs were put in place to develop new leadership skills to support these values. Recognizing that workforce diversity was becoming increasingly important in this changed environment, the HR team put in place new flexibility and work-life balance programs.

Our study of human resource strategy followed these companies for almost a decade. During this time we saw some of the HR teams actively strengthening alignment and enactment across the three dimensions. Here is how they did it.

Strengthening Vertical Alignment

Getting Quick Wins. Faced with the need to strengthen vertical alignment, the most successful HR executives decided on a few key areas. They judged that these were areas where they could quickly demonstrate a contribution, and where the positive benefits of change were readily visible to significant line managers. This was the dilemma faced by the new HR Director at the Chelsea and Westminster Hospital. As we saw earlier, she had joined a hospital with very poor HR processes. However, she scored a "quick win" by introducing a sophisticated workforce information database. This enabled line managers to quickly and easily access vital information about the profile of the workforce. By doing so, they were able to plan ahead for short-term cover and long-term recruitment. This new system soon won plaudits from the managers as it helped solve a difficult and ongoing problem.

Prioritize Resource and Effort Allocation Around Organizational Needs. The temptation for many HR departments is to focus on their own needs first and the needs of the organization second. We often heard HR executives say, "We could do so much more if only we had more resources," or, "We can't be strategic, we don't have time". However, the way that the most successful HR departments in our study secured the resources they needed was by doing what the line executives wanted them to do first. From this vantage point they were then able to create the reputational effectiveness[7] they required to be deemed worthy of further resources. A counter example to this was in one of the organizations where the HR function failed over a long period of time, to achieve any reputational effectiveness. When we asked one line manager what he thought the HR department did, his comment was, "I think they do some administration and sometimes get things wrong." Needless to say, this particular HR department saw a steady dilution of its resource base over the 10-year period.[8] In GSK, the HR team, as we saw earlier, took the decision to focus its efforts and attention during the time of the restructuring and merger around its role as change agent. This meant that their efforts were concentrated where the senior executives most needed it, around crafting people strategies aimed at bringing the newly emerging business together. This phase was followed by a second phase aimed at embedding these new strategies and ensuring horizontal alignment.[9]

Build a Business-Focused HR Team. In those organizations where the HR team was located and structured around the line, then we found that vertical alignment was stronger. We observed many instances where the entire HR team sat along one corridor, rarely venturing forth to visit the business units alongside whom they were supposed to work. Consequently, line managers or employees were unable to describe HR's contribution to their unit. In Kraft Foods, the HR staff were devolved to the business units to work alongside line manager as they made and implemented strategic decisions. The same was to be true at the Chelsea and Westminster Hospital. One of the early decisions the new HR Director took was to co-locate the HR nearer to the line executives. While this may seem to be purely symbolic value, in fact it went much deeper than this for the line managers. As a director at the Chelsea and Westminster said, "We have benefited enormously as a directorate by having people seconded from the HR department centrally to come and work with us and work with us only." It is only by sitting alongside the line executives, and taking part in their day-to-day decision-making about the running of their units, that these HR managers are able to alter their mindset and view human resource strategies from a line perspective.

Look Up and Out. The tendency in those organizations with weak vertical alignment was for the HR executives and managers to focus inward on themselves, the HR department, their processes, and policies. This was in stark contrast with those who were willing to extend their horizons. They were prepared to look up at what was happening at the top of the organization, and out, into the world, to see what was happening in their industry, their profession, their neighborhood, and the world.[10] We are thinking particularly here of the HR executives at Kraft Foods, who took the most active part in our Leading Edge workshops held over the course of the ten years. They attended more diligently than representatives from any of the other organizations, often with a large, international team, and contributed enthusiastically to the discussions and co-production of knowledge that was at the heart of our research endeavor. They were willing to invest considerable time in engaging in an open and frank dialog with their peers from other organizations and with the research team, and to learning without a particular end game in mind. Similarly, this senior HR team worked closely with the senior executive group, actively participating in strategy formulation for the entire firm, as well as being responsible for working out its people implications.

Strengthening Horizontal Alignment

Think Systemically. One of the challenges of horizontal integration is the sheer complexity of representing the various HR interventions and their potential relationships, intended and unintended consequences. As a result, the human resource strategy document, if it exists at all, does so as a simple, linear description of interventions. Not so at Kraft Foods. Here the HR team worked with the line managers to create a more complete picture of what the organization would look like if it was to have innovation as a key business goal. The cross-functional team worked together to create a systems map. This mapped the key practices and processes, the relationships between the process, and the intended and unintended consequences of the behaviors and value which these practices and processes would reinforce. This visual picture of the horizontal alignment of the policies and practices created crucial insights for the management teams. For example, they began to understand that if they wanted teams to be innovative, then it would not simply be sufficient to reinforce innovative behavior with reward. They would have to do more to encourage innovation through the way in which they created and structured teams, in the way they encouraged personal autonomy and risk taking, and in the coaching and support they gave to managers.[11]

Foster Creative Dialog. The conversations that enable the continual, mutual adjustments that are crucial to horizontal alignment are an important feature of the most successful companies we looked at. It was through these conversations that the HR teams and the business executives were able to design, plan, and make decisions. We found these companies fostered a context for great talk by creating time and space for conversations and by legitimizing big, broad questions.[12]

Time and space were particularly important in creating the conditions for real conversation to take place. In some of these companies, we saw both space and time fragmentation within the HR function. The experts in each of the functional processes remained isolated; the pay experts rarely talking with the career or the performance management experts. In those companies with strong horizontal alignment, we saw the HR team working closely together, even if they were geographically dispersed. We also saw that when they did meet it was not simply the reiteration of known facts, but rather exploration of big, broad questions. The same was true of the relationships and conversations between the line and the HR function. It would seem that there is a fine balance to be created between HR functioning as a cohesive team and as a business partner. In Kraft Foods much emphasis was focussed on achieving this balance. They devolved HR staff to the business units to work alongside line managers as they made and implemented strategic decisions. At the same time, they kept the HR team together through regular meetings, sharing of best practice initiatives, and e-communication. HR team members were appraised, and rewarded, for their achievements in support of the business and for their contribution to the HR team.

Draw Road Maps. Horizontal integration was consistently the strongest in Kraft Foods and, at the same time, this was one of the few organizations in our study that, from the beginning, had a written human resource strategy statement. This statement mapped the strategic aims of the company against a series of clearly stated HR interventions designed to support them. The document was frequently updated and shared both amongst the HR team members and with line managers. In 1997, the HR team began a more formal process of strategy creation, using visioning techniques to identify future trends, and systems mapping to describe and document the key aspects of horizontal integration between the HR elements. This process became embedded by 1998 and has been used ever since. The discipline of having to write down how the diverse elements of the people strategy interconnect quickly uncovers any hidden conflicts and tensions.

Avoid Black Holes. We saw two errors in horizontal alignment. The first was the error of not having sufficiently developed people policies across the whole remit of the people strategy. We saw this in the Chelsea and Westminster Hospital in the early 1990s, where the ad hoc arrangements inherited by the incoming HR Director meant that few clearly articulated policies were in place. Consequently, critical success factors such as the recruitment and retention of key staff fell down into black holes between the policies. It was only when she specifically focused on horizontal alignment that the source of these problems became apparent and could be addressed.

Avoid Initiative-itis. The second error that militates against strong horizontal alignment is having too many people policies. As we saw earlier, in the case of BT, the plethora of initiatives, programs, and activities they had developed under the banner of their human resource strategy floundered because of their sheer complexity. This was compounded by the starkly conflicting messages being sent out by the enormous redundancy program on the one hand, and the value change program on the other. The edifice crumbled because it was constructed on weak foundations. Having too many initiatives on the go simultaneously means that it is impossible to track their interactions.

Strengthening Action Taking

Focus on Doing. In those firms most successful at achieving a strong degree of enactment, we observed a clear ability to translate policies and strategies into action plans. While many of the companies in our study were adept at managing business processes, few were equally adept at managing people processes. Our study revealed HR teams developing a plethora of unrelated people process projects with limited integration. We witnessed projects begun and never completed. We saw unsophisticated tracking processes and ambiguity around budgets and timescales. Of the companies we examined, Kraft Foods and Hewlett Packard had developed and implemented the most sophisticated enactment project management practices. At HP, the people strategy was part of the whole "Hoshin" business strategy process and, from this, came a number of people imperatives. These imperatives were then treated to the same project management practices as any major project. Project plans were created, outcomes agreed, and timelines discussed.

Keep the Best. In the most successful firms we observed, there was a clear focus on the importance of continuity of people and process to ensure enactment was sustained over time. At Kraft Foods, for example, the basic structure of the key performance management practices remained intact throughout the time of our study. Within this time, the focus of the process changed (with a greater emphasis on the behaviors and values that reinforce innovation), but the structure of the process remained rock solid. In this subtlety we are reminded of the words of a Kraft manager, "Remember, you only need a very small amount of pressure applied to a rudder to turn a boat around." Thus, employees were not bogged down by complex, conflicting messages or constant distracting changes in the way that things were done. Instead they were able to accommodate the changing needs of the firm through an altered emphasis within a well-understood framework.

While continuity was crucial in Kraft, we saw in other companies continuity lost and, with it, the strong backbone of vertical alignment. Sometimes this reflected a change in philosophy. At HP, for example, the departure of the HR head in 2000 and the resulting amalgamation of the HR function with finance function, led by the previous finance manager, created a perceptible break with the past and the beginnings of the breakdown of vertical alignment. More often, this disconnect occurred as a result of mergers and acquisitions. This was particularly visible in the Citibank/Travelers merger that resulted in the complete disintegration of the previous senior HR team and the loss of knowledge and expertise with their demise.

Build a Holistic Picture of Reality. Each of these companies had built a realistic picture of financial capital that they presented to their employees and shareholders. This picture was created through a process of triangulation of many discrete financial measures. Few used the same rigor when contemplating the human asset base. In those companies with stronger enactment, we saw the HR teams working to collect and review data with executives at three levels of description:

- through a review of all HR documentation and communication of strategic intent to measure the degree of alignment between the stated HR objectives (of the people strategy) and the business goals and needs.
- by measuring the enactment of the people practices.
- by measuring and appraising the behavior and values of managers.

The triangulation methods involved data from employee surveys, focus groups, interviews, data from appraisal, and exit interviews. In our study, HP was particularly adept at this. Their complete picture of reality was built through multiple tools, while their HR audit involved consulting multiple stakeholders. For example, they made active use of peer assessment when teams from another business came to assess and comment upon the design and enactment of HR policies and practices.

Human resource strategy may indeed be an unknown quantity. But we have seen companies who have actively built and implemented strategies that add real value. They do this creating vertical alignment, building horizontal alignment, and ensuring enactment. For them, thinking about human resource strategy in three dimensions has made a real difference.

Endnotes

1. The cases presented in this article are drawn from a ten-year study in which a consortium of researchers and practitioners examined people management issues in the UK businesses of seven large, complex organizations: a telecommunications company, the BT Payphones business of BT; a food company, Kraft

Foods, a business of Philip Morris; a pharmaceutical company, Glaxo Smith Kline: GSK; a high-tech company, Hewlett Packard: HP; a large public hospital, The Chelsea and Westminster Hospital; and two financial institutions, the UK retail bank Lloyds TSB; and the global financial institution, Citibank. Four of these companies are headquartered in the UK, and three in the US. In each of the studies, we used a questionnaire, surveying the same business unit on three occasions. In 1994, a total of 1,764 individuals completed the questionnaire with a response rate of 52 percent; in the 1997 study a total of 1,592 completed the questionnaire with a response rate of 56 percent, and in 2000 a total of 1,248 employees completed the questionnaire with a response rate of 38 percent. Within each of the three studies, we also interviewed twenty to thirty-five employees in each company, ran a series of focus groups with the HR team, and collected extensive policy documentation. We also actively engaged the HR teams in each of the companies in the co-production of knowledge by designing a series of workshops in which the outcomes of the studies were described and debated.

2. Scholars working within the so-called High Performance Work Practices literature have used quantitative techniques to identify a range of HR interventions that, if bundled together, might be considered to contribute to firm performance. Reviews have shown, however, that there is considerable variation in the propositions put forward. See, for example, Becker, B. & Gerhart B. 1996. "The Impact of Human Resource Management on Organizational Performance: Progress and Prospects." *Academy of Management Journal*, 39 (4): 779–801. See also Baron, J. N. and Kreps, D. M. 1999. *Strategic Human Resources*, New York: Wiley.

3. This perspective has been referred to as the "fit" approach, which has been contrasted with the "best practices" approach described above. These various theoretical frameworks on strategic HRM have been reviewed in Delery, J. E. and Doty, D. H. 1996. "Modes of Theorizing in Strategic Human Resource Management: Tests of Universalistic, Contingency and Configurational Perspectives." *Academy of Management*, 39 (4): 802–35.

4. Some of the findings of this study are written up in Gratton, L., Hope-Hailey, V., Stiles, P. & Truss, C. 1999. *Strategic Human Resource Management: Corporate Rhetoric and Human Reality*, Oxford, UK: Oxford University Press.

5. This point is debated further in the Leading Edge book (op.cit) and in Truss, C. (2001) "Complexities and Controversies in Linking HRM with Organizational Outcomes." *Journal of Management Studies*, 38 (8): 1121–1150.

6. The literature of process fairness has explored this in great detail. For a useful overview see Greenberg, J. & Cropanzano, R. (Eds.) 2001. *Advances in Organizational Justice*. Stanford, California: Stanford University Press.

7. Tsui, A. 1984. A Multiple Constituency Framework of Managerial Reputational Effectiveness. In J. Hunt, C. Hoskin, C. Schriesheim & R. Stewart, *Leadership*. New York: Pergamon.

8. Baron and Kreps (op.cit.) similarly argue that many HR managers are perceived as divorced from the needs of the business by their line colleagues.

9. Quinn, R.E., Spreitzer, G.M. & Brown, M.V. 2000. "Changing Others through Changing Ourselves," *Journal of Management Inquiry*, 9 (2): 147–64, have shown that major organizational change efforts frequently fail through not altering the human system. This is where the people strategy can play a vital role.
10. Amabile, T. M. 1998. "How to Kill Creativity," *Harvard Business Review*, 76 (5): 76–87, highlights the importance of allowing people to have a large "network of wanderings", or intellectual space to explore possibilities and solve problems.
11. The visualization of horizontal alignment has been described by Lynda Gratton (2000) in *Living Strategy: Putting People at the Heart of Corporate Purpose*, London: FT Prentice Hall.
12. The role of conversation as a tool of mutual adaptation is described in "Improving the Quality of Conversations," by Lynda Gratton and Sumantra Ghoshal: *Organizational Dynamics*, 2002, 31 (3): 209–223.

Jac Fitz-enz PhD

"Dr. Jac" as he is known worldwide, is acknowledged as the father of human capital benchmarking and workforce analysis. He carried out the original research on human resources measurement in the 1970s and followed that by publishing the first human capital metrics in 1985. He was the founder and chairman of Saratoga Institute for over two decades. An award-winning author of seven books on human capital and organizational development, Dr. Jac has also published over 160 articles, reports, and book chapters covering human capital valuation, leadership, human resources structuring and benchmarking, team effectiveness, performance measurement, and employee retention. Prior to founding Saratoga Institute in 1980, Dr. Fitz-enz held human resource vice presidential positions at Wells Fargo Bank, Imperial Bank, and Motorola Computer Systems. He holds degrees from Notre Dame, California State University San Francisco, and USC. Dr. Jac can be reached at jac@drjac.com.

one : 3

Human Capital Branding:
The New Organizational Effectiveness Model

> A company's brand is not a product. The brand is the human capital that makes and services the product.

If we were to ask people to explain what branding is they might claim it is an advertised feature of a product. One of Chevrolet's brands is Corvette. Another is Nova. So what does Chevrolet stand for? The brand images of Corvette and Nova could not be more different. Pontiac on the other hand is a clear brand. For 30 years Pontiacs have stood for power, speed, excitement. The first issue with branding is, what do we stand for?

Branding is about establishing an image in the mind of the customer. Depending on the type of product, the image could be qualitative, such as creamy taste, high fashion color, luxury accommodation, safety, speed, excellent service; or a quantitative feature such as cost, economical or expensive. Companies spend millions of dollars trying to drive a positive image into the mind of the buying public. Assuming for the sake of discussion that the product feature that marketing is attempting to impose on the public is actually true, how does that feature appear in the product? Is it a result of the advertisements or the marketing brochure copy? Most emphatically, no!

The Truth about Branding

There is a subtle but extremely profound truth about brands. The true brand of your company is not the product or a feature of the product you sell. Fundamentally, it is the performance of your employees—your human capital—who design, build, sell, and service your offering. What the buying public sees is the direct result of the character and behavior of your human capital.

Your employees' behavior determines the buyers' perception of the brand, good or bad. All other things being equal, the product the buyer sees or the service she experiences is the result of employee effort. The thing customers purchase or the service they desire is totally a function of the innovation, productivity, quality, and service outputs of the people you employ. Therefore, by definition, your brand image is the mirrored reflection of your human capital. No amount of cash, no facility full of equipment, and no stockpile of material create a product.

The basic point for this premise is that all resources are inert, with the exception of human resources. It is people who put other resources into play and produce something. How that something tastes, looks, feels, and what it costs is the direct, singular result of the human input. There is no product without people. Therefore, without people there is no feature for marketing and advertising to attempt to turn into a brand image. That is why human capital equates with brand.

Important Distinction

Are we just playing a semantic game here? Why is it important to think of branding as starting with employee behavior rather than as an image in the mind of the buying public? The point is two fold. First, there is no brand until the employees produce it. Second, how they produce it shapes the product's features. What difference does this make, even if it is true? If we want to gain and sustain competitive advantage this is a very important distinction that should drive execution.

According to marketing guru Al Ries, a brand is nothing more than a word in the mind of the customer.[1] Brand is a noun. A noun is a person, place, or thing. That is, it is inherently fixed, yet changeable. How does a fixed thing change? If the product feature is a perception that a buyer has of say, the quality of a product, does that perception ever change? Of course, products are modified and "improved." As the modified product hits the market, the buyer might change her perception of the brand. How does the change occur? It can come about from without or within the product. Since perception is a selective judgment that the buyer makes, the change in perception can be relative. That is, a new product can come into the market and the buyer can perceive it more favorably than the old product. Or the buyer's needs or sophistication can change thereby modifying their perception of the old product's qualitative value. On the other hand, the product itself can change, either deliberately through a planned improvement or accidentally through a production mishap. In every case the change is a result of human behavior. The buyer's judgment changes or the producer's performance changes. Ultimately in the marketplace the brand image is a function not of marketing copy but of human behavior. A Corvette is a sports car. That has not changed in fifty years. But the perception of the car has changed due to competition, product innovation and quality, durability and service, and the changing demographics of the buying public. Branding is first a human issue, and only secondarily a product issue.

Applications

Marketing and advertising attempt to fix or change the buyer's perception in favor of the product. Production and service functions attempt to maintain or improve the product or service upon which the buyer will cast judgment. Sometimes companies spend millions of dollars on branding without making the product that they advertise. Let me explain it like this.

A pragmatist once said to me, "We can make it like this, or we can say we make it like this. To actually make it like this can cost a lot of money. To say we make it like this costs a lot less."

The first path is production. The second path is advertising. In both cases the decision to offer a product in a certain way is a function of human values, attitudes, and beliefs.

Product. The manufacture of every product varies over time. Even products as distinctive and automated as Coca-Cola depend on the human capital of the company to produce it at a competitive cost, according to Coke's quality standards, and service it effectively at the wholesale and retail levels. If the product doesn't taste like Coke because someone mixed it incorrectly, didn't clean the apparatus, put too much or too little carbonation in it, or let it sit in a hot truck or warehouse until its freshness diminished, the consumer will reject it as not being the brand that they know and want. Although the inputs are unchanged, still the product that reaches the consumer is variable. You say that can't happen with Coke because it is made to a formula. Then why does the company have a quality control function? Soft drink Odwalla is also made in an automated factory according to a recipe. Still, one time something went wrong and the output was contaminated. Automation has never insured perfection. If product quality becomes inconsistent, the brand takes on that aspect as its image.

Service. When it comes to service businesses the brand perception of the company is almost 100 percent the result of the behavior and performance of employees. The market confirms this by attributing as much as 80 percent of a service company's market capitalization to human capital over book value. Likewise, it can go the other way in a hurry. Consider what has happened to the brands of Arthur Anderson, WorldCom, Enron, or any of the other service company scandal cases. The image of those companies was destroyed not by lack of resources but by the actions of senior executives. The decades old, world-renowned company Anderson was snuffed out. WorldCom had to revert to a previous name to shake its brand stigma. Enron is being rebuilt on a much smaller scale with a quite different public persona.

We don't have to go to extreme cases to make the point. The cynicism that exists in the marketplace today is a direct result of attempting to market brand images that are not produced by the company's human capital. Banks advertise "your personal banker" who turns out not to know us or have the authority to do anything out of the ordinary for us. The telephone company trumpets its latest technology, but we can't find a service person to fix our system on the first visit. The popularity of Dilbert rides on an exaggeration of basic truths.

Human Capital Branding Elements

Building and maintaining a premium marketplace brand depends on employee response to and subsequent behavior regarding four factors. They are:

1. A clear vision of the essence of the company that is acted out by everyone, everyday. This is the heart of the brand image that the company wishes to portray to the public.

2. An alignment of individual and business unit objectives with the corporate brand goals. Masses of research have shown that in many companies over 50 percent of the time there is discontinuity between goals, objectives, and behavior.

3. Clear responsibility, authority, and accountability at each and every position linked to the brand. To be effective each employee needs to know not only what he or she is supposed to do, but is also given the authority and held accountable for meeting performance standards.

4. A tangible and intangible human capital effectiveness measurement system. The old saying that, "what gets measured gets done" is true. The measurement system has to be consistent, relevant to the brand goals and objectives, and function organization wide.

In summary, a human capital branding system is holistic, humanistic, and honest. Sustainable branding requires companies to focus on their human capital brand internally so that it will support the brand image they promote externally. Advertising a brand feature that is not being delivered wastes money, infuriates customers, and makes the organization the butt of late night show monologues.

Figure 1 shows the characteristics of a human capital alignment system. It is simple, open, logical, strategic, and effective.

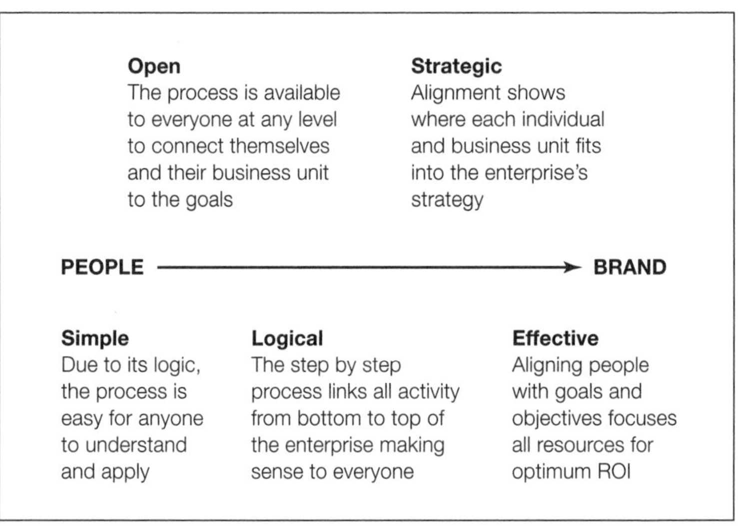

Open
The process is available to everyone at any level to connect themselves and their business unit to the goals
Strategic
Alignment shows where each individual and business unit fits into the enterprise's strategy
PEOPLE
BRAND
Simple
Due to its logic, the process is easy for anyone to understand and apply
Logical
The step by step process links all activity from bottom to top of the enterprise making sense to everyone
Effective
Aligning people with goals and objectives focuses all resources for optimum ROI

Figure 1. Brand alignment characteristics

Human Capital Brand Map

Vision

It is the responsibility of the CEO to set the corporate brand image by articulating the characteristics through a vision statement. The vision must be more than a slogan such as "We're Number 1." Statements such as that are hopes, not visions. A vision statement that supports the corporate brand goes beyond a slogan and includes the following:

- Who are we—vision of the enterprise; what we aspire to be, employer of choice, supplier of choice, market leader, etc.
- What we do—our product and service lines
- Where we do it—geographic markets, niche markets, corporate customers, individual consumers
- How we do it—expected productivity, quality, and service level targets
- How much we do—market share, gross revenue, and revenue by product/service

Once published there has to be a plan for monitoring it. If the vision is going to live, it has to be reinforced in every possible medium. Pep rallies do not sustain either visions or strategic plans. The pep rally might kick off a new strategic branding plan. But a system must be built to ensure that everyone is living the plan everyday. Its first application is in recruitment. It is both a statement and a screening device. The vision tells an applicant what this company is all about. It is also used by recruiters and hiring managers to explain the company and determine if the applicant is a good fit, particularly for the who and how part of the statement.

The vision has to be monitored for its vitality and realization otherwise it will be overrun by daily crises. It should be the first topic at every management review meeting. An extensive research project covering 1,000 companies revealed that the top 10 percent of performers continually reinforced their vision in all-hands messages and meetings, performance reviews, and most importantly through executive behavior.[2]

Alignment

Alignment is critical for two reasons. First, it promotes efficiency by driving behavior, and therefore job performance, directly at the operating objectives and corporate goals that embody the vision. Second, it promotes effectiveness because it shows us the what, when, where, and how that we need to focus on to achieve the objectives and goals, thereby reinforcing the vision.

Generally, most companies are proficient at strategic planning. Where the plan falls apart is when it moves across boundaries from corporate level to functions, strategic business units, departments, teams, and individuals. Alignment is a much-talked about and seldom-realized topic. Although most organizations claim there is alignment from top to bottom they know that often this is not true. It is common to have gaps, barriers, misunderstandings, and even deliberate breaks between enterprise goals, business unit operating objectives, individual objectives, and resource investments. These misalignments are the cause of most malfunctions. No brand can be sustained consistently if these gaps continue. If the goal is timely performance, then every objective at every level all the way through the organization should have a time component and every job should have time objectives.

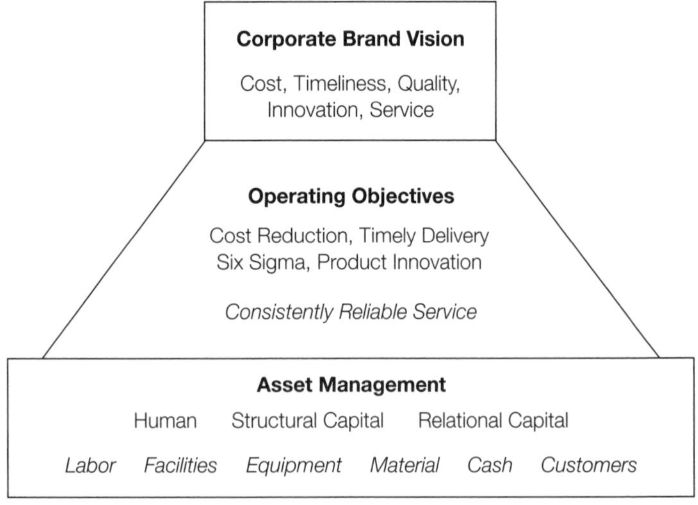

Figure 2. Vision alignment

Figure 2 shows how to align each employee and all non-human assets with the brand vision. The brand features will be expressed in one or more: cost, time, innovation, quality, or service categories. This is the foundation of the brand. With human capital alignment all operating unit objectives mirror the dominant brand feature. Then, investment in and management of corporate assets are applied to the desired feature. All individual tasks and subsequent performance measures are directly and unequivocally connected to the branding goals of the enterprise. It is also the test for new project proposals. Given data from within the enterprise as well as from outside entities such as customers, competitors, and regulators, management is able to forecast more effectively and invest with less risk.

Application

Application is the execution step of the alignment model. Asset management is a function of human, structural, and relational capital investments. Labor, facilities, equipment, material, cash, and customer attention are focused on the brand goal. One might ask how employees and customers come to be listed as assets since the corporation does not own them. Although they are not owned in fact, only employees and customers are active assets. They are the only factors than interact to create value. All other so-called assets are actually inert and depreciating. Even unemployed cash depreciates due to inflation.

Given that we know the alignment from vision to asset management now we can begin to manage our resources. Unfortunately, due to the massive disruptions that started with the layoffs at the beginning of the 1990s, the subsequent infusion of technology, as well as ongoing market uncertainty, many people—including executives—are confused. As Deming pointed out nearly 25 years ago, management often unknowingly inhibits performance.[3] The volatile world market makes knowing where to invest resources difficult.

We believe that almost everyone wants to do a good job, but they need the type of guidance and system that human capital branding offers. Line managers know they need help in managing and evaluating their human capital through this chaotic marketplace. Performance planning, objective setting, communications, process management, problem solving, and performance measurement and rewards are facilitated through the application of the brand alignment principle. In addition, the relevance and utility of scorecard systems are improved.

In this system there is absolutely no room for equivocation. Every decision must be made on the basis of how it is going to enhance the brand. With this approach we can invest cash in facilities, equipment, and material that are necessary for brand production so long as the connection from vision to asset management is intact. We can assign human capital to brand value work. Responsibility, authority, and accountability can be set with fairness, consistency, and efficiency. As individual and team assignments are made they can be tested against the brand goal. This system avoids the traditional performance review problem that too often is subjectively based. It provides unbiased objectivity and insures the ability to design administrative programs, production processes, and performance management systems confident that they support the branding goal.

Measurement

When we measure, we understand what is being produced and offered to the marketplace. When we understand that, we can improve and sustain our brand. Once the performance path is clear, it must be backed by training and underpinned by a reward system that fits each and every position. We need to build performance management systems that truly pay for performance. What we have to avoid is what we call the peanut butter compensation model. In this method pay increases are spread evenly across the organization, regardless of performance, with a variance of only 1 or 2 percent from best to worst.

People need to see how their pay reflects their performance. This implies an objectively driven assignment and review of work. In the human capital branding model every position has a set of personal and team objectives that are directly derived from the branding goal and other key corporate goals. For example, if timely service (responsiveness) is the branding goal, then every position inherits objectives that have time as a key imperative. In addition, if there are other strategic corporate goals such as cost reduction, quality improve-

1. **Vision.** Management's brand goal is clearly communicated and thoroughly understood by our associates. There are regular communications, meetings, and discussions regarding the brand. We periodically check associates' comprehension and commitment to the goals using the surveys and other polling methods.
2. **Structure.** We are structuring the company to support the brand. The structure promotes interaction and collaboration across business unit boundaries to foster teamwork and innovation.
3. **Culture.** The corporate culture supports collaboration in pursuit of the brand. It is clear how we are to communicate and work with each other, customers, competitors, suppliers, the community in which we operate, and regulators.
4. **Attraction.** The characteristics of the brand help in sourcing and selecting talent. The brand's characteristics are prominently displayed in recruitment advertising and serve as the focus for applicant screening and interviewing.
5. **Careers.** We have established a career path and development system that promotes development of the talent needed to deliver the brand. Associates are informed as to the skills, knowledge, and attitudes required to build a career in this organization.

Figure 3. Macro target scoring

ment, or service enhancement, each position will have objectives linked to those goals.

As we measure performance at the individual level it rolls up to teams and SBUs. These in turn roll up to functional levels such as overall production, sales, service, and support. Finally, the performance results culminate in the corporate branding and strategic goals. This system holds the entire organization together and serves as an early warning siren as deviations occur. It is basically the human capital brand assurance system.

Branding Targets. Each level has its targets, the objectives and goals toward which it is committing its resources. Typical organizational targets are financial, production, quality, service, innovation, employee development, and retention. These are set, reviewed and reset periodically. In addition to these typical measures there is a set of macro human capital targets that can be watched to ensure that your human capital is focused on the branding goal. Examples of these are seen in Figure 3.

Action Example

Assume for the sake of an example that the brand feature we truly want to develop (remember: do versus say we do?) is perfect service.

The first step is to put it into a vision statement, such as "on time, every time". This is quite clear. It is short, to the point, and unequivocal. The vision then has to be expanded with the who, what, where, why, and how much factors listed above. Then, it is objectified with a number. While we tell the market that our brand of service is to deliver on time, every time we know that we are not perfect. So we might set an internal target such as six sigma deliveries. This equates to no more than three late deliveries in one million attempts.

The second step is to align the organization to perform at that level. Each function, business unit, team, and individual has a time element in their set of operating objectives. Figure 4 is a brief example of the types of objectives by function. These cascade to business units, teams, and individuals.

Next, each supervisor meets with employees singly and collectively as a team to clarify responsibility, delegate authority, and establish accountability. In every case the people are bound up with objectives that are identifiable in terms of their effect on the corporate brand and other key support goals. Again, the effects are described in terms of cost, time, quantity, innovation, quality, or human reaction; i.e., employee or customer satisfaction.

Finally, the system is completed with the design of the measurement system. The top management team sets the macro measures. These relate to the enhancement of the brand as well as support of other key enterprise goals. These latter may have to do with such high level matters as research for future product innovation or market entry, becoming a supplier and employer of choice, corporate governance, and citizenship. There should also be macro human capital indices such as human capital value added and human capital ROI.

Based on those macro indices functional and divisional executives set operating objectives that directly relate to the branding goal. Also, they will set operational objectives for the other enterprise goals. The top executive team must be consistent with their brand characteristics and operating demands in order for second level executives to align their units with the strategic goals. Typically at the operational level, objectives will be measured by that now familiar combination of cost, time, quantity, quality, and human indices. In the last case the human factors relate to customers. They might be measures of customer acquisition, satisfaction, retention, share of wallet, and referrals.

Figure 4 provides an overall view of brand alignment and how targets are set at each level from the top corporate brand vision all the way through the organization to the resource management level.

BRAND VISION

On Time Every Time

FUNCTIONAL OBJECTIVES

Production and Distribution	**Sales and Marketing**	**Customer Service**	**Administrative Support**
Improve uptime of equipment 98 percent	Get timely market data to R and D first of each month	Anticipated needs of customers. Input information to Knowledge Base	Finance: Have funds available Maintain cash and borrowing sources
Reengineer to reduce rework Six sigma quality	Bring customers in to work with R and D Set quarterly visits	Refer emerging needs to sales Monthly meeting of service, sales, and production	Shorten process cycle times 48 hour turnaround time

HUMAN CAPITAL MANAGEMENT OBJECTIVES

ACQUISITION	MAINTENANCE	DEVELOPMENT	RETENTION
Shorten start time by 20 percent	Shorten pay actions by 15 percent	Deliver service training in 30 days	Involve employees in "timely" solutions

Figure 4. Brand alignment systems targets

At the resource management level we will measure the acquisition, maintenance, utilization, and retention of facilities and equipment and employees. In the case of employees, utilization refers to productivity, quality, and service levels. Also for employees we will add measures of employee development. For the human resources department we will design measures such as hiring costs and time to fill jobs, pay and benefits transaction costs and time cycles, employee turnover rates, and costs. We will also track investments in employee development and the return on those investments in terms of improved performance. One more time: All measures will relate to their impact on the brand. If the brand is perfect service then we hire, pay, train, and retain on the basis of service capability.

Conclusion

At last, through human capital branding we are dealing with the strongest, biggest, highest potential lever that management has, namely people, to improve corporate profits. By driving planning from a human direction (the only active asset) rather than a financial or technological direction (inactive assets) we take advantage of employee motivation and commitment. In short, without motivation and commitment, what do we have? At best, a mass of expensive depreciating assets and a disgruntled, disenfranchised, expensive, under performing workforce.

Human capital branding does not change the structure of organizational management. We still have to plan, organize, direct, and control our investment in various resources. However, human capital branding drives all of this by setting and reinforcing the corporate brand through emphasizing and focusing on how our human capital, will be employed as the catalyst. That is the operative term: catalyst. People are the only catalyst in an organization.

Consider this analogy: We have a match, an ordinary, what used to be called, kitchen match. Its components are a wooden shaft that supports a tip mixture of sulphur and phosphorous. The match is like an asset of the corporation. It contains all the elements needed to generate heat and light. So, why doesn't it just do it? Obviously, it is missing the activator, a human being. No only that, but the human being must know how to use it. If you never saw a match before and didn't know anything about chemistry and pyrotechnics, what would you do with the match to make it light? Would you roll it between your palms? Would you hit it with something, or throw it? Would you bite it? Hopefully not. Which end would you work on if you never saw this thing before? Again, because we know what a match is and how it is to be employed, we rub the mixture end briskly against some abrasive material to create sufficient heat through friction to ignite the chemicals in the tip. But even here, it isn't that simple. Have you ever broken a match by putting too much pressure on it? Have you ever rubbed off the chemicals by repeatedly rubbing the tip with too little pressure? The point of all this is that even some piece of technology as simple as a match requires human intelligence, experience, motivation, and determination to optimize the potential of this tool, the match. How much more important is human effort and commitment for optimizing corporate effectiveness? We can buy the most expensive matches in the world, but if we don't have a knowledgeable workforce committed to igniting these tools, all we have is a factory filled with depreciating, under performing assets.

Endnotes

1. Ries, A. and Ries, L., *The 22 Immutable Laws of Branding*, New York, Harper Collins, 1998, p. 5.
2. Fitz-enz, Jac, *The 8 Practices of Exceptional Companies*, New York, AMACOM, 1997.
3. Deming, W. Edwards, *Out of the Crisis*, Cambridge, MA, MIT, 1986.

CHAPTER TWO

Measuring the Impact of Human Capital

Dave Ulrich PhD

Dave Ulrich is Professor of Business Administration at the University of Michigan. He was named in 2001 as the number one management educator in the world by *Business Week*. Dr. Ulrich is currently on sabbatical serving as president of the Canada Montreal Mission for the Church of Christ of Latter-day Saints. A prolific author and public speaker, Dr. Ulrich has helped generate multiple award-winning national databases that assess organizations' alignment between strategies, human resource practices, and HR competencies. Dr. Ulrich can be reached at dou@umich.edu.

Norm Smallwood

Norm Smallwood is co-founder and President of Results-Based Leadership Inc., which provides education, tools, and consulting services that increase organization and leadership capacity to deliver the right results the right way. He and Dr. Ulrich are the authors of "Why the Bottom Line Isn't: How to Build Value Through People and Organizations" and, with Jack Zenger, of "Results-Based Leadership." Mr. Smallwood can be reached at nsmallwood@rbl.net.

two : 1

Building Intangible Value from the Outside In

Recent history demonstrates that the intangibles of business—quality of leadership, the ability to make things happen quickly, a clear growth strategy, strong functional competencies, and brand recognition—matter in both bear and bull markets. When the dot-com bubble burst, stories of corporate dishonesty grew, and the economy tumbled into recession, some firm's market value fell more than that of others in the same industry. We believe that firms that survived the market credibility crisis did so because their leaders had made the intangibles tangible.

Intangibles show up in business by boosting—or undercutting—investor's confidence in a firm's performance. Baruch Lev, an accounting professor at NYU and the leading thought leader on intangibles, has shown the importance of intangibles as indicated through the market-to-book value (the ratio of capital market value of companies compared to their net asset value). According to Lev, the market-to-book value of the S&P 500 has risen from 1 to over 6 in the last twenty-five years—suggesting that for every $6 of market value, only $1 occurs on the balance sheet. This data shows that the value of many firms comes as much from perceived value as from hard assets. Value, like beauty, is in the eye of the beholder. Firms like Coca-Cola and Merck have high market value from brands and patents. Technology-based firms like Amazon and Exult have high market value with relatively little in the way of either hard assets or patents. And even traditional companies like General Motors and 3M are increasing market value by focusing on brands, ever-aging the Web, and restructuring. Understanding and leveraging intangibles are powerful tools for leaders. When intangibles are defined and operationalized, leaders can make choices that affect not only what happens inside their firm but also how investors value those decisions. While Baruch Lev has offered a precise financial definition of intangibles, for our purposes we define intangibles simply as the value of a company not accounted for by current earnings. This definition suggests a new bottom line. The old bottom line consisted of current earnings on the standard P&L statement. The new bottom line includes current earnings as well as the confidence of investors, customers, and employees in the firm's ability to deliver in the future. The traditionally hard fields of accounting and finance are now coming together with the softer fields of organizational behavior and human resources to help us understand the new bottom line, focused on financial results intangibles. (See "Measuring the Value of People," *Leader to Leader*, Number 27, Winter 2003.)

Intangibles are most clearly visible when comparing firms within an industry, not across industries, and the variations in P/E (price to earnings) ratios of firms within an industry offer evidence of leadership intangibles in both up and down markets. Companies with high intangible value have higher P/E multiples than their competitors in the same industry. Their leaders have earned the perception that they can be trusted to deliver on their promises about the future. Companies with low intangible value have lower P/E multiples than their competitors because of erosion in confidence in the firm and its leadership.

The good news is that leaders can build higher intangible value for their organizations in both up and down markets. Intangibles become visible when they are understood and managed, allowing specific leadership actions and choices to define and deliver them on demand. When this is done, employee commitment, customer intimacy, and investor confidence rise. To illustrate how to build an intangible capability, we will explore the concept of performance culture. We will demonstrate the value of clearly describing what this intangible is and discuss practical ways leaders can build it. In *Why the Bottom Line Isn't* we offer detailed theory and tools for building this and other intangibles that increase organization capability and value.

Building Culture from the Outside In

Organization culture is rightly the focus of many change efforts. For example, organization cultures that are entitlement oriented or too internally focused lack competitive zeal. Most definitions of culture suggest that it is more than random or isolated activities. Your organization begins to have a culture, a unique identity, when its management approaches outlive any one executive and involve more than any single management practice, fad, or era. We prefer to use the term *shared mindset* for this phenomenon because it represents the essence of what's really happening. First, *shared* implies something common among a group of people that holds them together. A *mindset* represents an enduring thought pattern or framework that you bring to all your activities. When truly and deeply shared, a mindset becomes the enduring identity of the firm not only in the collective mind of employees, but also of customers and investors. A shared mindset exists when customers and investors outside and employees inside have a common view of the organization's identity.

Why do we include customers and investors in our description of a shared mindset? Focusing only on the patterns inside an organization that affect employee behavior ignores how customers and investors perceive and respond to the culture. Dell's commitment to rapid service, for example, affects customers as much as employees—and the perceptions and expectations of Dell's customers also affect employees. Merging internal and external views of identity means that customers perceive the firm in ways that match how employees perceive the firm. *Shared* mindset also shifts focus away from what executives *say* is important in generic value statements to what employees, customers, and investors *demonstrate* is important through their actions.

How A Shared Mindset Creates Intangible Value

A shared mindset produces intangible value when it creates an identity or positive reputation in the mind of employees, customers, and investors that is tied not to a person or product but to the firm itself. This mindset becomes a self-fulfilling prophecy when it affects how each stakeholder behaves toward the firm.

Employees will be attracted to firms where they perceive a fit between their personal hopes, values, and skills and the existing mindset at the firm. Employee commitment, productivity, and behavior both shape and are shaped by the identity of the firm. Employees who choose to work for Marriott must realize up front that they will be expected to provide exceptional customer service. Once hired, they accept management practices that reinforce the customer service mantra. Employees who don't fit with the service agenda are likely to leave. A shared mindset changes and reinforces employee thinking and action.

Customers also demonstrate their commitment to a firm's mindset or identity. When a firm develops a reputation for quality, service, or price, customers begin to rely on this identity and do business with the firm based on it. This identity of the firm in the mind of its best customers becomes a firm brand and demonstrates the impact of mindset on customer value. Firm brands are tied not to a single product but to the identity of the firm. Recent research shows that firms with strong and visible brands such as McDonald's, American Express, Harley Davidson, Herman Miller, and so forth create higher shareholder value in part because they have a positive identity as a firm in both up and down markets. Possessing a firm brand becomes even more important for Web-based sales. Firms on the Internet with a known identity and positive reputation attract customers much more than unknown firms do.

Shared mindset also affects investors in two ways. First, investors have a mindset that defines a company and its overall intangibles. Investors may gravitate toward firms with positive identities (as with the run-up on Cisco stock in the dot-com bubble) or rush away from those with negative reputations (as with the explosive run-down on Enron stock). Second, investors may be affected by the extent to which employees have a shared mindset. When every contact with a company reveals the same set of values and goals, it sends a powerful message. On the other hand, if what you hear depends on whom you talk to, the overall message may be one of confusion.

Creating a Shared Mindset

How do you create this outside-in shared mindset? We propose a four-phase process that creates a shared mindset that affects employees, customers, and investors:

1. Create the desired identity.
2. Determine how to make the identity real to customers.
3. Determine how to make the identity real to employees.
4. Build an action plan for implementation.

Phase 1: Create the Desired Identity

We have worked with more than a hundred executive teams to create a desired identity or shared mindset. Some were creating a desired identity for the entire organization; others were representing a division, a plant, or a function. Regardless of scope, the process for crafting a shared mindset is similar.

First, ask each individual to write a response to the question "What are the top three things we want to be known for by our best customers in the future?" This question turns attention outward rather than inward by seeing the organization through the eyes of the customers. It highlights the best customers, not the average ones. It focuses attention by asking for three answers, not an unlimited number. It emphasizes identity by asking what the unit is known for, not what it does. And it points toward the future, not the past or present.

Second, collect the responses and categorize them. For example, a team of ten people will give you thirty total items. Sort the thirty into common answers. Of the thirty, you might have seven that address service, six that focus on value, and five on reliability, with the other twelve scattered over other categories. It is important to sort rigorously. For example, some people will write things like service, reliability, or ease of doing business and imply that they all mean the same thing. This is not a safe assumption. At this point in the exercise, the goal is to see the extent to which a shared mindset exists among the top team, which requires rigor of language and ideas.

Performance appraisal questions show what your firm really values.

Third, add the total number of responses in the top three categories (eighteen in this example) and divide by total responses (thirty) for a rough measure of shared mindset (67 percent in this case). Our rule of thumb is that a desired level is 80 percent—which is rare on the first round. Generally, even when firms have strong cultures, executives use differing language and even differ in the aspects of the company they regard as crucial to its success when seen through the lens of customers.

Fourth, talk about themes in the results. Cluster and define themes that emerge from the responses and redo the exercise to see if an 80 percent consensus on the top three items can be reached. Reaching 80 percent consensus generally takes a couple of hours at most. After debate and dialogue, company leaders can usually agree upon what they want to be known for by their best customers. Fifth, put the themes into words that resonate with customers. For example, at Domino's Pizza in the early 1990s, we did this exercise with the top fourteen executives. When asked the top three things they wanted to be known for, responses included service, reliability, good product, good value, talented employees, easy access, and many more. The unity score was about 40–45 percent after Step 2. On discussion, they came up with themes around quality, service, and talent. Then they lowing desired mindset: *hot, fresh, tasty pizza delivered on time by friendly people who drive safely.*

Sixth, test the articulated mindset with customers to make sure it is right. This final step in building a shared mindset˜making sure it resonates with target customers' is probably the most important. If the desired mindset will not cause customers to pick your firm over competitors, it is the wrong one. This means having executives share their mindset with customers in one-on-one meetings, in focus groups, and in other customer contact and research methods to assure that it will influence their buying choices.

Phase 2: Determine How to Make the Identity Real to Customers

When you are confident that the desired identity will have meaning and impact for targeted customers, the next step is to find ways to make the stated identity real to those customers in their terms. (Phase 3 is a concurrent effort to make it real to employees so that employees have the right mindset and skills to deliver on the customer promises.) To make the identity real to customers find points of contact—touch points˜between the firm and the target customer and create ways to make the desired identity real in each one.

For example, at Domino's Pizza, executives picked four touch points between the firm and the pizza-buying customer: the call, the delivery, the pizza, and the box. To communicate service during the call, they worked to answer the call by the fourth ring, have a friendly greeting, use caller ID to verify name and address of customer, and make sure staff thanked customers for their patronage. To ensure on-time delivery drivers had maps and drove in areas they knew. In addition, the drivers were friendly people who dressed in clean uniforms, had correct change, and used a positive script in communicating with the customer.

The pizza was hot, fresh, and tasty because it was made of good quality ingredients, packed in heat bags to maintain warmth, and delivered quickly after cooking. But as executives thought more about the customer contact, they realized that the call lasted about 30 seconds, the delivery exchange about a minute, and the meal about 10 minutes, but the box often sat around customer kitchens for hours (and in many cases for days). So they chose to use the box for advertising their firm brand and identity. Rather than merely have the box give their name and say "our drivers carry less than $20 in change"—which might communicate an attitude of suspicion toward customers˜they placed coupons, slogans, and commitments about the pizza on the box itself.

Phase 3: Determine How to Make the Identity Real to Employees

To make the identity real for customers, companies need to put plans and systems in place that ensure that employees' daily actions reflect the shared mindset. We have found several critical factors for leaders who want to make the mindset real to every employee, including treatment of talent, reward systems, and training and development.

> *Points of contact*—touch points—
> *let you make the desired identity*
> *real to your customers.*

Talent Flow. How a company moves talent into, up, through, and out of the organization sends a powerful message to employees, customers, and investors about the company's values and identity. Hiring new people who embody the right mindset and promoting employees who live the mindset — removing those who don't— become critical tools for embedding culture. Employees observe what is happening and adapt their behaviors accordingly. Southwest Airlines rigorously screens flight attendants. It looks for employees who have technical skills, but even more it seeks those who are predisposed to engage with passengers, doing the required job with humor and enthusiasm. And in mergers and acquisitions this type of screening becomes critical—for the survival of the combined company, it's essential to assess talent and ensure that the right talent stays and the wrong talent, the talent that doesn't fit, leaves.

Rewards. Reward systems both change and reinforce behavior. The goal of a reward system is to turn goals into measures of behavior and outcomes, and then allocate rewards based on the extent to which employees behave in the right way and deliver the desired outcomes.

For a quick look at your firm's current mindset, take a look at its performance management system. The appraisal questions show what your firm values as defined by what it rewards. This reveals its real mindset—which may be quite different from the one fondly espoused in vision statements and other earnest pronouncements. It's also useful to invite customers to review the performance management process and report the extent to which the behaviors and outcomes on the appraisal document reflect what they as customers want from the firm.

Training and Development. Designing and delivering training courses sends messages about what matters. At the same time, it offers leaders messages. An audit of the content of training and development experiences should show that these investments focus on the desired mindset, both conceptually and pragmatically.

Phase 4: Build an Action Plan for Implementation

Developing a shared mindset will change how employees, customers, and investors think and act. When your employees behave in ways that customers would like them to behave, employees, customers, and investors are all well served. In the fourth phase, the ideas from preceding phases are translated to action. To be successful, action plans need to be specific, start small, and have leadership support.

We often ask leaders to look at the ways that they could make the culture real to customers and employees and pick two or three specific areas they could focus on. Prioritizing a few things and getting them done is more useful than talking about a lot of things and accomplishing little or nothing.

Hire new people who embody the right mindset, promote those who live the mindset, remove those who don't.

Conclusion

We have described four steps necessary to achieve a shared mindset: articulate your unity of identity (what you want to be known for by your best customers); make this identity real to customers at every touch point; make this experience real to employees through selection, development, bonus, and performance management processes; and finally, build an action plan for implementation.

When a strong and desired shared mindset exists between your firm and its customers, tangible and intangible value is created. Customers are more likely to do repeat business, the right kind of employees are more likely to be attracted to your firm, and investors have greater confidence that the growth plans of the firm will materialize in the future.

Developing a shared mindset is just one example of how an intangible can add value to an organization. When leaders understand how they can build intangible value, they can begin to identity specific actions they can take to strengthen their firm brand and market value.

Recently, we have witnessed how business leaders, impact on the market value of their companies can be a double-edged sword. Some executives inflated market value through deceit and manipulation and ultimately devastated their companies. Real leaders built tangible and intangible value and increased the market value of their businesses for the long term.

Leaders' impact on the market value of their companies can be a double-edged sword.

John Boudreau PhD

John Boudreau PhD is Professor of Human Resource Studies and the Center for Advanced Human Resource Studies (CAHRS) at Cornell University. Dr. Boudreau is also a visiting professor at USC. He is recognized worldwide for breakthrough research on the bridge between superior talent and sustainable competitive advantage. A Fellow of the National Academy of Human Resources, Dr. Boudreau has written more than 45 books and articles. His research findings have been published in such noted publications as *Management Science*, *Journal of Applied Psychology*, *Organizational Behavior and Human Decision Processes*, *Personnel Psychology*, *Human Relations*, *Industrial Relations*, and *Journal of Human Resources Costing and Accounting*. Dr. Boudreau can be reached at jwb6@cornell.edu.

Peter Ramstad

Peter Ramstad is Executive Vice President for Strategy and Finance at Personnel Decisions International (PDI). Prior to joining PDI, he was a partner with a public accounting firm focusing on financial, operational, and systems consulting in high tech and service environments. A Certified Public Accountant, Certified Management Accountant, and a member of the AICPA, Mr. Ramstad holds degrees in Math and Accounting with minors in Economics and Computer Science. He speaks frequently at professional conferences in human resource management, finance and accounting, and designs and conducts both public and firm-specific executive education. Mr. Ramstad can be reached at pete.ramstad@personneldecisions.com.

two : 2

Tapping the Full Potential of HRIS:
Shifting the HR Paradigm from Service Delivery to a Talent Decision Science

Introduction

The technical capabilities of human resource information systems (HRIS) are undeniable. HRIS vendors, service providers, and their customers constantly find new ways to enhance the speed, capacity, accessibility, and global reach of their systems. It is increasingly possible to capture HR data as it is entered into the system, making instantaneous data updates possible. Data warehouses are increasingly flexible and responsive, making it possible for a growing array of HR and business decision makers to have deep access to the information, on a real-time and global basis. Data interfaces are increasingly web-based and intuitive, allowing users to easily construct custom reports that slice and present HR data in virtually any form desired. A dizzying array of statistics, ratios, and descriptions of the HR function, HR processes, and employees are potentially available to virtually anyone at any time. Organizations are investing millions of dollars on HRIS design, implementation, and service.

Perhaps this is all quite justified. It is no secret that the human element of organizations is increasingly important to global organizational success (Boudreau, 2003; Boudreau & Ramstad, 2002; Boudreau, Ramstad & Dowling, 2003), and there is an increasingly rich array of measurement products designed to organize and interpret the data from HR information systems (Boudreau & Ramstad, 2003). Organization leaders increasingly encourage and support efforts to make the human element of the business more quantified, precise, and numerical. There is huge pressure to reduce unnecessary expenditures in HR, and if better HRIS can identify where those cost savings can be attained, the sizable investment in them can be justified.

Yet, the promise of HRIS remains in many ways unfulfilled. The most recent data from an ongoing study of the evolution of the HR profession by the Center for Effective Organizations at the University of Southern California (Lawler & Mohrman, 2003) suggests that while HR professionals largely believe that their activities and role have changed in the last five years, and that they have shifted toward more strategic and less administrative tasks, when they are asked to indicate the percentage of time they spend on various HR activities, the proportions have changed very little. For example, the time spent maintaining employee records was 15.4 percent in 1995 and 14.2 percent in 2001, and the time spent in the role of strategic business partner was 21.9 percent in 1995 versus 23.2 percent in 2001.

The table on the next page lists the highest-frequency HR measures, according to a Conference Board study (Gates, 2002).

While these measures are certainly relevant and potentially valuable, they hardly seem to reflect the depth and sophistication of today's global human resource data warehouses. Perhaps even more important, the measures listed in Table 1 largely reflect descriptive information about the workforce, rather than information relevant to the role of talent in achieving business success. For example, how should average seniority be interpreted? In some organizations or jobs, higher seniority may well indicate greater learning, experience, and value to the organization. In others, higher seniority may indicate a failure to move

Highest-Frequency HR Measures	
Turnover (96%)	Voluntary resignation (84%)
Average compensation (82%)	Average workforce age (77%)
Diversity (76%)	Compensation/total cost (76%)
Average seniority (75%)	Work accident frequency (74%)
Percent with variable compensation (71%)	Percent with stock options (71%)

Source: Gates, Stephen (2002). "Value at Work: The Risks and Opportunities of Human Capital Measurement and Reporting." Conference Board Report # r-1316-02-rr. New York: Conference Board.

Table 1.

talent to higher-level roles, or to bring in newer workers who have needed external perspectives or knowledge. Similarly, low turnover may indicate that the organization is retaining talent that is key to its success, but they may also indicate a failure to act decisively to remove low performers.

In short, for all the promise and investment in HRIS, their potential remains largely untapped. Today's HRIS usually automate and accelerate the traditional HR activities and functional services. This is not unimportant, but it is certainly not tapping the full potential of information systems to support decisions about talent that directly enhance the strategic success of the organization. The dilemma is that strategic decision support cannot be achieved by incremental improvements in traditional HRIS applications to HR activities and functions. It requires a fundamental shift in our perspective about human resources and in our approach to the design and use of HR information.

We can learn a great deal about how to accomplish this paradigm shift, but we must look beyond the HR function to the information systems in functions such as finance, marketing, and supply-chain management. In this article, we will describe some of these lessons, and suggest how HR professionals can embark on a path that will tap the strategic decision power of their HRIS. To gain a perspective on the development of HRIS systems, it is helpful to contrast their development with financial systems. Each revolution in computer technology (mainframes, minicomputers, networks, large scale data base servers, PCs, graphical user interfaces, internet, etc.) arrived at the same time, affecting both the HRIS and financial information systems. The difference is that finance and HR were at very different stages in their maturity, when technology arrived.

Automated Financial Information Systems Quickly Became Effective Decision Support Systems

When large-scale automation became feasible for bookkeeping, accounting, and finance functions, there was already a very clear distinction between the transactions (bookkeeping), professional practices (accounting), and the decision science (finance). The initial benefits came from automating the operations, with efficiency gains achieved in the transaction (bookkeeping) activities, where labor had historically accomplished the routine bookkeeping tasks of processing purchase orders, receipts, accounts payable, inventory, invoicing, and accounts receivable. Long before computers arrived, there were well-understood distinctions and contributions from bookkeeping, accounting and finance, and a clear link from the data to strategic organizational decisions. Bookkeeping practices were well established, and the results of these activities were logically linked to accounting (capital market reporting, management accounting, auditing) and to the decision models of finance (return on investment, portfolio analysis, capital budgeting). When the bookkeeping was automated, the efficiency immediately improved. More important, however, was that as this information became available faster and with deeper detail, it flowed almost immediately into more timely and accurate finance decisions. This is because the logic of the financial decision models that used the transaction information was already well-understood and firmly established within the organization. Similarly, the accounting system had established processes and practices for consolidating information from bookkeeping since the early 1900s, so the frameworks necessary to have broad and diverse business units using common transaction and reporting standards existed long before the first computers showed up on the scene.

Why HR Information Systems Have Yet to Become Effective Decision Support Systems

Computerized financial information systems rather quickly became a decision tool, but HRIS has still largely failed to achieve the same deep and logical connection to decisions that drive strategic business success. The history of automation in the finance discipline provides some important contrasts with the history of HRIS in the HR function. For example, the HR transactions that usually benefited from automation first were in payroll and benefit processing. Unlike automation financial systems, payroll and benefits transactions had relatively little connection with the HR professional practices of staffing, development, performance management, compensation, labor relations, etc. In fact, the information required for effective payroll and benefits transaction processing was more closely linked to accounting, such expense codes, overtime authorization, tax tables, etc. Before automation, payroll and benefits reporting frameworks were largely used for accounting control and compliance, so automated HR systems emphasized such things as pay grades, exempt/non-exempt, union/non-union, etc. Automating payroll and benefits increased transaction efficiency, but the information arguably created far more value for the management accounting systems, through more accurate labor cost data, than for improving HR processes or enhancing strategic talent decisions.

This is not to diminish the significant efforts to enhance decisions using the results of payroll and benefits automation. However, the lack of a deep, logical, and clear connection between transactions, professional practices, and strategic decisions is a key reason that improved data collection through HR automation have often yielded disappointing results.

Turnover reporting provides another good example. The payroll system tracks the transactions when employees leave the organization, so automating payroll provided an opportunity to automate, collect, and process turnover events. Existing payroll system separated voluntary from involuntary turnover, because these classifications were already important for external reporting regarding unemployment compensation, so their meaning was relatively clear. Typically, however, the new automated system added turnover classifications, in a turnover cause table. In the late 1990s business leaders felt the pain of increased talent mobility and shortages in key roles, and looked to HR professional to help. HR professionals turned to their HRIS, and often found ten, twenty, or more system codes for reasons why people leave (retirement, take another position, family issues, relocation, etc.). The modern computerized reporting system allowed analysts to calculate the number of separations in each category, even sliced by any number of demographic or business unit variables. Yet, this yields little insight into whether this was significant for business success. Several CFOs we worked with have noted that, "we have ten to twenty turnover codes in the system, yet no one can tell me whether turnover is hurting or helping my business units."

What is the key difference, then, between the rapid advancement of automated financial systems as strategic decision tools, and the less-than-rapid advancement of HRIS?

The Importance of Decision Science for Talent . . . Talentship

We have noted (e.g., Boudreau & Ramstad, 2002) that in the financial and customer/product markets, there is a clear distinction between the professional practices required to operate in the market and the decision science which supports analysis and deployment of the resources from that market. For example, there is a clear distinction between accounting (the professional practice) and finance (the decision science). Accounting for revenues, costs, taxes, and interest is important but very different from financial tools to decide about appropriate debt structure, internal rate-of-return thresholds, etc. There is an equally clear distinction between the professional practice of sales and the decision science of marketing. Excellent sales practices are critical, but very different from the decisions about customer segmentation, market position, product portfolio, etc. The examples above show that the clarity of this distinction, and the shared frameworks that integrate professional practices and decision sciences were key to the rapid evolution of automated financial systems into strategic decision tools.

We have coined the term "talentship" for the decision science applied to the human element of organizations, and defined the goal of talentship as "to increase the success of the organization by improving decisions that impact or depend on talent resources" (Boudreau & Ramstad, 2002). Talentship reframes HR beyond excellent service delivery to excellent talent decisions, just as finance reframes capital management beyond excellent accounting practices to excellent decisions about money. This fundamental shift in perspective has significant implications for the role of the HR function in organizations (Boudreau & Ramstad, 2002), for HR measurement (Boudreau & Ramstad, 2003); for how HR defines its processes and accounts for their contribution (Boudreau & Ramstad, 2001); and for the design and assessment of global talent and leadership systems (Boudreau, Ramstad, & Dowling, 2003). For more information about talentship and the HC BRidge® framework, please visit: http://www.hcbridge.com.

The shift toward a decision science for talent has equally important implications for the evolution of HRIS. Automated financial systems advanced quickly in part because of the logic linking bookkeeping with accounting (capital market reporting, management accounting, auditing) and accounting with financial decision models (return on investment, portfolio analysis, capital budgeting). For HRIS to advance as a decision tool, we will need a similar framework for talent resources. Next, we consider such a framework, called HC BRidge®, and its implications for HRIS evolution.

HC BRidge®: Connecting Talent to Sustainable Strategic Success

The HC BRidge® framework, in the diagram below, describes the elements linking talent and sustainable strategic success. The framework is not a rigid set of rules, but can be adapted to different business or competitive situations. It is based on the three generic elements: Impact, Effectiveness, and Efficiency, that are common to successful existing decision frameworks like finance and marketing. In the

HC BRidge® framework, each of these fundamental questions is broken down further into a set of linking elements that can be used to articulate it more explicitly. HC BRidge® is an outline, like EVA or ROIC, in which each linking element also represents deeper logic and analysis. For example, the linking element of resources and processes represents more detailed analysis of the value chain and unique organizational capabilities that support sustainable strategic success.

We find the HC BRidge® model useful as a planning tool, working from sustainable strategic success at the top, to derive implications for HR practices and investments at the bottom. We also find HC BRidge® useful in guiding execution, starting with HR investments and practices at the bottom and exploring how well and how clearly they link upward to sustainable strategic success. We also find the framework useful when talent questions start in the middle, as when HR professionals are confronted with a client request such as, we need to get our manufacturing employees to be more innovative. The model can guide a dialogue that begins with human capacity (in this case innovativeness) identify its links to key actions, talent, and business processes (moving upward). If it is indeed determined to be a high-impact capacity, the model can help to guide a discussion of the appropriate HR practices that will most enhance it (moving downward from the human capacity element).

A good point of view encourages and enables everyone in the organization to ask great questions about talent. Questions that identify the most important talent issues, the most promising talent investments, and the best use of scarce talent resources. So, a powerful way to evolve toward talentship is for HR leaders simply to begin asking questions using this point of view as part of everyday work with their constituents.

The HC BRidge® framework is built on the three major anchor points, and their associated fundamental questions.[1] We will illustrate the framework using an example of Federal Express in the Asia-Pacific region, because it is a familiar organization that offers some interesting insights into the model.

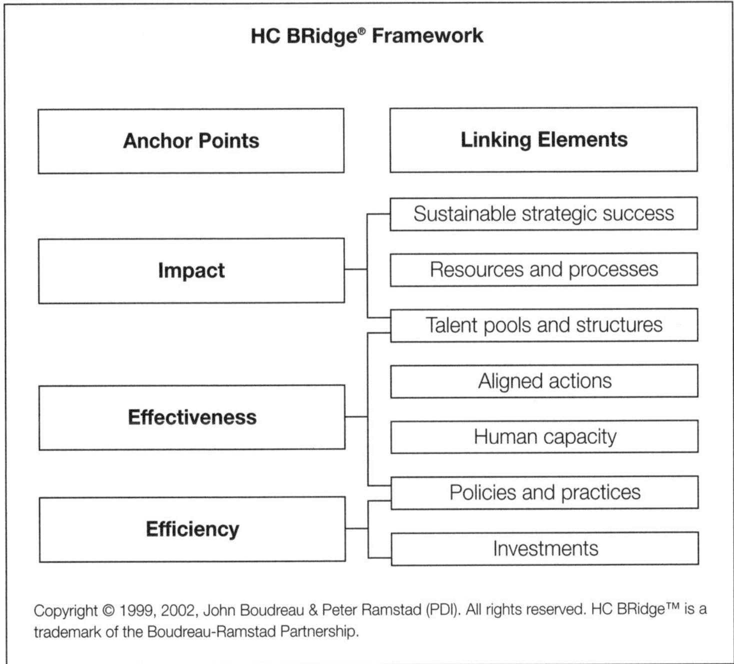

Table 2.

Impact asks, "For which talent pools do quality differences have the biggest impact on our competitive success?" This question, and the tools that support it, often unearths surprising talent potential. For example, with Federal Express Asia-Pacific, some of the largest opportunities to improve on-time performance and customer satisfaction might lie with a relatively undervalued talent pool—couriers and dispatchers. In our investigation of the talent issues at Federal Express, we found that it was not unusual for couriers to encounter a customer who said, "Can you wait fifteen minutes, because I will have twenty more packages for you." The quality of responses, multiplied across hundreds of incidents every day, contributed significantly to the effectiveness or ineffectiveness of the entire system. Waiting at the wrong time could cause a truckload of packages to miss the timing window at the airport hub, and be delivered late. Not waiting, when time is available, caused needless customer dissatisfaction. We find that most HR and business leaders searching for the key talent at Federal Express will identify pilots, logistics designers, and top leaders, which are undeniably important. Yet, in terms of strategic success improvement, changes in the quality of the courier-dispatcher talent pool was even more pivotal. Organizations that systematically consider the Impact anchor point often discover their own examples of previously overlooked key talent.

Effectiveness asks, "Do our HR practices make a significant difference in the strategically-important talent pools?" This gets at the effect of HR programs on capability (can employees contribute?), opportunity (do employees get the chance to contribute?), and motivation (do employees want to contribute?), which are the elements of Human Capacity in the HC BRidge® model. At Federal Express Asia-Pacific, the aligned action would be the response to the customer request. Understanding the importance of this action would reveal new opportunities to direct HR programs to create more aligned actions through capability, opportunity, and motivation. For example, couriers in Asia have very different social status compared to their customers, than in the US. In Asia, it is much more typical for couriers to defer to the customer. Thus, saying "No" to a customer request to wait would be very unusual. Yet, given the strategic impact of this action, it may well make sense to invest in ways to change the motivation and capability to say "No." In fact, it may also make sense to change opportunity, perhaps by providing increased alternatives to the couriers, such as additional shipping trucks that are available to handle overflow. Couriers could then say, "No, I can't take your additional packages now, but I can send someone who can." Thus, the talent issue reveals implications for logistics design.

Efficiency asks, "What is the level and quality of HR practices we produce with the resources that we spend?" In the courier-dispatcher example, HR might have benchmarked its efficiency by measuring couriers and dispatchers in terms of cost-per-hire, pay-per-employee, or time-to-train. Usually, such benchmarking suggests where costs/time can be reduced, and/or where volume of HR activity can be increased, without spending more. Yet, the more complete analysis of Federal Express suggests that it might make sense to spend more resources than their competitors, to get the right couriers and dispatchers, precisely because of their strategic importance. Competitors battling to reduce HR expenses may actually be a symptom that they have overlooked the strategic opportunity. The existing point of view about HR typically reflects mostly efficiency, because the existing organizational decision systems (accounting, budgeting, operations) can only see the cost and time spent on HR programs and employees. These existing systems are not wrong, but they are myopic to the connection between HR investments and organizational outcomes.

The key is not to rigidly adopt HC BRidge®, or any model, but rather to develop the point of view about talent that best supports a collaborative decision process, that clearly connects talent with organizational strategic success, and that enables a reliable, consistent, and productive approach to talent analysis, decisions, and evaluation. The best organizations integrate the HC BRidge® framework into their other management systems (strategy, capital budgeting, operational budgeting, financial reporting, product line analysis, etc.), so that the talent decisions are directly linked to the critical decision making processes and frameworks used within the organization. Whatever the final form of the decision model, it appears useful that it reflect the three anchor points of Impact, Effectiveness, and Efficiency.

The Next Evolution of HRIS

The evolution and decision influence of financial reporting systems has been fundamentally assisted by the clear and logical frameworks that connect data from bookkeeping and accounting to the decision science of finance, and this suggests that similarly clear connections will be necessary for HRIS to evolve to be a useful decision tool, and not simply a process for automating HR data. The HC BRidge® framework offers a model for logically connecting HR policies, practices, and investments, and the fundamental processes, resources, and competitive challenges facing organizations. So, we can use the HC BRidge® framework to suggest a path toward the next evolution of HRIS, as true decision support systems for talent.

Decisions, Not Data

It may seem counterintuitive to suggest that information systems emphasize something other than data and information. Yet, history in all fields of business and science show that information systems achieve their potential only when they improve decisions. HHC BRidge,® like EVA and ROI in finance, provides an example of a decision-based framework. It describes the logical connections between the elements that define both the investments and the returns to the talents of the organization. Today's HRIS are typically designed and organized to reflect the data and reports typically required or requested of human resource managers. Such data and reports were developed at a time when the HR profession was defined by its programs and practices. Organizing HRIS to reflect decisions has significant implications for both the design and accountability of such systems. Today, HRIS are largely evaluated based on their efficiency, the amount and breadth of data they can access, their accessibility, and their usage levels. In fact, none of these directly measures the most important outcome of an HRIS, improved decisions about organizational talent that enhance strategic success. Future HRIS evaluations should track not only usage levels, but the perceived and actual quality of the decisions they support. Moreover, the concept of pivotal talent suggests that not all talent decisions are equal. Truly strategic systems will not only improve talent decisions, but they will help to identify where and why talent contributes to strategic success, and target their effectiveness to those talent areas.

Necessary and Sufficient Conditions, Not Just HR Techniques

Today's HRIS, like the HR profession they support, focus largely on tracking HR techniques, such as tests, recruitment sources, training programs, performance assessment processes, and incentive systems. Many HRIS are devoted primarily to automating these processes. They provide compelling statistics showing the costs, activity levels, and the numbers of individuals affected by each technique. Techniques are evaluated with data, including the correlation between test scores and job performance, or the number of candidates generated by different recruitment sources. Some advanced HRIS go even further, providing process maps that describe and track activity levels across related techniques. One example is tracking the number of individuals who flow through the different stages of a staffing system, from recruitment, to selection, to offers, to hires, to retention.

Yet, information systems that support finance, marketing, and other disciplines go further. The financial system not only tracks each element of cash flow, it provides a framework that defines the requirements for high returns on cash investments, and diagnostic conditions that can pinpoint where those requirement are not being met. Future HRIS should learn from this perspective, to incorporate what we have called necessary and sufficient conditions for process success (Boudreau & Ramstad, 2001). The HC BRidge® framework provides one high-level set of such necessary and sufficient conditions, by defining the three anchor points of Impact, Effectiveness, and Efficiency. Within the Effectiveness element of HR policies and practices, there are important opportunities to take the concept even further.

For example, we have suggested that the staffing process can be conceived through the lens of a supply chain. This perspective suggests the importance of tracking not only the cost, volume, and quality of each separate technique that is a part of the staffing process, but the conditions that the staffing process must meet (Boudreau & Ramstad, 2001). These conditions include generating a sufficient quality and quantity of applicants, identifying the most appropriate candidates, constructing attractive and competitive employment offers, ensuring that offers are accepted by the best candidates, orientation of the new hires to ensure that they are retained, and then long-term employment relationships that encourage the best to stay and those who don't fit to leave. These conditions are well known in both the professional and scholarly world of HR, but it is surprising how difficult it is to collect and analyze data to reflect them. Typical HRIS are simply too rigidly defined to generate standard reports on each staffing technique, with little integration across them. Even when users attempt to analyze the entire system, they often find that key data (such as the qualifications of applicants) is only associated with one element of the process, and cannot be retrieved or linked with other elements. As a simple test, imagine trying to examine the qualifications of a sample of your own employees, taking when they were job applicants, and compare a group who stayed for at least three years, to those who left in the first three years. Typically, the applicant qualifications are available only at the time of application, to generate standard recruiting reports, but are not easily connected to subsequent stages of the staffing system.

Such necessary and sufficient conditions exist not only in staffing systems, but in other key areas of HR management, such as motivation, engagement, learning, labor relations, etc. For future HRIS to achieve true decision support, such frameworks should be used not only to explore the existing data, but also to design the data elements that define the system in the first place. In that way, like financial information systems, the logic of the decision model enhances the information system, and the data from the information system improves the logic.

Synergy, Not Silos

Recent research suggests that HR programs work as bundles, with the effects of one program affecting another, either in concert or in conflict. The HC BRidge® framework reflects this in the Effectiveness anchor point, and in particular in the connection between HR programs and human capacity. In our work with organizations, the COM concept (Capability, Opportunity, Motivation) provides a useful organizing framework for measuring and diagnosing the underlying cause of variations in employee performance and aligned actions. Decades of literature suggest that an appropriate balance of the COM elements is key, and that if any one of them nears zero, then performance is impossible. These two ideas—HR programs as interrelated bundles that contribute to a necessary balance of COM elements—have significant implications for HRIS as well.

Future HRIS must do better at reflecting the interactions between HR functional systems. For example, organizations that employ team-based organizational structures perform better when reward systems reflect team outcomes. While it seems obvious that the systems should compliment each other, it is not unusual for organizations to implement team-based performance structures, but to maintain performance management systems that focus on individual achievements, or worse, that actually create zero-sum outcomes (such as forced-distribution performance ratings). Viewing HR investments, programs, and practices as a portfolio is more appropriate than viewing them as separate services, and future HRIS may do well to draw on portfolio theory and financial systems for their inspiration.

A significant connecting point between HR activities and their ultimate outcomes, is how they affect the level and balance among three fundamental components of human capacity: capability, opportunity, and motivation (COM). Today's HRIS often focus on one or another of these outcomes, and most frequently contain data on capability-related elements such as skills, knowledge, competencies, etc. Employee motivation and engagement are increasingly available through attitude surveys, but they are surprisingly rarely linked to the capability elements. Opportunity is least-often reflected in today's HRIS, though the raw data reflecting organizational structures and reporting relationships is usually available. There is a very deep history of research on organizational structures, both informal and formal, and their effects on knowledge (Boudreau, 2003) that can be used by future HRIS. However, the most critical change for the future is that HRIS must develop systems and structures that reflect not only the level of each of the COM components, but their balance as well.

Self-Service Based on Capability, Not Just Cost

Future HRIS will increasingly create value through their ability to efficiently deliver HR activities through self-service platforms such as web portals and voice-response systems. Today, the promise of such delivery is largely expressed in cost savings that accrue from the reduced need for administrative time and effort within the HR organization. Certainly, such self-service delivery has enabled many HR organizations to reduce their functional budgets and headcount, and to successfully shift responsibility for data entry and even report generation to employees and managers. Certainly, such systems can achieve significant benefits for HR leaders, employees, and business clients, through greater data accuracy, timeliness, and speed. However, when self-service is driven largely by cost savings, it can be seen as a shell game in which HR cleverly shifts their functional budget items by increasing the workload of busy line managers and employees. We are rapidly reaching the point at which much of the low-hanging fruit has been taken, by shifting appropriate tasks from the HR function to employees and managers. Pressing for further cost savings is likely to increase the chances of being seen as merely cost-shifting.

However, future HRIS can avoid this problem by redefining the basis on which self-service applications are built. Rather than only cost-reductions and efficiency, future self-service applications can be based on the capability and expertise of the clients they are designed to serve. We can see early examples today, in the combination of online training and artificial intelligence built into many benefits enrollment systems, that help employees understand the implications of the benefits choices they are making. Yet, it seems fair to say that the link between user capability and HRIS applications today is largely focused on preparing users to work with the application. There is much greater potential in this connection in the future.

Financial systems educate by their very nature. Users learn relationships between financial ratios and money flows by using the system itself. Users are expected to become more sophisticated in concepts such as ROI, NPV, and EVA, so that the systems can be designed to allow them to do more sophisticated analysis and vary their assumptions. Finance professionals often educate users, not so much on how to use the applications, but on the principles that underlie the financial decision concepts on which the applications are based. In the same way, we envision that future HR professionals, particularly those with strong functional expertise, will so much more than service design and delivery, becoming expert educators on the principles, necessary and sufficient conditions, and frameworks that help business leaders and employees understand the connections between talent and business outcomes. The role of decision scientist for talent will not be limited to HR professionals, so redefining self-service to include user education will be essential.

Talent "Decision Scientists" Not Merely HR Partners and Clients

Virtually every proposal or evaluation of HRIS investments includes the idea that such systems will not only increase transactional efficiency and speed, but that they will also free the HR organization from its administrative burden, to allow it to spend more time on its important strategic role. Yet, the capability of HRIS to truly support HR professionals in this role still significantly lags the rhetoric. More evolved decision systems like finance have much to teach us about the evolution of HRIS on this domain. A good decision science has its greatest value in framing and structuring the questions, not in simply providing answers to existing questions. Our work with the HHC BRidge® framework in many companies demonstrates this. The most tangible value of the framework is that it provides an organized way for HR professionals, business leaders, employees, and others to sensibly and logically understand information about talent, just as financial systems help leaders sensibly and logically understand the vast array of information about money and financial capital.

Conclusion

Information systems are ultimately for decision support, and decision support requires deep and logical decision models. Building better decision models for talent will require that HR professionals move beyond defining their roles in terms of their activities, services, and clients. They must shift the paradigm to build on a logical decision science for talent, and shift from thinking only of client service to a partnership to help those within and outside the HR function make their greatest contribution to that decision science. The table below captures some of the key distinctions. The HR profession must drive this evolution, or others will do it for them.

Traditional HRIS	Future HRIS
The sytem gathers and delivers data, reports, and information about programs and their effects to HR leaders and their clients in a timely and useful manner.	Decisions about our pivotal organizational talents are much better when decision-makers have and use the HRIS.
Key service level measures:	Necessary and sufficient conditions:
• Amount of data in the warehouse	• Necessary data are in the system
• Number of reports generated or available	• Clients use the system
• Usage rates of clients	• Users understand which decisions matter most
• Client satisfaction	• Users apply a valid decision science logic

Table 3.

References and Further Reading

Boudreau, J.W. (2003). "Strategic Knowledge Measurement and Management." In S.E. Jackson, M. Hitt and A.S. DeNisi (eds.). *Managing Knowledge for Sustained Competitive Advantage.* San Francisco: Jossey-Bass/Pfeiffer, pp. 360–396.

Boudreau, J.W., Dunford, B. B., & Ramstad, P. M. (2001). "The Human Capital Impact on e-Business: The Case of Encyclopedia Britannica." In N. Pal & J.M. Ray (Eds.) *Pushing The Digital Frontier,* Chapter 10, pp. 192–221. New York: Amacom.

Boudreau, J.W. & Ramstad, P.M. (2001). *Beyond Cost-per-hire and Time-to-fill: Supply-chain Measurement for Staffing.* Working Paper 01-16, Center for Advanced Human Resource Studies, Cornell University. Ithaca, New York.

Boudreau, J.W. & Ramstad, P.M. (2002). *From "Professional Business Partner" to "Strategic Talent Leader": "What's Next" for Human Resource Management.* Working Paper 02-10, Center for Advanced Human Resource Studies, Cornell University. Ithaca, New York.

Boudreau, J.W. & Ramstad, P.M. (2003). "Strategic HRM Measurement in the 21st Century: From Justifying HR to Strategic Talent Leadership." In *HRM in the 21st Century,* Marshall Goldsmith, Robert P. Gandossy & Marc S. Efron (eds.), pp.79–90. New York: John Wiley.

Boudreau, J.W., Ramstad, P.M. & Dowling, P.J. (2003). "Global Talentship: Toward a Decision Science Connecting Talent to Global Strategic Success." In W. Mobley and P. Dorfman (Eds.). *Advances in Global Leadership* (Volume 3). JAI Press/Elsevier Science, pp. 63–99.

Gates, Stephen (2002). "Value at Work: The Risks and Opportunities of Human Capital Measurement and Reporting". Conference Board Report # r-1316-02-rr. New York: Conference Board.

Lawler, E.E. III & Mohrman, S. A. (2003). *Creating a Strategic Human Resources Organization.* Palo Alto, CA: Stanford University Press.

Endotes

1. A more detailed application of the HC BRidge® framework to the strategic challenges of the internet can be found in Boudreau, Dunford, & Ramstad (2001).

Harry Osle

Harry Osle, Managing Director of Global HR Transformation for Answerthink, Inc., has more than sixteen years of experience in human resources and transformation consulting and has worked with General Electric, Citigroup, Johnson & Johnson, FPL, Gap, and other industry leaders. Osle specializes in HR strategic planning, HR organizational effectiveness, applying best practices, and HR technology to streamline processes, increase effectiveness, and reduce costs. A member of the International Human Resources Information Management Association (IHRIM) and the Society for Human Resources Management (SHRM), Mr. Osle can be reached at hosle@answerthink.com.

John Cooper

John Cooper, Director, HR Services Practice, Answerthink, Inc., has over twenty years experience in the human resources, reengineering consulting, and information technology areas. He specializes in the use of automated solutions to streamline business processes and has led many projects involving the selection and implementation of integrated ERP and tracking systems. A frequent speaker and lecturer on human resources trends and technology, Mr. Cooper is a member of the Society for Human Resources Management (SHRM), the International Human Resources Information Management Association (IHRIM), and the Institute for Electric and Electronic Engineers (IEEE). Mr. Cooper can be reached at jcooper@answerthink.com.

two : **3**

Structuring HR for Maximum Value

During tough economic times, human resources organizations are often required, as are other functional areas, to increase the value of their bottom-line contributions. Many HR executives struggle with these situations and choose to respond with stand-alone initiatives like sweeping staff reductions, drastic process re-engineering projects, hurriedly establishing Shared Service Centers, or new technology implementations. While these individual efforts can offer some improvements in HR performance, world-class HR groups use a holistic, best practices-based approach that simultaneously addresses all four key business dimensions—people, process, technology, and information.

Research from The Hackett Group, an Answerthink company and the world's leader in benchmarking and best practices research, has shown that failing to take a coordinated approach can reduce ROI on key performance improvement initiatives by as much as 78 percent. (See Figure 1.) Further results show that while HR technology, spending has increased 40 percent over the past four years, administrative spending has also increased by 16 percent, which clearly indicates that HR's non-coordinated, technology-centric approach has failed to deliver the necessary ROI.

Failing to take a coordinated approach can reduce ROI on key performance improvement initiatives by as much as 78 percent.

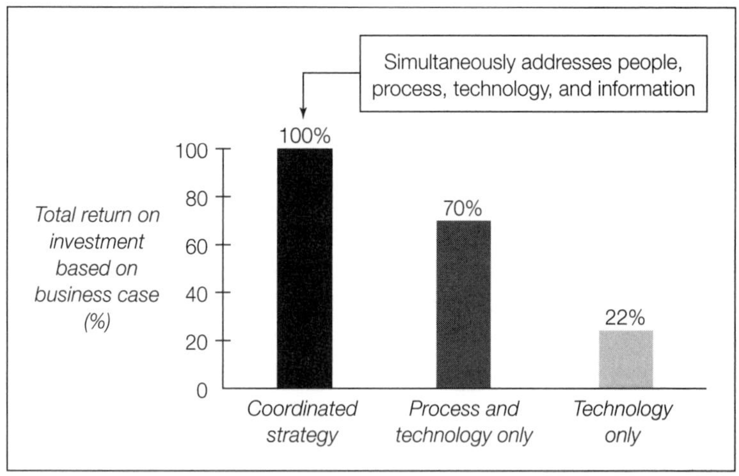

Figure 1. Research from The Hackett Group shows that companies can realize maximum value only through a coordinated strategy for performance improvement.

Successful HR Organizations Gain the Greatest Total ROI

For top-performing HR groups, it all starts with defining the right service delivery model for HR. The ideal model facilitates a greater focus on value-adding activities, as opposed to simple "paper pushing" and low-value transaction processing. The results are not only cost savings and productivity gains, but also increased satisfaction among business units and key stakeholders. It is through the development of highly effective service delivery models that HR organizations will maximize their bottom-line contributions and come to be viewed by key stakeholders as valuable strategic partners.

Given the amount of new technology on the market today, increasing customer demands, regulatory changes, an ever-changing pool of workers, competitive changes, and the number of mergers and acquisitions, it's no wonder many HR groups have been so reactive and overlooked the hard work of service delivery modeling efforts. The result is that they are left with HR organizations that don't match up to corporate objectives or business unit needs and services that cannot be measured to stakeholder satisfaction. How important is the development of a service delivery model? According to Hackett, average HR organizations waste up to 56 percent of their budget on initiatives or policies that are not directly linked to the company's priorities. Undoubtedly, this is among the reason total HR costs have increased in the last few years. The most effective HR groups long ago embraced the best practice of closely aligning HR activities to core business goals.

Other significant bottom-line benefits of a well-defined HR Service Delivery model include:

- increased flexibility and responsiveness to a range of business and organizational conditions, like mergers and re-organizations.
- increased focus on high-value activities and de-emphasis of routine transaction processing.
- improved focus on mutually-determined service level commitments that address business and operational needs.
- greater use of enabling technologies, like self-service, business process management, and portals, to improve the efficiency and effectiveness of core HR processes.

- decreased HR operating costs.
- enhanced integration of information and applications around core technology.

In short, the proper HR Service Delivery Model adds discipline, organizational clarity, and acts as the enabler that allows HR to execute its strategic plan. The driving force behind HR service delivery models is to generate outstanding performance in terms of both administrative excellence and strategic consulting—the two pillars of world-class HR groups today. The good news is, with the right approach and the application of best practices, it can be done.

Building the Right Service Delivery Model

Building the right service delivery model for your organization is an evolutionary process that should incorporate proven components and best practices. As with any well-defined plan, a focused approach should be taken in defining the HR Service Delivery Model.

There are three major steps in defining the right HR Service Delivery Model:

1. Understand the effectiveness of current services and how they're delivered:
   - benchmark costs, processes, cycle times, volumes, error rates, etc.
   - conduct stakeholder surveys to measure satisfaction
   - inventory organizational structure
2. Define a service delivery framework based on business objectives and proven best practices:
   - Develop a HR Strategic Plan based upon the HR objectives and drivers
   - Design a service delivery framework that may incorporate:
     - standard processes for efficiency
     - HR relations teams to be aligned with business units
     - standard technical infrastructure

3. Create Migration Plan to drive to the HR service delivery model:
   - Identify gaps between current and end-state models
   - Establish initiatives and migration steps to address gaps
   - Prioritize initiatives with a balanced approach (organizational, process, technology)
   - Create a communication plan to address migration steps and upcoming changes

As you can see, with every step it's vital to address people, process, technology, and information. Separating them will lead to diminished ROI. Throughout the entire process, it is important to maintain a clear and highly detailed understanding of what HR work is being done, who is doing it, and how effectively it's being done. The objective is not only to discern the role that HR plays today, but also to determine what is the best positioning for tomorrow. A thorough benchmark is crucial to understanding where changes will deliver the highest returns on investment. Similarly, a stakeholder survey can further uncover strategic opportunities. Without this level of insight,

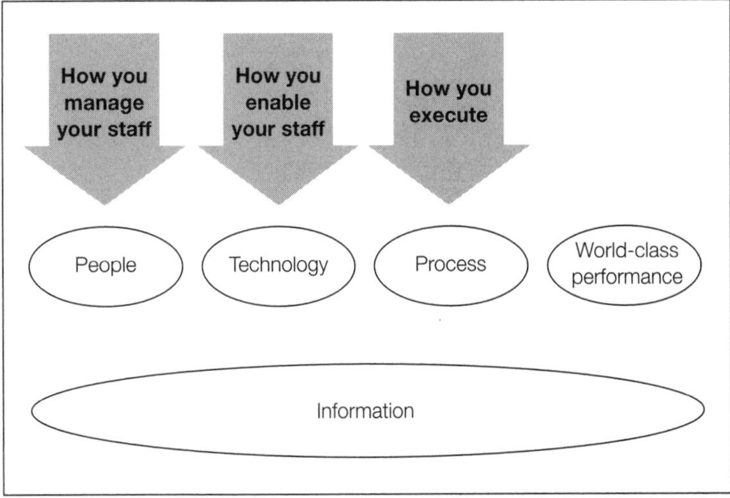

Figure 2. To develop and deploy the right end-state HR service delivery model, companies need to follow the three-step process while maintaining a big picture perspective that incorporates people, process, technology, and information.

companies will continue to make decisions about resource allocation, head count and services without considering the financial or strategic implications of those decisions. This step can be completed in as little as four to six weeks.

Defining the right end-state service delivery model involves aligning HR investments and resources to support core business processes and therefore, core business objectives. Most HR groups will need to balance two key business drivers, administrative excellence, and business unit needs for strategic consulting. The business case for a new model should be based on empirical cost data from the benchmark. Administrative excellence typically involves eliminating, simplifying, automating, or outsourcing low-value transaction processing. For those firms that have not implemented it already, self-service technology usually has an important role to play in this area.

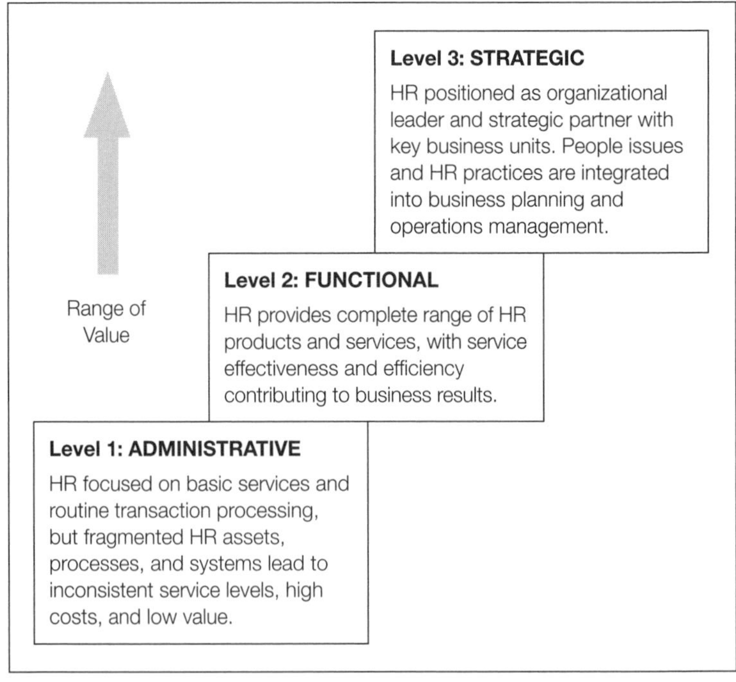

Figure 3. As HR groups more clearly define their service delivery models, the more value they can add to the organization.

Establishing a mission for HR, on which the service delivery model must be based, requires input from senior management. It's key that HR align itself to core business strategies at the highest levels. Also, validation from the top helps ensure the future success of organizational changes. It's important for HR to present a formal, documented strategy to the Board and position themselves as trusted advisers to the business units. Again, this represents a significant change for HR, which not too many years ago was strictly focused on benefits administration, performance appraisals, and hiring and termination paperwork. It's no coincidence that 89 percent of world-class HR groups have an explicit workforce strategy, while only 41 percent of average HR groups do. Similarly, world-class HR groups maintain high-levels of support for long-term organizational objectives, as compared with only medium or moderate levels at average firms.

Eighty-nine percent of world-class HR groups have an explicit workforce strategy, versus only 41 percent of average groups.

Developing Support

Once the service delivery model is in place, how can you ensure it's embraced across the organization? We already mentioned the value of senior-level support for conceptual buy-in. Many organizations overlook the value of change management and communication plans, which can be vital to realizing full benefits and maximum ROI from HR transformation efforts, as well as enterprise-wide change initiatives and technology implementations. HR has a leading role to play in these efforts, of course. As a result, the ways in which a company manages its human resources will strongly determine its ability to transform successfully.

Execution of the new vision will largely be determined by how well the benchmark and service delivery modeling were carried out. A thorough benchmark and stakeholder survey will make clear the gaps between performance and end state, while business cases should facilitate the prioritization of initiatives. For most organizations, initiatives will likely occur in multiple phases.

To ensure the changes hold on an operational level, the redesigned HR group should reinforce its vision, as well as core company objectives, through targeted performance measurement and management and compensation and rewards. To facilitate continuous improvement, the model should be linked to clearly measurable objectives around critical success factors, including:

- sustaining a service focus on key stakeholders needs (employees and management).
- supporting key outcomes, like increasing talent management activities, achieving higher levels of performance, and increasing the speed of change implementation.
- enhancing performance capabilities without significantly increasing size.
- establishing a core HR management team with effective spans of control.
- reinforcement of connectivity between HR and allied organizations, such as IT.
- formation and support of cross-functional HR teams to manage global processes and reduce organizational coordination points.

This model is the way to make HR a force for best practices deployment across the enterprise. The key is that a properly designed HR Service Delivery model provides HR staff with the time needed to focus on more value-adding activities. A well-designed service delivery model will provide HR with the time to develop innovative and responsive products and services and commit to continuous change and innovation that drive to true key stakeholder needs.

Service Delivery Models In Action

Let's look at how several organizations put the process into action. When a large waste management organization with 60,000 employees asked Answerthink to help design and deploy a new HR service model, shared services played a huge role. The decentralized culture presented some challenges, but by creating an empirical case for linking transaction processing for finance with employee data management, the new strategy gained momentum. A regional piloting program helped work out the bugs of the system, but also helped demonstrate the benefits, as did service level agreements. Ultimately, payroll, benefits administration, and time and attendance, all of which had previously been handled by the business units and usually through inefficient pencil-and-paper systems, were all centralized. With the new centers in place, both costs and error rates went down. Instead, highly skilled managers who had in the past been forced by faulty systems to focus on transaction processing were freed up to work on higher value activities.

A global retail organization recognized the need to offer more effective support to its various brand units, but wasn't sure how to get there. They started with a benchmark, which provided much revealing data. From there, they set out to define the best way for HR to organize, govern, and resource itself in the future. Balancing short- and long-term needs against financial restraints, they developed a tiered plan with immediate initiatives to support longer-term objectives. Because of the benchmark data, they were able to develop solid business cases for each component of the delivery model. Their initiatives addressed three main business drivers—administrative excellence, strategic consulting services, and the creation of a best practices environment that supported ongoing innovation in a changing environment. Long-term objectives emphasized succession planning, as well as development and retention programs to support increased productivity and employee satisfaction. Furthermore, the HR group sought the development of clear metrics and better use of systems for decision support. To promote efficiency in transaction processing, the company identified areas to implement increased use of self-service functions.

To support this "brave new world," HR designed an organizational structure featuring dedicated teams led by senior generalists responsible for managing relationships with business units. Centers of Excellence assumed enterprisewide responsibility for the key issues of compensation and workforce development. A shared services organization handled compensation, payroll and benefits administration, and other tasks. Underlying the HR organization was an integrated information and technology architecture, as well as standardized HR policies, process, and procedures.

The company expects to reduce overall HR costs by up to 30 percent, while increasing performance and contributions to key stakeholders.

As the initiatives are rolled out during the course of the next few years, the company expects to reduce overall HR costs by up to 30 percent, while greatly increasing transaction processing performance and its strategic contributions to key stakeholders.

Balancing Flexibility and Proven Best Practices

Today's HR organizations have many opportunities to add value to the business—which gives them flexibility in defining service delivery models that best fit their company's unique needs, objectives, industry, and competitive landscape. But the following questions must always be addressed: Where is our company today? What is the desired positioning for tomorrow? What level of investment can be justified?

While there is no one single best way to organize an HR operation, some best practices trends have emerged in the last few years. Typically, leading HR groups centralize some functions, such as compensation administration, payroll, benefits administration, diversity programs, policies, and HRIT. These organizations also standardize many of their HR processes holistically across varying brands, businesses, and operations. Leading companies have an innate ability to standardize process while maintaining flexibility to meet special local needs. They invariably understand that standardization allows for clarity in the organization and frees up time for HR to concentrate on more value-creating activities. The most frequently outsourced functions include 401(k) savings plans administration, employee assistance programs, relocation services, benefit administration (excluding defined contribution plans, management development programs, skills training, payroll administration, recruiting). That many of these functions are also commonly handled in a centralized environment speaks to the complexity of the decisions involved in designing effective service delivery models.

The centers of excellence and shared services models have brought a great deal of credibility to HR organizations in the past few years. Centers of excellence can be established for certain planning-focused activities within recruiting, benefits and compensation planning, training and development, and regulatory reporting. A large utility and energy firm was able to increase its effectiveness while reducing its HR staff by more than two-thirds by disassembling its regionally-dispersed HR organization and implemented centers of excellence in key planning areas. While cutting staff is never easy, it was a strategy necessary for this company and likely prevented further job cuts in other areas.

The centralization question is at the heart of designing service delivery models, and there are no easy answers or silver bullets. Some organizations with strong business unit leadership may prefer decentralized, but standardized HR operations, with each business unit maintaining their own HR functions, information and control systems, and only informal reporting relationships to corporate HR. The advantage to this approach is that HR is where the people are, especially for critical HR functions like recruiting and training. Similarly, some performance management processes are rolled out by corporate HR, but are managed and tracked at the business unit HR level.

While decentralized models give management maximum control and the likelihood that they will hire exactly the skills they need, there is the risk that costs will be higher than more centralized operations. The natural tendency of this model is to have standardized processes at the beginning, but then drift toward highly customized models. Another potential downside of the decentralized model is lack of information sharing and silos of employee data.

Naturally, many companies will seek to leverage the best of both of these models, and thus find a happy medium on the centralization continuum. By assigning HR generalists from a corporate unit to support business units, corporate HR units can serve as consultants or advisors to the business units, while still managing key functions. While it's part of their jobs to serve as advocates, sometimes these generalists have greater loyalty to the business they support than to corporate HR, making policy enforcement more challenging.

Whatever strategic delivery model your organization adopts, it will need the following characteristics if it is to drive world-class HR performance:

- HR strategy aligned to key stakeholder needs
- Leverage model for high volume transaction processing
- Maximize use of technology and increased use of self-service
- Highly efficient administrative processes
- Centers of Excellence focused on planning functions

The Value of Best Practices

Many HR best practices are both cause and effect of establishing the right HR service delivery model. For example, world-class HR organizations have a staff mix dominated by more professionals and fewer clericals. Moreover, 58 percent of their team is focused on such value-adding employee life cycle processes as staffing and selection, learning and development, and organizational effectiveness. Similarly, learning and development costs plummet by 60 percent when employees have individual plans tied to company strategy, and companies benefit further by being able to promote internal candidates 230 percent more often. These are benefits from strategic alignment that can deliver near-term impact on the bottom line. Higher retention rates at the professional, managerial, and hourly levels allow world-class companies to have approximately $2 million lower turnover costs per 1,000 employees.

Looking at technology, Web-enablement and self-service are two effective strategies for creating more value with lower costs. One of our larger clients, an international financial services organization, has used portals to put more control in the hands of managers and employees. This reduces duplicate entries and lightens HR's transaction processing burden. Executives at world-class HR groups can also be more effective because they use online modeling tools to more efficiently develop compensations plans.

Failure to deploy technology-enabling employee self-service has been demonstrated to raise health and welfare administrative costs by as much as 69 percent. Centralized, automated processing of employee data leads to administrative error rates that are three times lower than decentralized, manual HR process administration. The high level of error rates at the latter can result in a 98 percent increase in transaction costs. Thus, companies aiming both for lower costs and greater HR value would be well advised to bite the bullet and invest in technology that allows employees to access benefits options, obtain answers to common questions, and manage benefits online. Companies with enterprise-wide consistency in data structures and an ERP system spend 23 percent more on technology than average, yet with these enhancements they are actually able to reduce HR administrative costs by 38 percent.

Again, this empirical best practices data from The Hackett Group's comprehensive research into HR performance.

Average vs. World-Class HR

Average Profile

- Decentralized administration
- Manual administration support
- Multiple HRIS systems
- Multiple plans, eligibility criteria, etc.
- Limited self-service available
- Limited functionality leveraged
- Unstructured development program

World-Class Profile

- Highly centralized administration
- Simplified, automated administration support
- Single HRIS system
- Standardized plans, eligibility criteria, etc.
- High level of self-service available
- Functionality leveraged
- Targeted development plan

Conclusion

In the next decade, HR will continue to expand its strategic role. It's also uniquely positioned to become a force for the deployment of best practices, particularly through the leveraging of integrated systems, frameworks, and enabling technologies to reduce costs. The big picture view of service delivery models will continue to identify opportunities for improvement either through outsourcing, elimination, or process redesign. Creative HR leaders will find hybrid models that leverage the considerable cost benefits of centralization, while still meeting business unit needs through strategic consulting. One factor that is unlikely to change, however, is the underlying importance of a strategically aligned service delivery model, which should be driving the design of HR service delivery models today, and will continue to do so moving forward.

| CHAPTER THREE |

Bridging Technology and People—Driver of Corporate Success

Bob Stambaugh

Bob Stambaugh, President of Kapa'a Associates, has been involved with HR, IT, and HR systems for over thirty years. His practitioner experience includes career stops at SRI International, Crocker Bank, Intel Corporation, and Atari. He has also served time as a consultant at VRC Consulting, Hunter Group, and HRchitect. Mr. Stambaugh has been associated with IHRIM since its first organizational in 1979. He served ten years on IHRIM's Board of Directors, including a year as IHRIM President. He is a co-founder of the *IHRIM Journal* and is a member of the Journal's editorial board, the editor of the new *IHRIM e-Journal*, and a columnist for SHRM's HRTX PEG website. The author of more than 200 columns and articles and a frequent speaker on HRIS futures and organizational effectiveness around the world, Mr. Stambaugh can be reached at bobstambaugh@earthlink.net.

three : 1

Hard Systems, Soft Systems:
New Challenges for Twenty-First Century HR Systems, Stakeholders, and Vendors

Introduction

Most of what we have been doing in the HR and the HR systems world for the past two or three decades has been focused on creating structures within which we try to manage and control people and costs in organizations. As HR grew, evolved, and assumed new roles and responsibilities, we expanded and fine-tuned one basic IT portfolio upon which we rely to support those activities. As long as the basic corporate business model remained substantially the same as the model we began to support with rudimentary automated systems in the 1970s, the upgrades we made in response to HR's evolution were incremental, not revolutionary.[1]

Yet even before the dot.com bubble of the late 1990s, there were indications that the old model was breaking down in the face of an increasingly heterogeneous workforce, the demands of globalization, the impact of the internet, and myriad other forces.[2] When the pace of such changes slowed after 9/11, many observers interpreted the slowdown as an indication that another management fad had ended—that it was time to get back to the meat and potatoes of HRIS functionality. In fact, what they interpreted as the end was just a pause and a regrouping before new systems approaches and issues reappeared in the workplace.[3]

Signs of strain are reappearing now and will accelerate as the economy improves, the scope of connectedness and mobility in the workplace increases, and the availability of highly qualified workers shrinks. New approaches to HR and HRIS will be further magnified by management demands for speed, often at the expense of accuracy, and a growing understanding of the role of intuition and fuzzy logic as tools in the overall manager portfolio.[4]

Structure is just not the priority anymore. Nothing fits cleanly into old categories, and it has become increasingly expensive to develop work-arounds that pave over the potholes in organizational effectiveness. Systems solutions—upgrades and enhancements in vendor parlance—are stale before they are complete. The new forces are creating an HR workspace—not a workplace—in which the key focus of attention is no longer the old structure model, replete with predefined competencies and role-based activity, but a new flexible framework that emphasizes capability.[5] This transition from stability—the machine view of the organization to responsiveness—a holistic or organic view—is an established phenomenon and a critical factor in the forward-looking organization of 21st century.[6]

It's critical to recognize the challenge these shifts present for HRIS professionals and managers, vendors and consultants. On the one hand, we need to maintain and even strengthen the old structures and methodologies that form the backbone of what we can now view, metaphorically, as a living organization/organism. On the other hand, we have to create spaces in that organization[7] where old structures and practices do not squelch the flexibility and ambiguity needed for knowledge creation and employee growth.[8] Without such flexibility, we risk morphing from lean and efficient to anorexic and ineffective.[9]

There are no tested paths and proven approaches for this journey: after all, the central component of the new posture is an awareness that detailed plans are no longer possible in many parts of the business. No one can give you predefined programs, actionable items, or guaranteed strategies for the shifts that are taking place. In fact, action plans as opposed to a bias for action are part of the problem, not part of the solution. It is possible, however, to identify a set of concepts and behaviors that you can adopt and apply in the HRIS arena.[10] Some seem counter-intuitive, even counter-productive in familiar HR settings and systems. Not all of them work all the time. Nevertheless, they are a first step to creating tomorrow's workspace, without destroying the key components of yesterday's structure in the process.

There are eight such concepts and behaviors discussed in this article, along with a mention of four other important new ways of looking at the emerging 21st century workspace. Given the nature of the problems we're addressing in the new HRIS world, they're just a start, but they offer a way to begin understanding what we should ask of packages and systems, and what we should not attempt with structure and engineering. There are some areas we should set aside for human intervention, in many cases insulated from the structures and strictures current systems prescribe.[11]

Tools and Techniques for the Capabilities-Oriented HR Workspace

These eight criteria, many of which have their origins in the life sciences rather than the engineering disciplines, are a yardstick: They can be used to measure and highlight what belongs to the structured world and what belongs in the organic, developing part of the organizational environment.

Holism: You Can't Understand Your Whole System by Looking at the Parts

The corollary to this statement is that, "you can't understand the whole HRIS environment by identifying and analyzing the components of the environment."

At a basic level, we often suffer the fallout from this whole/parts approach when we conduct needs assessments, gap analyses, and requirements definitions. We identify separate functions, with or without interfaces, and then address these functions and the proposed system's stakeholders in isolation. We decide how to weight or prioritize different activities and data needs, and we expect that these optimized individual reviews will deliver the best overall system. But like a dissected frog that is probed and examined organ-by-organ, then reassembled, the recombined parts of systems and work processes lack the life that existed in the systems as a whole before they were torn to bits.

We identify separate functions, with or without interfaces, and then address these functions and the proposed system's stakeholders in isolation.

At a higher level, our whole vs. parts approach usually misses many of the soft issues like corporate culture whenever we try to apply purely rational measurements of the HRIS problem we want to address. Fuzziness—or intangibles—have been roundly derided by the systems engineers for years, but there's a change in the wind, and it's reached HR.[12] In fact, the change has always been here: What we've told people is sound project management and scope control is usually an exercise in eviscerating what needs to be delivered in a new system in favor of what can be financially justified by conventional analysis. The people on most teams know this.[13]

Think of it this way. I describe a building in the following terms: "The object is a black polished granite wall, two hundred feet long and ten feet below ground at its lowest part, with approximately five hundred thousand characters in Trajan lettering—each about one inch high—etched into the granite. A sidewalk starts at ground level and gradually descends toward the middle of the wall, then rises again at the other end. The wall and the sidewalk are surrounded by grass."

You can probably close your eyes and see this structure because the description is fairly complete and precise. Some of you may guess that the object being described is the Vietnam Veterans Memorial in Washington D.C. Anyone who has been to Washington and seen the memorial will tell you about its overwhelming emotional power: Many people have written about the impact of the wall. Yet no one I know will claim that the description above begins to capture the whole of the experience.[14]

As more and more of what we do at work drifts toward the soft areas of business and goes beyond repetitive processes and reporting, we need to remember this example.[15] We need to be careful that the demands we place on our systems are in fact amenable to systems thinking.

Diversity: Organisms—and Organizations—Cannot Survive without Requisite Variety

This concept, borrowed from biology and evolution/natural selection, tells us that a species has a higher probability of surviving the constant and inevitable changes in its environment if it hasn't overspecialized—if there are enough different individual behaviors in the overall species inventory to increase the odds that one or more will thrive in the new, changed environment. When there's not enough give in the inventory, a species either reaches an evolutionary dead-end or, like the dodo, disappears entirely and abruptly because it is not equipped to deal with a new addition to its space.[16]

In our traditional HRIS environments, we have specialized by streamlining and rationalizing processes and programs, using tools like process re-engineering and standard data or business models. We have done this to increase the efficiency and ROI demanded by finance and executive management. But we run the risk, as did many of yesterday's biological successes, of becoming so specialized that even a minor change in business practice will undo the houses of cards we have created. More and more, we're deploying those specialized processes in an artificial world as well—the ERPs we've built around our activity.[17] Like a greenhouse in the winter when the power goes off, one blip in the ERP umbrella and we're in big, big trouble.

We need to look carefully at when and where we standardize. Engineering makes sense in those parts of the system where work is repetitive and predictable. We need to continue pressing vendors for better solutions in this problem space. But where we want to encourage creativity and innovation, a little slack is wise. The higher the human component in any part of the ecosystem, the higher will be the risk of the standards approach, and the more benefits we derive from softening models and allowing generality.

Disorder: Life and Messiness Go Hand in Hand

We have been conditioned to view precision and order as the prerequisite to HRIS credibility and the basis of good project planning and management. HR systems designers and government economists share an unfounded belief: People behave rationally and consistently. That's the theory, but we all know that the moment a plan is complete or a project is finished, things begins to deteriorate: Life gets messy. As behavioral economists (they've won a Nobel Prize or two in recent years) are now discovering, people don't behave like robots: They are inconsistent. They behave like, well, people.

Just like things in the real world, it is virtually impossible to isolate one part of a working system from all the other parts of the system—there are too many links and interrelationships, and as we can see from the spread of SARS, West Nile Virus, and other natural plagues, human boundaries are porous unless we take heroic (and costly) measures to maintain them. The only neat system is a system in which the people component is missing—payroll comes close, but there are exceptions in that area too.[18]

In most systems and packages we have implemented to date, the human component has been relatively minimal: We have been dealing in transactions, financial measures, ratios, and explicit knowledge. Once again, the foundation is based on structured approaches, and the structure is designed to deliver data or information about tangible issues.

Accepting messiness does not mean acquiescing to chaos.[19] It does mean accepting evolution and drift of ideas and practices, and in today's global business climate, the evolution is both accelerating and punctuated. Acceleration is a fairly straightforward and familiar concept, but the punctuated part needs a little more explanation. Experts in evolutionary biology tell us that our traditional view of things (species) changing over thousands of years isn't quite right: Things actually stay much the same for most of those long stretches, and then suddenly, when a change of climate or similar blip occurs, there's a flurry of adaptation, selection, and—voila—new species.[20]

The Internet is the blip that's responsible for the accelerated changes we are experiencing now. It allows information sharing, and whenever two or more orderly but different views or data models collide, there will be ambiguity, questioning, changed viewpoints—messiness. It's a flexible alternative to all the formal communication channels we have imposed upon what are, at their essence, our informal organizations.[21, 22] Once the ease of information transfer is present, many other parts of the systems that have been limited by information availability themselves begin to evolve.

We can see this phenomenon at work everywhere. If you have been to San Francisco, for example, think about the old Ferry Building at the foot of Market Street: Back in the frenzied days of freeway construction—with a lot of similarities to the equally frenzied era of BPR and ERP—engineering demands and efficiency dictated a freeway that ran along the waterfront and cut the Ferry Building off from casual traffic. People hardly realized it was there, and the whole area was lifeless and dead. When the freeway was razed after the 1989 Loma Prieta earthquake, locals and tourists alike were amazed by the sweeping vistas and aliveness that resulted.

We need to make sure our HRIS initiatives create or reinforce order in a few core areas, but we also need to make sure the demands for stability and definition don't undercut inquiry, evolution, quality of work life, and creativity: After all, it's the human capital we need to nurture, not just the financial and structural capital components.[23]

Multiple Futures: Strategies with Measurable Goals Won't be Relevant by the Time You Realize Them

The real world very rarely cooperates with human strategy, and the more finely we tune and measure strategic goals and objectives, the less likely we are to satisfy our aims. This may sound like semantics, but there's a difference between strategy and strategic readiness or strategic capability.[24] If a company strategy changes, much of the rationale for systems and practices may change too. But where the flexibility of systems and availability of data for visioning is easily available, such a change of strategy is a gift, not a death sentence.

If you spend time and resources developing elaborate benchmarking, reporting, and measurement structure for tracking the multiple components of a strategic plan, you'll be paying attention to what used to be rather than what is and what can be. Constructing metrics and then extrapolating into an uncertain future to see whether we'll meet strategic goals only works when the goals are tangible, countable, and stable. The alternative, in an uncertain world, is to decide where we want to be, focus on the capabilities we need to move in that general direction, and then identify half a dozen or more situations that might cause us to change or abandon the goals entirely.[25]

If a company strategy changes, much of the rationale for systems and practices may change too.

Peter Schwartz and Shell Oil did exactly that when they created a set of scenarios for the oil business prior to the OPEC embargo a generation ago.[26] Scenarios have become a big part of military training for the U.S. Marines and Army. Many businesses employ scenario planning all the time. Their objective—and the objective we need to support in HRIS activity—is sensitizing our employees and managers to possible events and groups of events in the future, and then providing a set of forecasts and easy to access information that allow them to improvise when one of the alternative futures starts to occur.[27]

Mother Nature builds and plays out scenarios all the time: Mutations in a species don't all make it to the mainstream. Most are scenarios for possible future climate changes or ecosystem evolution, and if circumstances aren't right, the mutant strains disappear. The point is, if an unforeseen change in the external environment does occur, local adaptations and mutations are already right there, prepared to exploit the change. It's not strategy, it's flexibility and opportunity.

Remember the story about the race between the tortoise and the hare? In today's business climate, the hare wins and goes home, and the finish line has disappeared by the time the tortoise comes into view.

Hierarchy and Democracy: You Can't Control Living Systems

Writers from Margaret Wheatley[28] to Warren Bennis have made this point over and over again.[29] Their reasoning is closely connected with the messiness issue already discussed, but bears repeating because some of the authors mentioned here go a little farther. Their comments are important for anyone whose systems have been justified and optimized for efficiency, standardization, and stretch behavior from our employees.[30] These authors and others call into question many of the traditional approaches and ideas about employee motivation: One of the most interesting new approaches in this area is illustrated in Miguel Premoli's recent HR.com article—and reader comments—on "Motivation: The Polynomial Theory."[31]

While you can't control the external environment or the human beings who make up the living systems in these businesses, you can influence the people in your organization through a variety of approaches.[32]

You can supply them with information and suggest interpretations they can apply to their jobs. That means tying the information to ideas and metrics that are meaningful to the people, not to executive management. (If you give people meaningful work, responsibility, and information, they'll generally perform at a level that will delight executive staff.) Much of this activity stands outside the reach of HR systems software: We need to create these capabilities specifically for a company and a culture, not sell them off the shelf.

You can also create chat rooms, support blogs, enhance portals, and otherwise broaden employee access to information and connections to other employees.[33] IT may howl about the bandwidth demands your projects make, but bandwidth expansion is a lot cheaper than missing the next uptick in the economy and the hiring demands you need to face. I think one of the roles HR and HRIS will play in the future is that of a knowledge yenta: We'll look at different individuals or groups within the company and, depending upon their interests and availability, snoop around a little and then introduce them to each other. The result may not be marriage, but unless the introduction takes place, there won't be any result at all.

Non-Numerical Realities: Pictures Are Worth a Thousand Words and Stories Are Worth a Thousand Pictures

Most of the old printed transaction listings that formed the meat of yesterday's HRIS report libraries are gone. So are the line-by-line employee detail lists and departmental/division roll-up reports. First-generation metrics have been relegated to the backroom in many companies. There's a clear trend toward bigger-picture, more relevant information delivery, and it is often tied to data mining, multiple-source input, and combined human and machine interaction.

More and more vendors and HRIS departments are discovering graphics as a reporting medium Even at their most primitive levels, the advantages over yesterday's statistically-oriented packages are easy to see. First, a little bit of missing data doesn't undermine the integrity of the trend lines and big picture. (Again, context matters—missing data does undermine financial reporting, but in the human areas it is less relevant.) Second, users don't get hung up with questions about a pet department's details or a specific data element. Third, big picture approaches highlight key connections and links that would be submerged in an avalanche of numerical detail with standard reporting. Fourth, graphics travel well—we don't lose a lot because of semantic difficulties. (Although there are some graphical dialects that don't travel well, either.) Last, management decision makers get the information they want at the level where decisions occur: Despite what some vendors want us to believe, most executives don't make decisions by looking at details—they apply experience and intuition to the big picture.[34, 35]

The next punctuated leap in the evolution of reporting will take us beyond the graphics and business visualization approaches we are just beginning to use today and into a world that is still very unfamiliar to HRIS professionals: storytelling and narrative. This shift is already underway in many other parts of business, but it has been slow to penetrate HR awareness as a tool we can wield.[36]

And yet we are all familiar with the use of story in organizational settings. We insist on case studies (stories) at conferences. We like narratives about best practices at comparable companies. We learn from presentations that recount the ups and downs of an implementation project. In his book, *The Springboard* and in its forthcoming sequel, *The Squirrel*, Steve Denning discusses multiple approaches and strategies for storytelling.[37]

We have a real opportunity to contribute to corporate performance if we can learn to apply some of these story-telling techniques. Done correctly, management dashboards are a first step in this direction. If they are grouped in a meaningful manner and accompanied either by descriptions, commentary, interpretation, or related questions, they have enormous power.[38] If we build and comment upon a series of three or four related high-level graphics such as those used lavishly in *Fortune* or *Business Week* magazines, we provide added value to our customers.[39]

In the real world, as Von Frisch discovered, bees invoke a complicated and complex dance to give other bees in the hive the directions to a source of nectar—a goal. Human beings have been responding to pictures, stories, and narrative for millennia, from the cave art at Lascaux to the murals of Diego Rivera; from Homer's *Iliad* and *Odyssey* to today's romanced novels. Given the power of computers and networks today, there is no reason why HR systems products and services should not also employ similar powerful approaches to information sharing and productivity.[40]

Limited Horizontality: If You Want Innovation and Creativity, You Need Boundaries and Walls

In our love affair with engineering and efficiency, IT and its HR counterparts have been in the forefront of a sustained effort to knock down the boundaries between what have been characterized as the silos in the corporation. That's a necessary component of the modern approach to management and a prerequisite to the kind of IT infrastructure we chose a decade ago.[41] But there is a big difference between silos, on the one hand, and boundaries or walls on the other.[42]

In nature, there are all kinds of boundaries between parts of an ecosystem. In fact, it's the boundaries that allow the creation of a vibrant ecosystem: They isolate and insulate species from predators and conditions that would compromise their viability. In nature, these boundaries may be separate microclimates, streams and rivers, the tree line on a mountain, or the desert that separates oases. All of these create buffer zones behind which nature experiments—many new species don't make it, but a few do, and they can then branch out and influence other parts of the bigger system.

What goes on *at* the boundaries also acts as a buffer between the outside and the micro-environment. Think of the wetlands along the upper Mississippi that for thousands of years acted as a sponge to soak up much of the snow melt that poured into the river and, cumulatively, made downstream water levels so high the river overflowed its banks.

Courtesy of the US Army Corps of Engineers, we drained and filled in the wetlands, the snow melt went south, and entire communities downstream were inundated by what the Corps had promised would be hundred year floods. Boundaries do more than we know.[43]

When we knock down the silos in and around HR, we have to be careful not to knock down all the walls or undermine all the boundaries. It is important to leave enough room and resources for new ideas and approaches—new analyses and metrics, stories and processes—to grow and gain strength locally, then test the wider waters of the company at large.

HR and HRIS need to develop a habit of conducting not just feasibility studies, but also full-blown environmental impact analyses before we launch new projects or reengineering efforts. We need to catalog rare, exotic, and desirable species in our organizations and make sure anything we do protects them. Such a practice will not be easy. We know that many of these exotics are linked in symbiotic relationships with other, perhaps more endangered individuals or groups. So when we start down a road to downsizing, mergers, or even transfers, we need to know in advance where the impact will be—or we need to identify sets of conditions that will act as a warning sign that our actions are compromising environmental integrity. Vendors and consultants need to insist that these activities take place before they deploy new systems.

Robert Frost was right. Good fences do make good neighbors.

Half-Life Measures: Stability Is a Sign of Sickness, Change Is a Sign of Health

If you see a landscape where there is little or no movement, it's a good bet it's not healthy. (Generalizations are dangerous—lots of ecosystems like the Sahara look pretty dead, but in the rainy season or in the cool of the night, they come alive. If you live and work in an organization that exists in extreme conditions, the Sahara model might well work for you, too.) In general, the more activity, the healthier things are. Species that exhibit variation are more adaptable, and the whole and the parts of a dynamic system are more resilient when stressed.

Likewise, if you see an HR landscape where every stakeholder wants the same report, when definitions and processes, and events don't change on a regular basis, either the HR staff have been lobotomized; something unhealthy is afoot; or the definitions, models, reports, and processes you support and access aren't reflecting the real world anymore.

I've advocated for some time an HR systems practice of stamping a "best if used by" date and message on everything we do—from data element definition, to process or analysis, all the way to standard reports, and even the HRIS package that drives our overall infrastructure. In their new book, *Why the Bottom Line Isn't!*, Norm Smallwood and Dave Ulrich talk about the half-life of processes. This is the same general approach to what we do in a real-world, changing business environment. If these authors are correct (and there are few people in HR who would bet against them), external investors will be weighing things like this when they look at the health and value of potential investments.[44]

These eight imports from other disciplines help us get started in a world that's alive, unpredictable, and increasingly intangible. There are many more lessons we can learn from sources similar to those introduced in this article. For example:

- **Good and fast is better than great and slow.** The window for identifying and assessing threats and opportunities, then acting and evaluating the results of our activity has shrunk from months and years to days and hours. As other non-native species invade our home environments, HRIS not only needs to build systems faster, but also has to deliver results in final form to our customers. That means we have to know the business. Using scenario planning, we can open a window into the future and do much of the identification and assessment before the event itself.

- **Tipping points are sensed, not analyzed.** Most instances of punctuated equilibrium, discussed earlier, don't seem to occur after a major, dramatic event like a meteor crashing into the earth and obliterating much of life as we know it. Instead, big change occurs as the result of an apparently insignificant event: Despite assurances from President Bush's advisors, a two or three degree change in overall global temperature may well be such a tipping point. This realization is now driving futures planning in the military and in big business and has been categorized by some as asymmetric threat. In brief, the impact of an event or change is often totally disproportionate to the size—or the intent. It's a sobering discovery for those of us who like to tinker and improve currently adequate processes.[45]

- **Everything makes sense, eventually.** Retrospective rationality, more and more, we realize that things are so complicated and so interconnected that they make sense only after the fact, when we can see what the results of our plans and actions really were. Sometimes, the retrospective component needs to be combined with dialog and discussion, since we may not have enough information individually to assess overall results. Sometimes we just don't have enough information period, and our rational explanations need intuition or jumps from one train of thought to another.[46] Such a realization may occasion a review of some of the claims for HR metrics and analytics.

- **From Biology to Anthropology, from action to observation.** As we move more and more to the soft side of the business, we also move away from the belief, fraught with hubris, that we can look at a work group as outside observers and in a matter of weeks or days identify the optimum systems and support infrastructure for the present and well into the future. Some leading-edge analysts are now shifting from the intrusive engineering paradigm to a hands-off, anthropological observation in the field stance. This approach, best described by Dave Snowden, entails observing and recording what happens in a group—not asking questions, interpreting, or otherwise contaminating the site. The observers make sense of what they see after the engagement. This approach preserves the environment under review.[47]

HRIS: Human Resource Intangible Support Systems

Systems that count—the tangibles era—aren't over (in fact, aberrations like Enron and WorldCom will make them a more salient part of our thinking for years to come), but competitive advantage from innovation and knowledge creation/application, combined with investors' awareness of the part intangibles play in a company's overall value, make what we have always seen as the soft side an increasingly important contributor to organization viability and perceived investment value.

Experts like Dave Ulrich and Norm Smallwood constitute a visible vanguard for the intangibles movement.[48] They're reinforced by studies on capability and the value of human capital, driven by people like Tom Stewart, Leif Edvinsson, and Edward Lawler. Hubert Saint-Onge even recreated the HR function as the Department of Strategic Capabilities at Clarica.[49] Throw in ideas about naturalistic decision making and intuition from people like Gary Klein. What results is the prospect of a new kind of HR and HR system, operating at varying levels of engineering, exactness, intuition, and the intangible. We're faced with a daunting challenge in years to come, largely because we have to balance the needs of the old and the new viewpoints and associated practices. We will not be successful with a least cost, lowest bidder approach. We're not going to flourish with an excessive emphasis on either effectiveness or efficiency.

Summary

Living here on this leeward side of Kauai, one of the driest microclimates in a very arid part of Hawaii, I know without a doubt that I could save a great deal of money by uprooting the thirsty grass and plants in my yard and replacing them with cinders and lava rock. I look at the water bill each month and, from an ROI perspective, I know I should uproot these growing things. But then the birds wouldn't appear as often and the trade wind breezes wouldn't smell like flowers, and my quality of life would be compromised. So I keep the grass, plant even more shrubs, and then add new trees—and the water bill goes up.

Everywhere I look here in Kekaha, people seem to be making similar choices. Intangibles matter in our daily lives. It's a part of traditional local culture: Hawaiians talk about *aloha aina*—love for the land—and *malama aina*—caring for the land. It's another intangible concept. And we don't ask the Water Department to deal with our intangibles. We know, and they know, that they're optimized to deal with the pipes and the water—the hard stuff.

Business gurus are telling us the soft stuff concepts are starting to matter in corporate and external investment communities, and when that shift becomes a little more apparent, there may be a willingness to entertain proposals for actually spending money to make things happen. We must work with vendors and consultants to develop new ways of working with the intangibles: We do violence both to the soft issues and to vendor effectiveness if we try to apply traditional engineering and efficiency-oriented thinking to these very different environments.

No one ever said quality of life or quality of systems is cheap. But they extend and leverage the value of the investments we have already made and the maintenance outlays we continue to make in the bricks and mortar part of our world. Isn't it about time we come alive and introduce intangibles into the HRIS world, too?

Endnotes

1. Looking at the progression or evolution of Dave Ulrich's vision of HR is a very good way to see how our function has changed in the past several decades. As you read some of the ideas in his writings, note that the older thoughts and precepts are not so much superseded as subsumed by the newer directives. You can start with some of the older books and trace the entire trajectory of his thought, but it's enough to weigh the shifts in the last five or six years. The sources cited here are a good beginning for such a review.

   Dave Ulrich, *Human Resource Champions*, Harvard Business School Press, 1997.

   Dave Ulrich and Dick Beatty, "From Partners to Players: Extending the HR Playing Field", *Human Resource Management*, Winter 2001 (Vol.40, No. 4).

Dave Ulrich and Norm Smallwood, "Building Intangibles From the Outside In," in *Leader to Leader*, No. 28, Spring 2003.

Dave Ulrich and Norm Smallwood, *When the Bottom Line Isn't!*, Harvard Business School, 2003.

2. Margaret Wheatley, *Leadership and the New Science*, Berrett-Koehler, 1999.

   Wheatley's book was for most readers the opening salvo in this new assault on an overly engineered workspace. See also her article "The Real Work of Knowledge Management," in *IHRIM Journal*, April-June 2001.

3. Look, for example, at the evolution of another well-known HR author, Jac Fitz-enz. Fitz-enz has moved from a focus on measurement of HR to a much broader view of the discipline—but measurement still has a basic role in his model. The greatest leap in his thinking seems to have come with the advent of the e-workplace. His books include:

   How to Measure Human Resources, McGraw-Hill, 1984 and 1995.

   Human Value Management, Jossey-Bass, 1990.

   Benchmarking Staff Performance, Jossey-Bass, 1993.

   The ROI of Human Capital, AMACON, 2000.

   The E-Aligned Enterprise, AMACOM, 2001.

4. McKinnon and Bruns (along with Henry Mintzberg) identified non-rational and collegial aspects of managerial decision-making years ago. More recently, work by Gary Klein and Flavia Cymbalista have carried those studies further—and into the realm of intuitive or naturalistic decision-making, which draw upon but are not limited to traditional data and metrics. Also, consider the following:

   Flavia Cymbalista, "Focusing: A Kind of Knowledge You Didn't Know You Knew" and "A Conversation with Flavia Cymbalista", both in *IHRIM* Journal, March-April 2003.

   Gary Klein, *Sources of Power*, MIT Press, 1999.

   Gary Klein, *Intuition at Work*, Doubleday, 2002.

   Sharon McKinnon and William J. Bruns, *The Information Mosaic*, Harvard Business School Press, 1992.

   Henry Mintzberg, *The Nature of Managerial Work*, Harper & Row, 1973.

   Henry Mintzberg, *The Rise and Fall of Strategic Planning*, Free Press, 1994.

   Kathleen Sutcliffe and Klaus Weber, "The High Cost of Accurate Knowledge," in *Harvard Business Review*, May 2003.

5. Edward E. Lawler III and Susan Mohrman, *Creating a Strategic Human Resources Organization: An Assessment of Trends and New Directions*, Stanford University Press, 2003.

   This new book combines longitudinal data from three studies of HR in large corporations with some excellent insights about overall trends in the business—and some misconceptions that may exist among HR managers and consultants today.

6. For a pair of excellent collections of essays on this topic, see:

   Subir Chowdury, Management 21C, *Financial Times*, 2000.

   Subir Chowdury (ed.), Organization 21C, *Financial Times*, 2003.

7. Making a space for creativity is similar to the Japanese concept of *ba.*

   Ickujiro Nonaka and Hirotaka Takeuchi, *The Knowledge-Creating Company*, Oxford, 1995.

8. These ideas fit with the emerging field of social network analysis, frequently covered by Valdis Krebs in his *IHRIM Journal.* See also John Seely Brown and Paul Duguid, The Social Life of Information, Harvard Business School Press, 2000; Ronald S. Burt, *Structural Holes: The Social Structure of Competition*, Harvard University Press, 1992.

9. The "anorexia" metaphor comes from Leif Edvinsson's new book Corporate Latitudes, Financial Times-Prentice Hall, 2002, and Edvinsson, "Intellectual and Knowledge Capital for the Longitude Wealth/Value of Both Nations and Corporations," in *IHRIM Journal*, March/April 2003.

10. For example, Michael McMaster suggests overloading systems from time to time to make them stronger and more responsive—the reasoning here is that improvisation and informal cooperation forge new connections and working relationships, then the infrastructure to support them. See Michael McMaster, *The Intelligence Advantage*, Butterworth-Heinemann, 1996.

11. The tension between the specificity we have been trained to demand and the alternative tolerance of ambiguity is captured in this excerpt from Ester Dyson's "blog" Release 4.0 (4/25/03):

    DW: ambiguity is good!

    ED: you mean the richness of human interaction, etc.

    DW: yes, but I want to get beyond that...

    ED: Ethics!...Without ambiguity, there is no free will.

    DW: Explicitness is an act of violence. You think it's archeological: You take something and dust it off, but in fact explicitness reduces things; it destroys....

    DW: But I'm ending with hope. That there's now hope for social software to move from its past—harsh and glaring and topdown—to a new, emergent, bottom-up form that preserves the ambiguity. There's an art to doing explicitness well, so that it's not destructive.

12. Dave Ulrich and Norm Smallwood, *Why the Bottom Line Isn't!*, Harvard Business School, 2003.

13. This topic is covered very well in Philip Streatfield's, *The Paradox of Control in Organizations*, Routledge, 2001. A different but equally challenging approach comes from Olivier D'Herbemont and Bruno Cesar in, *Managing Sensitive Projects: A Lateral Approach*, Routledge, 1998.

14. Maya Lin, *Boundaries*, Simon & Schuster, 2000.

15. Google the web for articles on "fitness landscapes". Some are very technical and don't apply directly to HR and organizational analysis, but there are new contributions all the time. The quarterly journal *Emergence*, available only as a web-based publication, is a good source of organizational thinking related to this topic.
16. Ernst Mayr, *This is Biology: The Science of the Living World*, Belknap/Harvard, 1997. Also, Lynn Margulis, *Symbiotic Planet: A New View of Evolution*, Basic Books, 1998. The Margulis nook has some interesting discussions of symbiotic relationships that can be extended to organizational thinking as well.
17. See Kevin Kelly, *Out of Control*, Addison-Wesley, 1994, for an excellent discussion of how inadequate engineering and planning are in the face of real complexity. In one particularly valuable chapter, Kelly discusses what went wrong with the Biosphere experiment.
18. See Margaret Wheatley (endnote 2) for a better understanding of these living systems.
19. In fact, the area of greatest creativity and innovation in a system is at the border between order or structure and chaos. Complexity specialists call this area the edge of chaos. You can find an excellent introduction to the entire complexity discussion in Arthur Battram, *Navigating Complexity*, The Industrial Society, 1998. There's also Richard Pascale et al, *Surfing the Edge of Chaos*, Crown Business, 2000. French speakers may also want to read *L'economie du chaos*, Christopher Laszlo and Jean-Francois Laugel, Editions d'Organisation, 1998. The message we need to take away from this approach is that getting rid of chaos is a lethal goal for a living organization.
20. Stephen Jay Gould, *The Structure of Evolutionary Theory*, Harvard University Press, 2002.
21. Geoffrey Moore, *Living On the Fault Line*, Harper Business, 2000.
22. Paul Wiefels, *The Chasm Companion*, Harper Business, 2002.
23. There has been a flurry of interest in this topic during the past three or four years. The best books include Leif Edvinsson's, *Corporate Longitude*, Financial Times-Prentice Hall, 2002, and Tom Stewart's, *Intellectual Capital: The Wealth of Knowledge: Intellectual Capital and Twenty-First Century Organizations*, Doubleday, 2001.
24. Hubert Saint-Onge, *Leveraging Communities of Practice for Strategic Advantage*, Butterworth-Heinemann, 2002.
25. Arie DeGeus discusses the concept in, *The Living Company*, Harvard Business School, 1997. I also like Gill Ringland's, *Scenario Planning: Managing for the Future*, John Wiley & Sons, 1998. For a slightly different perspective—the French approach to scenario planning—there's also Michel Godet's, *Creating Futures: Scenario Planning as a Strategic Management Tool*, Economica, 2001.
26. Peter Schwartz, *The Art of the Long View*, Currency-Doubleday, 1991; and Peter Schwartz, *Inevitable Surprises*, Gotham Books, 2003.

27. Another worthwhile set of materials is entitled, *Storytelling in Shell: Managing Knowledge Through New Ways of Working*, from Shell International Exploration and Production B.V., telephone +31 (0)70 311 2627. This eighty-page plus document is not by or about HR, but line engineers—and that makes the entire approach more credible in management eyes.

28. Margaret Wheatley has written extensively about these topics. Go to for a long list of articles available for download.

29. Warren Bennis, *Managing People Is Like Herding Cats: Warren Bennis on Leadership*, Executive Excellence, 1999.

30. The book from the biological sciences that started the whole biology/organization equivalence is Humberto R. Maturana and Francisco J. Varela's, *Autopoiesis and Cognition: The Realization of the Living, D. Reidel*, 1972; followed by their, the *Tree of Knowledge: The Biological Roots of Human Understanding*, Shambala, 1987. For much easier reads, see John Henry Clippinger III's, *The Biology of Business: Decoding the Natural Laws of Enterprise*, Jossey-Bass, 1999; Richard Koch's, *The Natural Laws of Business*, Currency-Doubleday, 2000; Tachi Kiuchi and Bill Shireman, *What We Learned in the Rainforest*, 2002.

31. See Miguel Premoli, "Motivation, the Polynomial Theory," and posted comments, June 2003.

32. Perhaps the easiest way to accomplish this in the modern HR environment is via the selective use of portals for introducing employees to ideas and approaches you wish to see them adopt. There's a trade-off, however: A great deal of valuable learning comes when employees look for information on their own and accidentally encounter unexpected but relevant information in the process.

33. See my article, "I Blog, You Blog, They Blog", at SHRM's HRTX Web page.

34. The best way to sense these ideas is by looking at biographies of new and old leaders. There are plenty of current leaders to choose from—Jack Welch for one. For the quintessential "old" leader, look for articles and books about Harold Geneen.

35. The most recent example of this trend is Todd Raphael's, "Think Twice: New Workforce Math: It's the In Thing," in *Workforce*, June 2003.

36. There are numerous workshops and seminars that provide training in storytelling and narrative. The masterclass led by Dave Snowden is the best. Google "Cynefin Centre" for more information.

37. Steven Denning is the best example of the storytelling/narrative movement (and a co-presenter with Snowden for the storytelling masterclasses). See his book, *The Springboard: How Storytelling Ignites Action in Knowledge-Era Organizations*, Butterworth-Heinemann, 2000; and watch for his new book, *The Squirrel; The Seven Highest Value Forms of Organizational Storytelling*. There is also a short but worthwhile article in *Harvard Business Review* (June, 2003) by Robert McKee, called "Storytelling That Moves People."

38. There are many sources of metrics and analytics available to HR professionals and managers, but not all can be placed into the contexts suggested in this article. I recommend looking first at the products and services from InfoHRM at for a wide variety of metrics that you can mix and match for the people and the context you want to feature.

39. *Fortune* and *Business Week* both employ the technique of lining up three or four very simple graphs and tying them together with a storyline that runs across the top of the sequence. It's the graphic equivalent of a thirty-second sound bite (compare it, for example, to the more traditional and meatier graphs in *The Economist*), and it delivers enough information to frame a problem very well.

40. For a very good introduction to these ideas in a mainstream context, look at J.R. McNeill and William McNeill, *The Human Web*, Norton, 2003.

41. "Conversation with Tom Davenport," in *IHRIM Journal* (forthcoming).

42. Tom Davenport and Laurence Prusak's new book, *What's The Big Idea?*, Harvard Business School Press, 2003, is a valuable study of ideas in business—which ones are fads, which ones aren't—and the people whose guru status makes the ideas credible. There is an especially worthwhile chapter about the whole re-engineering movement. (It was Davenport's before Michael Hammer made it popular.)

43. The main reason to build and maintain boundaries is to provide a shield behind which people have an opportunity to test new ideas and approaches without the fear of failures reaching management attention. In many instances, the test areas and the boundaries are both informal and existing in parallel with the modern, engineered, boundary-less, and horizontal enterprise. You don't have to de-engineer in order to create the space for experimentation, but you do need to set aside the space and time for it to occur. Look at articles like Howard Sherman and Ron Schultz's, "Open Boundaries: Creating Business Innovation Through Complexity" in *Emergence*, Vol. 1, No. 2 (9/99); Debra Amidon's, "The Emerging Community of Knowledge", at www.entovation.com; and Dave Snowden's, "Communication, Trust, and Privacy, Part 2: Discord and Harmony in eBusiness and Knowledge Management," at www.unicorn.co.uk/3in/issue4/2.asp.

44. See the books by Leif Edvinsson, Tom Stewart, and Dave Ulrich, noted above.

45. Malcolm Gladwell, *The Tipping Point*, Little, Brown, 2000; and Andrew S. Grove, *Only the Paranoid Survive*, Currency-Doubleday, 1996. We cannot deliver necessary and sufficient information to executive decision makers if we clean, standardize, and sanitize what's in our reports and metrics.

46. Dave Snowden, "Complex Acts of Knowing", at the web address mentioned above.

47. Dave Snowden, "Using Narrative in Organisational Change," and "Emergent Knowledge Management," a pair of CD's that capture Snowden's classes, are available from www.collaboration.co.uk, or contact Brad Meyer at

bradmeyer@collaboration.co.uk. See also the Snowden articles "Just in Time Knowledge Management" and "The Knowledge You Need, When You Need It," *KM Review*, Vol. 5, Issue 5, and Vol. 6, Issue 1 (respectively).

48. "Conversation with Norm Smallwood," in *IHRIM Journal* (forthcoming).
49. For more information and other articles from Saint-Onge, go to www.konvergeandknow.com.

Naomi Lee Bloom

Naomi Lee Bloom, Managing Partner, Bloom & Wallace, is a renowned consultant and recognized thought leader throughout the HRM delivery system industry. Ms. Bloom has worked as a change agent and process coach for many complex organizations, including Cisco, Suncor, Harvard University, General Mills, International Paper, and Hewlett-Packard, using information technology to achieve breakthroughs in their HRM business. She has been an advisor on product direction and positioning for most of the leading vendors in this industry. A frequent author and speaker, Ms. Bloom wrote "Human Resource Management and Information Technology: Achieving a Strategic Partnership" and writes a monthly column for *HRO Today*. Prior to founding Bloom & Wallace, Ms. Bloom, who holds an MBA from Boston University, was a Senior Principal with American Management Systems. Ms. Bloom can be reached at naomibloom@mindspring.com.

three : 2

Be Prepared When Your CEO Asks "Why Don't We Outsource HR?"

When we laid down our butter churns and stopped making our own clothes and candles (this actually was before my time), outsourcing became an integral part of business strategy and tactics. Every time we buy something, delivered as a product or service, we are engaged in outsourcing, so it should come as no surprise that all public and private sector organizations outsource extensively and are always looking at new ways of doing so. Within our own human resource management (HRM) domain, and consider here the broadest possible definition of HRM to include everything we do to organize, acquire, deploy, develop, assess, reward, lead, coach, support, inform, and equip a cost-effective and productive workforce, there are so many good reasons for outsourcing one or more functions, whole processes, or whole packages of processes with integrated delivery—always assuming that we select the right provider, negotiate the right contract, and manage that relationship effectively—that the only surprise is that we don't do more of it.

No chapter, not even an entire text, could provide all of the guidance you need to address the questions of what, when, how, to whom, etc. you should or should not outsource. Furthermore, every consideration of these questions must be grounded in the specific nature of your organization's business strategy, HRM strategy, HRM policies, plans and practices, HRM delivery system current state, and all of the issues/challenges you face in each of these areas. But we can certainly provide, even in a short chapter, guidance on how to think about the what and why of outsourcing and offer some of the questions whose answers will guide you to the how and to whom.

The "What" of HRM Outsourcing

Before we discuss the reasons for outsourcing (i.e., the why of outsourcing) and get prepared to address the questions about the what, how, and to whom of outsourcing that we're getting from senior management, we need to define the three major types of outsourcing that are relevant to HRM, (i.e., the what of outsourcing):

- HRM expert resources outsourcing (whether delivered as a finished product or as consulting services)
- HRM IT outsourcing (HRM ITO)
- HRM business process outsourcing (HRM BPO)

With HRM expert resources outsourcing, we may be asking a provider to help us design a compensation plan, develop a staffing strategy, or provide specific eLearning content. Whether delivered as a finished product (e.g., a stock training video) or via consulting services (e.g., actuarial consulting on our pension plan), essentially all organizations engage in this type of HRM outsourcing. However, there is little or no integration needed between these vendor-provided products and services and the overall operating model or delivery platform of the organization's HRM business except to ensure intellectual integration with the rest of our HRM policies, practices, and plans. An exception would be that eLearning content must be delivered across our eLearning infrastructure and, therefore, must comply with those technical standards.

Not so with either HRM ITO or HRM BPO, for here the products and services provided by the vendors are woven into the very fabric of how we do the HRM business and, therefore, into how the organization's overall business is conducted. With HRM ITO and/or HRM BPO, we are often betting the business on the performance of our selected vendors and, therefore, on how effective we are in selecting and managing those vendors. With respect to HRM ITO, we might outsource:

- Applications software development and enhancement via the licensing of packages or subscribing to relevant Web services;
- Applications software implementation and maintenance support through consulting contracts with systems integrators;
- Infrastructure management and maintenance when we use traditional IT outsourcers to provide that infrastructure on a utility basis or when we license or subscribe to applications software that is hosted either by its owner or by a third party ASP; and
- Pre-integration of application software components when we license not just a single HRM application but an entire suite of HRM applications and, perhaps, the rest of our business applications from a single enterprise applications suite vendor.

Many organizations that do operate their own HRM delivery system (HRMDS), and that's nearly everyone who doesn't move to integrated HRM BPO across many HRM processes, don't realize that, by licensing vendor software to create their HRMDS platform, they are adopting that vendor's vision of the HRM business. If that vendor hasn't provided for support to contingent workers or doesn't envision an individual holding two part-time positions with different but complimentary work schedules (as in retail, health care, and branch banking), then your ability to support such HRM practices will be hampered. Therefore, even when just outsourcing the IT work associated with your HRMDS, it's critical to get a good fit between your software vendor's HRM vision, processes, and data design, and what's needed to run your own organization.

But when organizations outsource at the HRM function or process level, the impact on their ability to execute HRM practices that aren't supported by their selected provider(s) is much greater.[1] The best licensed HRM software can usually be configured to do what you need it to do, but in their need to reduce their costs, few outsourcers provide that degree of flexibility as regards their offering. Thus, with outsourcing of business functions or processes, it's even more important than when licensing software to make sure that there is alignment between the HRM vision, practices, and processes supported by the provider and what you need to run your business. Here too, it helps to look at the different ways in which the business itself can be outsourced, to include:

- Functional outsourcing, in which discrete and usually narrowly defined functions, like applicant background checking or traditional payroll service bureau gross-to-net calculations, are performed by the provider in response to information which we provide, returning results that we approve and/or use as we choose, and for whose integration with the rest of our HRM process model and our HRMDS we are responsible;
- Business process outsourcing, in which more broadly defined and even grouped functions, like benefits administration or complete payroll processing, are performed by the provider with considerable control over how they respond to the relevant business events, a more extensive bi-directional information flow, the expectation of extensive customer contact support in addition to self service, the responsibility for acting upon the intermediate results as appropriate to the process and interacting as needed with other third parties, while we continue to take responsibility for data and process integration with the rest of HRM and the HRMDS, a particular challenge where employee and manager self service are involved; and
- Very extensive and integrated HRM business process outsourcing, where the breadth of data and processes supported by the provider are sufficient to shift to the provider—and this is a

MAJOR shift—the primary responsibility for the HRM delivery system's software platform (to include most but not necessarily all of the software involved), customer view (to include most but not necessarily all of the self service and customer care capabilities), and a good bit of the people and processes of the operating model view (e.g., the customer care center, shared services in support of the delivery system's software, and center of excellence in HR operations).

Although HRM functional outsourcing and BPO are well established, integrated HRM BPO is relatively new except for those smaller organizations that have always met their HRM needs via a PEO. Perhaps the most important development in HRM outsourcing over the last few years has been the growth in both the number of providers and breadth of covered processes being offered as integrated HRM BPO. But regardless of the success of integrated HRM BPO, and this is still a territory of early adopters, or how much they rely on HRM expert resources outsourcing, each organization clearly retains the responsibility for defining and executing its own HRM strategy, business rules, HRM practices, and key strategic processes (e.g., identifying high potentials), not to mention having to select, engage, and manage all of their outsourcing relationships. And the responsibility for determining by what metrics they will run their HRM business, regardless of who provides or manages the underlying data, rests squarely inside the organization.

The "Why" of HRM Outsourcing

With this greater precision about the various types, the "whats" of outsourcing, and always assuming that any outsourcing we choose to do will be done well (yes, there's always a catch, and the catch here is to do it well), we can begin to select the right type of outsourcing to achieve specific HRM objectives:

- Reduce HRM costs, make them variable with organizational activity, create predictable expenses and, in some cases, turn in-house facilities and intellectual property into revenue-generating assets;

- Gain access to best-in-class HRM consulting, products, and/or programs as well as delivery system capabilities whose costs are prohibitive if not obtained through HRM BPO for all but the very largest organizations;

- Move more quickly than we could on our own to implement specific HRM and/or HRMDS capabilities that are needed to run the organization,(e.g., widespread self service and/or the ability to handle important new programs in variable compensation or candidate sourcing);

- Achieve better service levels than we could on our own because that service will be delivered by a firm for which that HRM activity, function, or process is their core competency—but real care is needed here to select the right metrics and target values so that, for example, your selected provider of outsourced staffing processes doesn't help you to hire poor performers faster and at lower cost;

- Eliminate the capital investments needed every year to create and then maintain a state-of-the-art HRMDS, where the standard for what the workforce expects is being set by their experience with such commercial Web sites as Amazon.com and Landsend.com;

- Gain access to good HRM and HRM delivery system (HRMDS) practices—no one in their right mind shares with potential competitors a truly best practice because that's what creates competitive advantage;

- Gain immediate access to that state-of-the-art, highly automated HRMDS without having to construct it for the first time—and without having to understand in detail how it's constructed, supported, and evolved;

- Free up valuable management attention to focus on running the business; and, going a step further,

- Reduce the time, expense, risks, and distractions of managing directly a portfolio of outsourcing relationships and integrating a portfolio of HRM delivery system components through more integrated business process outsourcing.

So, HRM outsourcing can achieve many objectives, but only when the right type of outsourcing is selected for the benefits sought, when realistic expectations are set for those benefits, and when the selected provider really does deliver those benefits. With outsourcing on every business leader's mind, especially the more extensive, integrated HRM BPO, we need to be prepared to answer before our own CEO or HR executive asks, "Why don't we outsource HR?"

What Is the Total HR Outsourcing Question?

To answer this question, and not with outrage or fear, we first need to understand why we are even getting this question? One reason is that the real "costs" (total cost of ownership) of a contemporary and effective HRMDS have escalated tremendously as the performance bar has been raised. We've gone from having a back office system for personnel record-keeping, payroll, and some benefits administration to wanting and needing stronger HRMDS. Furthermore, as we've expanded our use of outsourcing across HRM, the portfolio management, vendor management, and systems integration challenges of piecemeal HRM BPO, to include acquisition of software and becoming our own systems integrator and shared services provider, are outpacing our capabilities in these areas, and the difficulties of coordinating and managing many standalone SLAs is becoming a serious business risk.

Perhaps even more relevant to why this question is being asked now is that the importance of excellence in the HRMDS has grown as self service exposes our HRMDS problems to every employee and management relies much more directly on strategic HRM processes and related analytics. As with corporate IT capabilities, HRMDS talent shortages and retention challenges have grown as talent moves to those vendors, consultancies, and BPOs which can offer greater career opportunities to the very best people in this field. Add to these consciousness-raising factors the broader discussion about doing more with less, aligning whatever HR does more closely with the business, and aligning HR's IT strategy with that of the larger organization, and no competent CEO can avoid asking about more integrated and extensive HRM BPO.

You Need Facts at Your Fingertips!

To address these questions, we need to have the right facts at our fingertips. Long before management raises these issues, and just to manage effectively our current state HRM business processes and HRMDS, we'd better have answers to the following:

- What are the HRM business outcomes to the achievement of which all HRM processes and the HRMDS must contribute? How are these intended contributions going to be made and by when? At what levels of investment for what target values of the HRM outcome metrics? And who is accountable for what outcomes?
- What would the HRM processes and HRMDS need to look like to achieve these business outcomes? How does this future state of our HRM business model compare to our current state HRM business model? How does this future state HRMDS compare to our current state HRMDS? How are we planning to close these gaps? What are the benefits of closing these gaps? Are they sufficient to warrant the planned effort? Can we afford that plan?
- What are we outsourcing now and to whom? HRM policy/program design? HRM program administration? Litigation support? Software development? Systems integration? Hosted delivery of software (ASP)? Individual or integrated HRM processes (BPO)?
- What are the total life cycle costs and expected benefits of each outsourcing arrangement? Have those benefits been realized and/or costs been exceeded or under run (as if this ever happens)? And don't forget the costs to enter into and then manage

those outsourcing relationships as well as to integrate the results of those outsourcing relationships into our own HRM business model (both current and future states) as well as into our own HRMDS (current and future states).

- What other services do our current providers offer that may be of interest? Have any of them expanded their services in areas where we now use a separate provider?

- Why would we continue using separate providers in place of a more integrated offering from a single provider? Why would we hesitate to put more eggs in the same basket? Do the benefits of a more integrated HRM BPO approach more than offset the risks? When you consider at what point an integrated approach assumes responsibility for the bulk of the HRMDS platform and much of the operating model?

- What processes aren't we outsourcing currently that could be candidates for outsourcing? Why are they being done in-house now? What would need to change (in our business, our thinking, our culture, our processes, our systems, etc.) for us to consider outsourcing these additional processes? Would such changes help or hinder us in meeting our business outcomes?

- What processes do we consider off-limits for outsourcing? Why? What would need to change (in our business, our thinking, our culture, our processes, our systems, etc.) for us to consider outsourcing these processes? Would such changes help or hinder us in meeting our business outcomes?

- What are our true, fully-loaded enterprise-wide costs for conducting the HRM business? Have we remembered to include all of the time spent outside of the HR organization by those engaged in the HRM business, (e.g., the time spent by managers to understand the practices involved, conduct, record, review, approve, etc.) performance reviews, and the time spent by employees to understand the relevant business rules, apply for, and schedule vacation time?

- What is the relationship between those costs and various surrogate measures of organizational activity, (e.g., headcount metrics), and organizational outcomes, (e.g., revenue metrics)? Between those costs and our required HRM business outcomes?
- Would more or less outsourcing affect those costs in a positive way without adversely affecting the quality, timeliness, or other important measures of process outcomes? Without adversely affecting our required business outcomes?
- What are our decision criteria for when, how, to whom, and with what service level agreements (SLAs) we will outsource each type of HRM process? Collections of HRM processes? Integrated collections of HRM processes to include shifting major responsibility for the overall HRMDS to the provider?
- Who makes these decisions? Any pending opportunities to influence them?
- How do we decide on the scope of each outsourcing relationship? Are we inclined toward one-off or more integrated arrangements? Why or why not?
- How do we manage these relationships? What are the performance incentives? Any problems with these relationships? What problem resolution techniques are we using?
- What's the HRM business model against which we consider processes for outsourcing? Does it match each SLA already in place? What, if any, changes are we or should we be considering in our HRM business model and, therefore, in the related outsourcing relationships?
- What's our process for monitoring the financial and market health of our providers? Are we the first to know if there's a pending M&A? A change in their offering? New providers that we should consider?
- Are we investing enough in our competitive intelligence effort versus the risk of not doing it well? Are we able to monitor

the financial health, market performance, and future direction as well as needed to ensure the success of our outsourcing relationships?

- Would we be better able to achieve our HRM business outcomes with the capabilities of our HRMDS enhanced by further outsourcing? By considerably further and/or more integrated outsourcing?

Bring On the Proposals!

With all of this information available as background, we're now ready to consider any and all HRM BPO proposals that surface, either ones which we've solicited in an orderly way or ones which have shown up, as such things do, from aggressive vendors soliciting business, as "bright new ideas" gleaned by our executives from the latest conference or trade show, or just out of the peer-to-peer interactions between our HR executive and a colleague who has just signed up for integrated HRM BPO and would feel a whole lot better if his decision were supported by the similar actions of his colleague. Unsolicited proposals or ideas can be quite vague as to the what, why, and how, and only formal proposals will contain a single to whom. Using the material discussed above, you now know how to get really clear on the what and why, but there remain many further questions for which answers are needed to explore the how and to whom and whether or not the overall proposal or idea is a good one.

Regardless of where the HRM BPO proposal or idea originates, and with the information described above truly at our fingertips, let's consider the broader issues before we get lost in the weeds:[2]

- Is this outsourcing idea/proposal compatible with our strategic business and HRM plans, (e.g., to improve our use of competencies in our strategic HRM processes), or is it intended to address temporary tactical problems, (e.g., our reluctance to invest in the next upgrade of our core HRMS during a weak economy)?

- Are the outsourcer's employees (or our employees sold to the outsourcer) going to give us better service that our own workforce did? Why? How? In the face of tight deadlines and downward pricing pressures?

- How will we develop excellent HR generalists, specialists and vendor life cycle managers if we accept this outsourcing idea/proposal? If the provider is hiring our staff, how will we gain an increase in their proficiency?

- How will we control costs with sufficient granularity if the provider bundles everything into one fee?

- What are the implications of this outsourcing idea/proposal if we merge with another organization our size?

- What are the implications of this outsourcing idea/proposal if another organization wants to buy us at an attractive price? Are there any unattractive contract buyout provisions?

- What are the implications of this outsourcing idea/proposal if we sell off peripheral businesses and focus on our core business(es)? How are contract fees adjusted when business activity slows and/or we downsize our workforce?

- How do we know that these financial projections are real and accurate?

- Since change is a sure thing, how can we be sure that the proposed outsourcing contract will protect us as much as it protects the outsourcing provider when change happens?

- What changes will our employees notice? Will our managers notice? Will these changes be received as positive? What's the upside and downside on their reactions?

- Will our best HR and HRMDS staff walk out on us the minute they sense the intent of this outsourcing idea/proposal? What's the upside and downside if they do?

- Why is this being discussed/proposed now? What's the impetus for this outsourcing idea/proposal? Is the timing convenient with respect to our HRMDS planning cycle, budget cycle, organizational change cycle, etc.?

- Who's going to manage the financial aspects of this outsourcing idea/proposal to ensure that we achieve the intended results? How? Do we have the people, processes and technology to do this effectively? What would it take to put those people, processes and technology in place? Has this been factored into the outsourcing idea/proposal?

- Who's going to manage the performance aspects of this outsourcing idea/proposal to ensure that we achieve the intended results? How? Do we have the people, processes and technology to do this effectively? What would it take to put those people, processes and technology in place? Has this been factored into the outsourcing idea/proposal?

- What if the outsourcing provider we like and select is then acquired by an outsourcing provider we rejected because of their management style, ethics, customer service track record, technology, geographic coverage, etc. How easily can we escape?

- Has our lawyer negotiated at least as many HRM outsourcing contracts as the outsourcing provider's lawyer? Do we have the legal and vendor management horsepower needed to make this work for us?

- Where will our HR executive, CFO, CIO, etc. be five years from now? Would he be as enthusiastic (or as unenthusiastic) about this proposal/idea if he were going to have to be judged long-term on how well this works for our organization?

- If we change our minds in two or three years, what's involved in bringing this activity, function, process, or integrated processes, along with the relevant HRMDS components, in-house?

- What impact would implementing this idea/proposal have on meeting our organizational and/or HRM business outcomes?
- Is the cost of getting there (i.e., to an improved HRM process or set of integrated processes and related HRMDS components) justifiable in terms of improvements to those business outcome or is this a cost of doing business (i.e., a fix the roof investment)?
- Is the impetus for this idea/proposal contained in an investment plan to bring our current HRMDS to the standard needed to sustain our business? If we took a hard, careful look at what's really needed in our HRMDS to support our business outcomes, would we be shocked by the investment needed?

Final Thoughts

I do believe that all but the very largest and most sophisticated organizations have much to gain from integrated HRM BPO, especially as the provider landscape matures, if—and it's a very big IF—they select the right vendor, enter into the right contract, and then manage the relationship effectively. However, just like the many in-house HRMDS implementations that overemphasized the administrative aspects of HRM and under-invested in the more strategic HRM processes, I am seeing a repeat of short-term thinking in the move to integrated HRM BPO. Presumably strategic, integrated HRM BPO deals are focused very heavily on the basics, at least initially, and that's absolutely understandable. Unfortunately, these initial business rule, data structure, workflow, and broader process designs, although able to deliver vastly improved administrative services metrics, are not always designed with sufficient attention to their foundational role in unleashing and supporting strategic HRM. The consequences of this shortsightedness are just around the corner for the earliest adopters. If you never enabled competency-centric HRM processes with your selected provider's platform, if you didn't design your data and coding structures with sufficient granularity to support teams and role-based processes, if you didn't lay out your strategic analytics as part of the service level agreement, you're in for some substantial rework. So my final thought here is that you consider your long term HRM business outcomes and their HRM business model needs sooner rather than later in considering any outsourcing activity.

Endnotes

1. For more insight into the importance of your outsourcers' platform, please consider reading my column, "Tech in Bloom", in each month's issue of *HRO Today*.
2. Some of these thoughts have been adapted quite loosely from an excellent article by M. Arthur Gillis, "Should You Outsource?", in *American Banker*, 2002.

Alexia (Lexy) Martin

Alexia (Lexy) Martin is Director, Research and Analytics at Cedar Consulting. Her work includes defining the value of workforce-oriented technologies through developing winning business cases for customers in all industries. Prior to joining Cedar, Ms. Martin held positions such as Vice President, Marketing at Co-Development Technologies and was a Research Fellow at the Institute for the Future, Management Consultant at SRI International, and Systems Manager at Stanford University. She holds a MA from the University of San Francisco in Organization Development and an undergraduate degree from San Francisco State University in Political Science. Ms. Martin can be reached at alexia.martin@thecedargroup.com.

three : 3

Justifying Workforce Technologies: ROI, JOI, HCM TCO Portfolio Analysis, and Post Implementation Audits

Investing in workforce technologies is not high on executives' lists of how to survive and excel in today's economy. Opening a new store and bringing in new revenue at Borders Group that runs Borders and Waldenbooks stores worldwide, upgrading St. Elizabeth's hospital facilities and adding new beds for additional revenue in Kentucky, or opening a new ski run and spa that pulls in more skiers and their families at Vail Resorts, one of the leading resort operators in North America, has a whole lot more sex appeal than upgrading their human capital management systems. On the surface, these investments bring more value to these organizations. But, being able to recruit, develop, manage, reward, and incent the best and brightest talent for high performance product and service delivery is how these organizations will survive and excel. So, justifying continued investment in the workforce technologies that support these actions is critical.

Conducting Rigorous Hard-Dollar Cost Justification Is Mandatory

In our business case work with customers such as Borders, CUNA Mutual, The Hartford, or St. Elizabeth's Medical Center, or with partners such as PeopleSoft, the final investment proposals that get approval require a hard-dollar justification. For example, at St. Elizabeth's no money can be spent unless some corresponding costs are eliminated from the following year's budget. While arguments such as "self service will improve productivity" or "workforce analytics will improve managers' decision making" are often key messages that support a business case, they are not acceptable by the investment approving body.

So, what are acceptable hard-dollar savings and how can they be developed?

The easiest hard-dollar justification is reducing the cost of labor resources, materials, and information distribution. These are direct, hard-dollar savings that will go straight to the organization's bottom line and ultimately result in increased earnings. For example, we implemented self service in an organization with 25,000 employees and were able to eliminate twenty-five HR staff—a huge savings on overhead salary expenditure. In addition, applications that enable online administration, such as pay advice, allow organizations to eliminate costs of paper, envelopes, and postage to distribute information including printed pay stubs.

The easiest hard-dollar justification is reducing the cost of labor resources, materials, and information distribution.

Organizations can also produce hard-dollar justification by consolidating reporting and data warehousing applications. For example, an international organization with operations in twelve countries can save by replacing local data warehouses with one global warehouse. This again, reduces staff to maintain the local site databases and also eliminates fees associated with ongoing software and hardware maintenance, license upgrades, and implementation services at each of the twelve local warehousing sites.

These examples, result in ongoing savings for the life of a new workforce technology solution.

Another hard-dollar justification is that of cost avoidance. For example, if an organization builds its own payroll solution, it will spend twice as much as if it buys a payroll solution and implements this package. Or, in the case above, if another five countries planned to deploy their own local data warehouse, that cost can be avoided with the deployment of the global warehouse. These hard-dollar savings are one-time savings that can also contribute to the justification.

In Tables 1 and 2, we show the hard-dollar cost savings associated with two of PeopleSoft's human capital management solutions: Core HR and the collaborative applications that provide for employee and manager self service (such as benefit or payroll services and employee change actions and salary management). These examples show savings that assume the organization has no automation, and pays its administrative, processing, and HR specialist staff national average salaries. If the organization already has some level of automation, the savings will need to be reduced accordingly.

How to Determine Hard-Dollar Savings

1. **Assess current costs of providing services without the workforce technology.** We use an activity-based costing approach to decompose how each service is delivered today. Who does each step, how much time does it take, what does that time cost, is there paper or postage involved in the step, and so forth. We focus on the steps performed by staff whose position can be eliminated such as administrative personnel, data entry staff, and HR specialists.

Hard-Dollar Cost Savings with Selected PeopleSoft Core Human Resources

PROCESSES	Current Costs	Costs with PeopleSoft	Percentage Savings
Applicant Tracking: Conduct Interview	$ 2.05	$ 1.90	7%
Personnel Administration: Personnel Action	$ .60	$ .40	33%
Personnel Administration: Off Cycle Pay Actions	$ 19.18	$ 12.42	35%
Compensation: Salary Budgeting—set up employee data	$ 18.43	$ 0	100%
Reporting: Obtain data for a headcount report, compile, distribute	$ 58.60	$ 9.21	84%
Interfaces: Build	$ 6,763	$ 3,540	47%

Table 1.

These result in hard-dollar savings. We also focus on those who may have time freed for other activities such as employees and managers, but their time and costs are merely productivity savings that we consider soft savings.

2. **Determine future costs of providing services with a technology solution.** Using the activity-based costing approach, we continue to assess who does each step, their time, the cost of that time, and any material or distribution costs in the future. We actually sit down with the technology and clock how long it takes to conduct a process in many cases.

3. **Summarize the savings between the current and future costs to get the resulting savings on a single transaction basis.** Then multiply that transaction savings times your volume of activity—for example, open enrollment savings is $80 per transaction, and 2,000 employees enroll each year, giving a resulting annual savings of $16,000

Hard-Dollar Cost Savings with Selected PeopleSoft Employee and Manager Self Service			
PROCESSES	**Current Costs**	**Costs with PeopleSoft**	**Percentage Savings**
e-Benefits: Enroll in Benefits	$109.48	$ 21.79	80%
e-Development: Enroll in Training	$ 17.77	$ 4.87	73%
e-Profile: Change Home Address	$ 12.86	$ 3.39	74%
e-Recruit: Apply for a Job	$ 21.31	$ 11.85	44%
e-Compensation Manager Desktop: Change salary	$ 44.67	$ 18.26	59%
e-Profile Manager Desktop: A-pprove Promotion	$ 48.64	$ 14.01	71%
e-Recruit Manager Desktop: Create Job Requisition	$ 36.89	$ 11.11	70%

Table 2.

4. **Assess and summarize the solution costs.** Both one-time investments such as license fees, hardware servers and public access workstations, training, internal and implementation services for development and customization; and ongoing costs such as IT support to maintain and upgrade the software, to manage the server systems and their upgrades, any help desk support, and ongoing customization and development. Areas that are often overlooked are business process redesign to take advantage of technology that streamlines business processes and change management—all those activities to ensure user adoption with the organization's culture—these latter two categories can be approximately 15 percent of the entire implementation costs.

5. **Calculate the return on investment metrics.** Net present value, internal rate of return, and payback period are typically required for a capital investment.[1]

In our experience, most workforce technologies can typically be paid for with staff elimination, error reduction and the risk of non-compliance, materials and distribution cost reductions, elimination of systems and their associated software and hardware maintenance costs, and outsourced service fee elimination.

However, staff elimination is sometimes not part of the organization's culture and policy—and, the HR function itself does not want to lose headcount as it has already been operating lean and mean for the past few years. But, if a move to self service identifies that the current data entry or administrative staff are no longer necessary, the organization must decide whether to eliminate the staff or undergo job redesign and transition the staff to more productive positions.

Thus, a result we see is that the identification of potential headcount reductions encourages management to use the information to manage resource levels of staff more effectively.

For example, at The Hartford, an ROI calculation identified a potential headcount reduction. This target staff elimination was used in determining staff resources for the following year. The various managers to be impacted by staff elimination agreed that they could eliminate only about two-thirds of the potential staff reduction— but, they had to justify why they still needed the other one-third staff they were not eliminating. In this case, the employees were used for new staff development (e-Learning) initiatives, but only under strict conditions that the contribution of these employees and the initiative itself were beneficial to the bottom line of the organization.

Soft savings made tangible can contribute to a winning justification.

Many executives consider anything other than hard-dollar savings unacceptable. The problem with this thinking is that some of the savings not being considered can actually provide a very compelling justification for strategic deployment of workforce technologies. In fact, some workforce technologies can actually contribute to improving shareholder value! According to Tom Pisello, president and CEO of Alinean, "Some CEOs and executives view intangible benefits as their most important decision-making criteria, and almost half look at both intangible and tangible benefits before giving the stamp of approval."[2]

The issue for those building justification arguments using soft, intangible savings is twofold: 1) converting soft savings to measurable, tangible savings, and then 2) convincing management that these are valid criteria to even use to justify an investment.

The first issue is easier to address than the second. According to Jack Keen, founder of The Deciding Factor, a consultant and author of an important book on building better business cases, "converting intangible benefits—payoffs with no measurable monetary value—into tangible benefits—payoffs with definable money value, can often make the difference between an accepted or rejected business case."[3, 4]

Everything that is real for a technology investment is measurable.

Mr. Keen's premise is that if a workforce technology is deemed as valuable it is valuable in some relevant way. If it is valuable in some relevant way, it is observable. If it is observable, it is observable in some amount. If it is observable in some amount, it can be measured. Everything that is real for a technology investment is measurable.

Converting Soft Savings into Measurable Savings

Cedar uses an approach that borrows from Keen's methodology, adding from our work in conducting and supporting numerous business cases in the human resources domain.

- **State the intangible.** For example, "HR self service, such as online benefit enrollment, 401(k) services, or online pay stubs improve employee satisfaction."
- **Define the cause and effect.** In many companies, HR service delivery creates frustration among employees. An organization that does not provide access to acceptable 401(k) services that enable an employee to manage this critical personal investment, can lead an employee to leave one organization for another that does provide good services. Acceptable services can improve employee satisfaction and the impact is reduced employee turnover. Reduced employee turnover, in turn, leads to reduced employee acquisition costs, which are a real, tangible hard-dollar cost savings. Consider that actually acquiring a new employee can cost from $500 to $100,000+ depending on the industry and the costs included.
- **Apply formulas to calculate the intangible into a measurable value.** In this case, we apply a factor that for every 2 percent increase in employee satisfaction, a 1 percent in turnover results.[5] The formula then is: Total number of employees times 1 percent times the average cost to acquire an employee. This latter cost can be comprised of recruiting costs, costs to bring a new employee up to speed, lost productivity costs of employees involved in on-the-job training and more.[6]
- **Provide citations of proof to support the claim.** When it was difficult to recruit high-tech workers, a broad spectrum of high growth firms used this argument to justify augmenting their employee self service offerings to employees as they needed to improve services to keep or attract employees. During that time, high-tech employees would migrate from firm to firm upon hearing of better services, such as "concierge benefits" at neighboring companies.[7]
- **Discuss and agree upon the impact potential.** For example, in the ROI calculators we build and use, we include numerous strategic savings but give the prospect the ability to state what

percent they will accept into their justification. Some organizations that we work with choose to augment their hard-dollar savings and ROI calculations with a small percentage of the employee acquisition cost reductions.

- **Define how to measure the impact after implementation and deploy the measurement approach.** To prove this particular case, organizations deployed two measures: employee satisfaction surveys to measure satisfaction before and after deploying self service, along with turnover.
- **Conduct post-implementation audit to assess actual impact.** Ideally, one year after deployment, results should be assessed.

The second issue, convincing management that the soft savings that have been turned into tangible savings are valid to *use* to justify an investment, requires a collaborative approach to workforce technologies justification as well as numerous examples of success using intangible savings. By collaborative approach, we mean that decision makers are involved in the business case development process and identify their expected outcomes and what will be their acceptable level of tolerance for measurable soft savings. In our experience, we find that because of the due diligence we have done to show the causal link between a workforce technology and potential soft savings (see Table 3), that management is willing to allow at least a small percentage of potential soft savings into the ROI calculation. However, so many workforce technologies can show hard-dollar savings, that this is not always necessary.

Acceptable services can improve employee satisfaction and the impact is reduced employee turnover. Reduced employee turnover, in turn, leads to reduced employee acquisition costs.

Soft Savings Made Tangible—A Few Examples

Soft Savings Statement	Rationale	Formula
Self service can improve employee retention thereby promoting customer loyalty which can in turn result in increased corporate profitability	Improving human resources services, by lightening the work burden through making administrative tasks simpler and more accessible through self service contribute to improved employee satisfaction. Employee satisfaction leads to improved employee retention. Research indicates that a 5 percent increase in retention can result in a 60 percent improvement in profits over a five-year period.[8] The rationale is that the longer employees stay with your company, the more familiar they become with the business . . . the more they learn . . . the more valuable they are . . . the more impact they have on customer loyalty. Therefore, if your employees' satisfaction with their work experience improves due to self service and employee retention improves by 5 percent, your organization might experience as much as a 60 percent increase in profits (or 15 percent for each 1 percent improvement in employee retention).	Current profit (or loss) x 1.6 = potential profit growth

(continued)

Table 3.

Table 3, continued

Soft Savings Statement	Rationale	Formula
Improved human resources record keeping can result in a decrease in workers compensation premiums	According to KPD Insurance, an organization focusing on workers compensation,[9] there is a 3 percent overpayment for workers compensation premiums due to job misclassifications. Improved human resources record keeping leads to correct job classifications. Note: This rationale can also be a true hard-dollar cost savings particularly if an organization's current processes contribute to considerable errors with workers' job classifications.	Number of employees times average salary = total annual payroll times 2.17[10] * 3 percent = potential savings in Workers' Compensation Premiums
Discrimination lawsuit risk can be avoided by deploying a global data warehouse and/or analytics software	Organizations can proactively identify workforce trends that indicate potential inequities in pay, promotions, or separation rates by race, gender, and age with operational reporting available within a data warehouse, or with trend analysis available in various analytical applications. Cedar's research indicates that .56 percent of an organization's employee population is awarded an average of $50,044 in a discrimination lawsuit.[11]	Number of employees times .56 percent times $50,044 = estimated value of avoiding a discrimination lawsuit

(continued)

Table 3, continued

Soft Savings Statement	Rationale	Formula
Use of performance management software can improve shareholder value	According to Watson Wyatt, superior human capital management practices are a leading indicator of financial performance.12 Companies with best human capital management practices provide three times the shareholder return as companies with weak practices. Specific practices drive shareholder value, while others diminish it. Among those that drive improved shareholder value, several are operationalized with performance management software: 1. Pay is linked to company business strategy (1.1 percent) 2. Top performers receive better pay than average performers (.8 percent) 3. Company promotes most competent employees (.9 percent) 4. Company helps poor performers improve (.7 percent) 5. Company terminates employees who continue to perform poorly (.6 percent)	Current shareholder value times 104.1 = improved shareholder value
Use of global warehouse can improve shareholder value	Watson Wyatt further reports that when increasing transaction accuracy/integrity is a key goal in implementing HR service technology, that this has a 1.9 percent positive impact on shareholder value.	Current shareholder value times 101.9 = improved shareholder value

Taking a Portfolio Approach to Justification

Recently we have begun conducting expanded return on investment analyses by assessing the total cost of ownership of the entire human capital management portfolio of workforce technologies. Rather than justify each technology on its own, we evaluate the impact of proposed, new workforce technologies against the total cost of ownership of *all* the human capital management (HCM) technologies in place at an organization. When a new technology is evaluated against the backdrop of the entire HCM portfolio, the result is a cost- and value-based view that encompasses our customer's long-term, HCM strategy. We thus show the total cost to deliver Human Capital Management services using a strategic technology portfolio that achieves the optimal balance of feature/functionality and return on total past and future investments.

At a leading, multi-national organization with over 100,000 employees engaged in the manufacture and sale of a broad range of health care products, we recently evaluated the contribution of a global warehouse—and associated analytical reporting—would have on the total cost of ownership (TCO) of the current portfolio of over 20 major corporate systems. In addition to a portfolio of over 20 major corporate systems, the organization has over 100 human resources-oriented systems in its various operating regions. To begin this process, we established a baseline of the TCO of the corporate systems. This is not always an easy exercise as the information resides with the system owners, finance, human resources, and information technology departments. We pieced together the initial capital and one-time expenses, including software license, hardware, internal and external implementation services, data cleansing efforts, and numerous other costs. We also determined the ongoing costs including internal labor from human resources and information technology, maintenance, upgrade, and hosting services, among others. With the initial costs and the ongoing costs, we were able to forecast TCO, with costs alone over a five-year period.

We then reviewed the potential savings for the global data warehouse against each of the 20 plus existing systems and determined the costs that could be eliminated or would be added.

We found the customer had no trusted global system of record for holding up-to-date compensation figures to support the annual compensation management process. Thus, they had established a process of feeding compensation figures from a global succession planning process and subsystem into the global compensation subsystem. Since the data warehouse could now serve as a global system of record that would be fed required compensation figures by the core HR system in domestic and international operations, there was no longer the need to have this extra integration between the succession planning and compensation subsystems. Thus, the cost for maintaining that particular system integration would be eliminated. We also found that while the current reporting process needed a new Export/Transform/Load (ETL) software facility, and the ETL software that comes with the global warehouse could be leveraged for this reporting.

The review process also helped us identify some data cleansing processes that could be eliminated—by transitioning to one global warehouse, the need to synchronize the 20 corporate systems was eliminated. Thus, reviewing the impact of a new system acquisition on *all* current systems helped us find numerous justification rationales. This process also built awareness among system owners of their current costs of ownership and the contribution the global warehouse could make. Given that our customer's long-term HR system strategy is to move from separate functional systems to a global, integrated system that supports performance management, this analysis also helped show management the value of this approach.

As mentioned above, we started this process by identifying the total cost of ownership of all current systems. Total cost of ownership can be just costs, or it can also be offset with savings that are possible with each system. In other words, subtract the savings to get a modified total cost of ownership—or perhaps a total value of ownership. Thus, in looking at the impact of the global warehouse, one-time and ongoing savings can also be reduced from the overall total cost of ownership. See Figure 1. For example, if the current cost to compile and distribute a global headcount report is $100,000 and the new cost with the global warehouse reporting facility is $10,000, then for each report, we can subtract $90,000 of compilation/distribution *savings* from the *costs* to yield a modified total cost of ownership that reflects more of the value of each system.

With a total cost of ownership baseline in place, all subsequent investment decisions can be made against their impact on the total portfolio costs and savings. By doing so, the organization takes a strategic view of workforce technologies investment and their contribution to services delivery. The expectation is that going forward, no further technologies will be evaluated individually, and thus fewer functional-oriented systems will continue to be implemented.

The approach takes into account and satisfies the perspectives of each key constituent: Human Resources that, in this case, has a vision of an integrated solution to support performance management); Information Technology that wants scalable, integrated, extensible technologies that will be supportable for the long term; and finance that needs to ensure that any investment creates acceptable economic value.

Continuing Post Implementation Audits Make Justifications Easier

The above approaches result in winning workforce technology justifications. But to be able to continue to garner investment dollars, you also need to prove your results. You need to be able to make sure you actually get the results you estimated in your justification and you need to know how to fine tune your approach for future justifications. Cedar has conducted numerous post-implementation audits at organizations where we also conducted their initial business case. We actually use our ROI models to collect baseline information, and then can summarize savings accumulated after the implementation has been in place for at least one year. The value of this process is first of all, that our ROI calculators become learning models that can be constantly

	Initial Capital Expenses	Initial One Time Expenses plus Upgrades	Ongoing Expenses Including Labor	Total System Costs	Direct Savings (One Time)	Direct Savings (Ongoing)	Total System Savings	TOTAL COST OF OWNERSHIP
Plan, Attract, Onboard								
Recruiting solution	$ 2,000,000	$ 500,000	$ 1,000,000	**$ 3,300,000**	$ 700,000	$ 150,000	**$ 850,000**	**$ 2,450,000**
Subtotal	$ 2,000,000	$ 500,000	$ 1,000,000	**$ 3,300,000**	$ 700,000	$ 150,000	**$ 850,000**	**$ 2,450,000**
Assess, Design, Develop								
Learning Management System	$ 300,000	$ 50,000	$ 500,000	**$ 850,000**	$ 100,000	$ 250,000	**$ 350,000**	**$ 500,000**
Succession Planning	$ 800,000	$ —	$ 300,000	**$ 1,150,000**	$ 250,000	$ 250,000	**$ 500,000**	**$ 600,000**
Subtotal	$ 1,100,000	$ 50,000	$ 800,000	**$ 1,950,000**	$ 350,000	$ 500,000	**$ 850,000**	**$1,100,000**
Optimize, Track, Monitor								
Core HR	$ 6,000,000	$2,000,000	$ 2,500,000	**$10,500,000**		$ 450,000	**$ 450,000**	**$10,500,000**
Data Warehouse and Reporting	$ 500,000	$ —	$ 750,000	**$ 1,250,000**			**$ —**	**$ 1,250,000**
Employee/Manager Self Service	$ 1,500,000	$ —	$ 200,000	**$ 1,700,000**		$ 225,000	**$ 225,000**	**$ 1,475,000**
Subtotal	$ 8,000,000	$2,000,000	$ 3,450,000	**$13,450,000**	$ —	$ 675,000	**$ 675,000**	**$12,775,000**
Plan, Incent, Reward								
Benefits	$ 7,000,000	$ —	$ 7,000,000	**$14,000,000**		$ 700,000	**$ 700,000**	**$13,300,000**
Compensation Planning	$ 2,500,000	$ —	$ 750,000	**$ 3,250,000**	$ —	$2,400,000	**$2,400,000**	**$ 850,000**
Subtotal	$ 9,500,000	$ —	$ 7,750,000	**$17,250,000**	$ —	$3,100,000	**$3,100,000**	**$14,150,000**
GRAND TOTAL	**$20,600,000**	**$2,550,000**	**$13,000,000**	**$39,950,000**	**$1,050,000**	**$4,425,000**	**$5,475,000**	**$30,475,000**
Proposed Investment								
Global Warehouse	$ 2,500,000	$ 750,000	$ 600,000	**$ 3,850,000**	$ 200,000	$3,000,000	**$3,200,000**	**$ 650,000**

Note: Depreciation has been excluded from the costs in order to show most of the model components.

Figure 1. Total Costs – Total Savings = Total Cost of Ownership

fine-tuned based on customer experience. We typically not only provide summary reports of savings achieved, but also do "go forward" analysis that then enable our customers to prioritize the next set of workforce technologies that can provide value.

To conduct a post-implementation audit for your organization, you need to collect numerous baseline data (see Table 4). This data can then be used to show current costs and operational effectiveness before and after.

Suggested Baseline Data for Post Implementation Audits

- Number of employees
- Employee satisfaction with HR services including perception of convenience, contribution to decision making, understanding of options and choices, image of Human Resources
- Operational metrics (these will vary by organization and department but might include revenue by employee, sales by employee, turnover, errors by employee, etc.)
- By process/transaction: volume, steps, cycle time, process time, hand offs, labor costs, material, and distribution costs
- Solution costs see discussion on ROI and TCO above for the components
- Numerous measures related to web usage including number of users who started a process and completed it, errors by day, transaction volume, etc.

Table 4.

Conclusion

Organizations need investment decision-making approaches that can encompass both hard- and soft-dollar justifications. The best approach, however, will evaluate the role of any workforce technology being assessed, against the whole HCM technology portfolio. By doing so, the organization moves from tactical ROI assessment to a strategic, value-based, assessment that will transform HCM services delivery.

Diligent organizations, on deploying any new workforce technology, will put in place metrics so they can audit results of their technology deployments compared to their predicted returns. A post-implementation audit can help them to learn and improve their next justification analysis as well as assist them in future prioritization of workforce technologies deployments. The end result of these justification approaches will blend an optimal balance of feature/functionality of an HCM workforce technologies portfolio and the return on total investments, past and future.

Endnotes

1. McCready, Scott (2002). *TCO, NPV, EVA, IRR, ROI—Getting the Terms Right*, white paper published by CIOview Corporation.
2. Pisello, Tom (2003). "The ROI for Human Capital Management Solutions," *IHRIM.link*, June/July 2003.
3. Keen, Jack and Digrius, Bonnie (2003). *Making Technology Investments Profitable: ROI Road Map to Better Business Cases*, New York: John Wiley & Sons.
4. Keen, Jack (2003). *ROI: Turn "Soft" Benefits into Hard Savings*—a top tip available on his web site; www.decidingfactor.com.
5. Talley, Jerry, 2001. Interview conducted with the President of Organizational Diagnostics, a management consulting firm in Mountain View, California, specializing in employee satisfaction research in high-tech firms.
6. Employee acquisition costs include recruitment and advertising fees that are costs that can be eliminated. They also include cost to train an employee and bring them up to proficiency, including lost time of other personnel spent doing on the job training. In our work with customers, we see a low end of acquisition costs ranging from $500 within the retail industry to a high in the $100,000+ range for a high-tech specialist.
7. Examples of concierge services included on the job dry cleaning; travel, hotel, and restaurant reservations; handling of house cleaner or child care arrangements; and other services that contributed to the quality of life for workers.
8. Rucci, Anthony J., Kim, Steven P., and Quinn, Richard T. (1998). "The Employee-Customer-Profit Chain at Sears," *Harvard Business Review*, January/February, 1998.
9. KPD Perspective (2002), newsletter published by KPD Insurance, Medford, Oregon.
10. BLS stat from HR Calculator.
11. Cedar research (2002). We collected settlement costs from organizations in different industries such as K-Mart, Coca-Cola, Waste Management, and University of South Florida and then averaged the total settlement amount and the amount awarded per employee covered by the settlement. With this information, we calculated the percentage of employees covered within each organization. By using the percentage of employees covered and the average settlement amount, we can

estimate a potential lawsuit amount for any organization. However, when applying this rationale, it is best to substitute your own organization's average settlement amounts.

12. Human Capital Index: Human Capital as a Lead Indicator of Shareholder Value, 2002 Survey, Watson Wyatt.

Tod Loofbourrow

Tod Loofbourrow is President and CEO of Authoria, Inc., the world leader in personalized, Web-based human resource communication. Today, over one hundred organizations worldwide rely on Authoria to dramatically improve employee communication while streamlining costs. Based in Waltham, MA, Authoria has been ranked three times by *Inc.* magazine as one of America's fastest-growing private companies. It has also been named three times to the prestigious Deloitte & Touche New England Technology Fast 50 and National Technology Fast 500 listings. The author of publications about knowledge-based systems and B2B Internet commerce, Loofbourrow's work has been featured in dozens of publications including *The Wall Street Journal*, *The New York Times*, and *Forbes Magazine*. He is a graduate of Harvard University and has performed graduate work at Harvard and Oxford Universities. Mr. Loofbourrow can be reached at tod.loofbourrow@authoria.com.

three : 4

The Role of Personalized Knowledge to Support Employee Self-Service Transactions

What can we expect next in the ever-changing world of service delivery on the Web? For one thing, we need more personalization and knowledge support before we can provide true end-to-end delivery of employee self-service, HR call centers, and associated infrastructures.

Consider the following: To date, self-service and portal deployments have not always yielded direct savings, and initiatives have often been hampered by limited budgets and anticipated high costs of ownership. In Towers Perrin's Web-Based Self-Service Survey, for instance, respondents acknowledged that the reality of web self-service has not yet fully lived up to its promise. While 80 percent of the survey group agreed that use of web self-service could lower HR operating costs, only 40 percent said it had actually lowered costs in their organization.

Similarly, while 96 percent said it would improve the quality and timeliness of services to employees, only 70 percent agreed the move to Web self-service had done so already. Nonetheless, in a demonstration of continued faith in technology, fully 76 percent said they planned to increase their investment in benefit applications, with the remainder saying they would hold their investment steady.

More Personalization Needed

These challenges indicate a growing need for more personalization of the information employees can now access on their own. Without the personalization needed to reduce the noise of the massive amounts of information available via the web, employees will be unable to focus on their specific needs and will continue to use other, more traditional means of obtaining information. Think about the kind of personalized information that cannot be delivered by the most sophisticated of today's self-service applications and portal capabilities. Even though self-service taps an employee's individual data in an HRMS database, most self-service web pages are simply predefined information from that HRMS, with the user seeing only the data displayed on the web pages. While that information is very valuable, what happens if an employee needs to know if he can receive long-term disability benefits due to a drug or alcohol problem? Or if her dental plan covers orthodontia? Or whether and how he can borrow from his 401(k)? What does the employee need to know for the birth of a child? These are the kinds of questions employees need tailored to their own personal situation before making a decision or transaction.

The need is particularly evident in the area of employee benefits. As confirmed in the 2002 Towers Perrin HR Service Delivery Survey, organizations need to find the right balance between high-tech transactional efficiency and high-touch personal contact within the employer-employee relationship. This is why the survey shows that the number of calls to HR service centers has changed in complexity but not significantly decreased with the use of web self-service. According to the study, most employees are still more comfortable calling the service center to get answers to their complex questions—those requiring the knowledge and expertise of the HR professional.

Knowledge to Support Transactions

By all estimates, the next major step is the use of HR knowledge applications—software that delivers HR-specific knowledge, configuration capability, a common repository of information, and personalized presentation to the employee. The knowledge application delivers immediate, personalized, intelligent answers to employee questions about benefits and HR policies, round-the-clock. Web-based by definition, HR knowledge applications can provide dynamic personalized answers to almost any employee benefits-related question—from, "Does maternity leave coordinate with FMLA?" or "Will I receive a benefit if I carpool to work?" to life events such as, "How do I enroll a new baby in my health plan?" or "What do I need to know about buying a house?"

HR knowledge applications craft plain-language answers to workforce questions by combining industry and company information with employee-specific data from an HRMS database, data mart, or other source. The result is actionable, personalized HR knowledge. The questions and answers can all be made via direct HR self-service access or from knowledge application access by service center representatives who relay answers over the phone. Knowledge applications can also provide detailed comparisons of benefit plans, and be implemented with over 80 percent of commonly asked HR questions installed as core content or domain specific knowledge.

This is a type of HR knowledge management that is situational in nature, derived from many sources, and only practical and possible with today's HR technology. It is not the application of technology to document management, text management, or case-based reasoning—the traditional foundations of static knowledge storing and sharing within an enterprise. Available on an installed or outsourcing basis, HR knowledge applications reduce administrative costs, leverage ERP systems, improve service to employees, and greatly enhance personalization, taking employees from self-service to a new degree of self-sufficiency.

The trend is catching on fast, with knowledge applications or knowledge-base technology already in use at a substantial number of corporations.

The Cedar 2001 HR Self Service/Portal Survey reports an increase of 100 percent over the previous year in the use of knowledgebases in North America to drive personalization and access to employee-specific data. The survey findings state:

> Another emerging key technology solution is HR knowledgebase products that deliver knowledge and content in a personalized format. Personalized knowledge is a driver to help employees understand and make decisions, which can then result in self-service transactions. Over 75 percent of all respondents report they use or plan to use a structured repository of HR-oriented knowledge to enable employees to access frequently asked questions, Summary Plan Descriptions, and data personalized to the specific employee and the role they play in the organization.

Towers Perrin's s 2001 HR Service Center Survey confirms this. Nearly 60 percent of the survey respondents reported they use a knowledgebase and find it both effective and critical to their operations because they can deliver informed, web-based answers to thousands of benefit and HR policy questions almost instantly. The survey showed that companies are turning to knowledgebase technology to meet the need to consolidate and personalize information and respond quickly and meaningfully to employees. The study noted that "...(a knowledgebase) allows employers to consolidate all of their HR information in a centralized online location and helps create a personalized experience for employees."

HR Knowledge Application Advantages

Here are just a few of the many advantages that HR knowledge applications provide.

Personalizing Content for Strategic Dissemination

Communications change, particularly in HR. Unfortunately, when people think of portals they think of the way that the worldwide web works. A portal provides the conduit by which employers speak to their employees. A knowledge application is capable of personalization, meaning that what appears in the portal allows the employer to speak directly to the intended audience (e.g., employee, service center representative, HR manager), in the appropriate format. A knowledge application enables you to transform how you say what you want to say, versus taking what you have today and reconstituting static text in a different location and format. Personalization means creating a portal that truly communicates.

Personalization in a knowledge application is important in employee self-service. It is also critical to drive how customer service representatives handle calls in an organization's service center. It is critical in how HR managers or other managers see information both on their own information as employees of an organization, but also how they access and view personalized information regarding those employees for whom they answer HR-related questions.

Centralization of Information into a Single Knowledge Repository

HR communications are complex, that's why HR communications cost so much to create. Documents exist in disparate locations and for even modest-sized companies, the question of how to assemble a meaningful answer from all of the facts on HR that exist in an average organization becomes a difficult one. A knowledge application provides a solution by transforming the communications challenge from one in which people create documents in serial fashion for discreet purposes into a scenario that fundamentally changes how you address the way you manage information.

A single knowledge repository becomes the standard and centerpiece—the single location—in which plan, policy, and life event design types are stored. These plans and policies appear differently for different audiences. They appear differently based on personalization. Characteristics may appear differently in a summary plan description rendered in a PDF than they would as HTML on the web. The information may appear differently if configured for a CSR on the web versus an employee using information as decision-support as part of a self-service transaction. Transforming and centralizing information into a knowledge repository means creating a strategy to disseminate a sanctioned answer in multiple formats. From one place, driving consistency, you gain usability across multiple channels.

Single Link to Virtual Content

Knowledge applications feature virtual pages versus actual pages. This means that you'll build and maintain fewer pages during construction of the web site. Over time, you'll have less to keep up to date year-to-year. Most importantly, you'll say more about benefits because personalization means you don't have to consider the business logic surrounding a particular web page as you would if you were posting static text or using a document management system. Instead, the knowledge application puts a filter on the content so that a single link goes to exactly that content that should be visible to a particular audience.

The knowledge application proposition is a single link to personalized content. That is, in other words, if one placed a link that stated "Annual Enrollment is underway," the link doesn't bring the employee to a single document or a series of documents that the individual needs to sort through. Instead, a page personalized to the individual's actual information. A knowledge application takes away the need to build logic on documents or create libraries of links because a single link will configure a page that speaks directly to the audience it is intended to address. Personalization within a knowledge application means that portal designers no longer need to think about the "what if's" around putting certain types of information out there—because the information will only appear to those who should see it.

Application for Content Configuration

A knowledge application is designed to manage and communicate HR information for organizations. The part that is most visible lies in how a knowledge application scales for presenting personalized content in different formats across multiple channels. Just as important is the second half of the equation, which is how a knowledge application *manages* information. When organizations turn to a knowledge applications, the business issue they are looking to solve often revolves around the complex nature of HR communications that breeds static text documentation—web sites, summary plan descriptions, annual enrollment brochures, instructions for transactional self-service web sites or IVR, call center scripts, and so on.

To create a single knowledge repository that contains the organization's sanctioned answer that feeds all of the channels listed above and more, a knowledge application needs a configuration tool that allows users to configure content in a fashion specific to their organization. One employer calls its employees "associates," another "team members." One employer refers to its 401(k) plan as the "Employee Savings Plan" and another calls it the "Retirement Savings and Investment Program." A knowledge application must allow configuration capability so that these differences may be represented from employer to employer from the single knowledge application.

Configuration must go even further than that. It also must represent differences within organizations, so that a category of plans such as medical may be represented differently depending on whether the plan in question is an HMO, PPO, POS, Indemnity, retiree, or other sort of plan. A compensation plan may grant bonuses based strictly based on performance or there may be strict guidelines in place based on broadbanding rules that govern an organization's compensation philosophy. One office location allows workers in Boston to take Patriot's Day off for the Boston Marathon versus another location that offers the Day before the 4th of July or floating holiday. All of these differences are centralized and configurable using the knowledge application.

Finally, it's important to note the difference between configuration and customization. Configuration means accessibility to the underlying knowledge repository to make point-in-time changes to communications in a scalable way. Customization means altering the structure of the knowledge repository itself or building a solution versus buying into the overall value proposition of knowledge applications.

Ability to Begin Your Project with Domain Knowledge in Place

HR's complexity comes from personalization and diversity of plan types. A knowledge application makes configuration and maintenance of different plan and policy design types easier by coupling configuration capability with built-in industry standard knowledge models. A knowledge application doesn't know what *your* medical plan looks like, but knows how the plan characteristics of an HMO differ from that of an indemnity plan, PPO, POS, and so on.

The structure of the plan type is in place in the knowledge model. Coupled with the configuration capability of the knowledge application toolset, you have a method and mechanism of speeding implementation by starting with industry standards and common features in place. You do not need to think about how communications about the legislative elements of FMLA work or where and how they should appear. You do not need to think of all the things you need to say about how a cash balance pension plan works versus a final average pay plan. The characteristics and standard structural elements of these plan and policy design types preexist within the knowledge application and are then configured to the specific communications preferences of your organization during implementation. You don't start with a blank sheet of paper or an empty web page—you start with a structure and organizing principle, then make it your own through configuration.

Facilitating Data Gathering through Built-In Intelligence

A knowledge application enables configuration with intelligence built-in. When using a tool without intelligence, you need to do all of the structural thinking that surrounds building the right answers to put on the screen, the format and order to place them in, the appropriate links to other content, the required characteristics that most usefully illustrate how the plan works, legal elements, and so on. There is a great deal of work involved in creating this structure for communications.

With a knowledge application, this structure already exists within the context of domain-specific knowledge. Knowledge applications then take the value proposition a step further by creating intelligence in how implementers collect, configure, and maintain information within the knowledge repository. In implementing a vacation plan, the system will ask you different questions, depending on whether the number of weeks is automatic based on years of service or earned over time in a time-off bank. If an implementer indicates that dependent children are covered under the plan, another question is asked regarding what the specific definition of a dependent child is.

Asking only the right question at the time of implementation and configuration is a critical component of implementing fast and creating a structure for rapid maintenance over time. HR's complexity means that there are a number of different ways in which an employer may offer a medical benefit, vanpool, dental plan, personal leave, and so on. Intelligent data gathering means getting more communications in place, because you only deal with what really matters to your organization. Intelligence takes the breadth of industry knowledge and allows you to focus on only that cross-section that applies to your organization today. By only asking the right questions, you dramatically speed the time it takes to get communications on the web or to generate a summary plan description.

Enabling Technologies Improve Your Technology Infrastructure

By choosing a knowledge application, you are making a choice to implement something that will fit into multiple formats and in multiple ways into the solutions that organizations are building. Just as importantly, the facts about your benefit plans and HR policies are captured in ways that allow the information to remain flexible as your web and HR communications strategies evolve. By serving as an enabling technology that powers and provides for communications needs across the entire lifecycle, knowledge applications are designed to change as your needs change—and fit into how your delivery system works today. This flexibility means consistency with what you have in place today and changeability that by nature assumes compatibility with where you wish to be in the future.

Limiting Interpretation and Maximizing Breadth of Understanding

Knowledge applications allow users to see exactly what they should see, plus give avenues into other areas of content that might be important to the individual. Knowledge applications feature intelligence that allows you to capture more information and make the information included personalized meaning more information with a greater focus across all of HR and benefits. This helps employees make informed decisions.

In addition, the level of detail, accuracy, and consistency that a knowledge applications provides will eliminate or reduce the interpretation of information. The complexity of information and the disparate sources in can be gathered from, open up the potential for misinterpretation and confusion. For example a CSR or employee may seek information about a benefits-related question from a SPD, static text on a website, or another benefit communication vehicle. Since these communication tools are not targeted to an audience of one, the answers they find may be vague, conditional in nature, inconsistent, or outdated.

Life Events Represent Information in Context

Content does not need to exist discreetly within a knowledge application, because employees do not think of these topics discreetly. In many cases, employee decisions are based on an enrollment decision or life event. In these cases, it's content from multiple areas that matters most—for example, if someone's child is going away to college, it's not just benefits decisions that matters. In addition to consideration such as out-of-area care under an HMO's provisions, also important are things like the existence of a company-sponsored scholarship, availability of loans from the Savings Plan, process for taking time-off to assist in the move, and so on. Each of these topics might be searched for and accessed separately. Knowledge applications eliminate these steps by bringing discreet but related topics together for easier accessibility and understanding on the part of employees, customer service representatives, and so on.

This capability transforms communications from a research process to a delivery scenario. Organizations want employees to appreciate what's offered to them. They want them to understand the value of the HR offerings available to them. Knowledge applications bring the right decisions and information before them at the time they need to make a decision. Searching through each disparate topic that might be related to a particular life event puts the research burden on the shoulders of employees and service representatives. Knowledge applications clarify this process by placing a contextual filter on what individuals need to know as they experience different situations in their lives.

Enable Intelligent Searches by Users

This single access point may either exist as a link directly to content or may take the form of a search generated via a question such as, "I got a 'C' in my MBA class, do I still get tuition reimbursement?" In the case of searching, the knowledge application provides meaningful search results that are specifically generated based on the appropriate and personalized information. Searching the web without context and personalization often leads to incredible diversity in search results rendered. Knowledge applications sharpen the focus on the targeted results and get users closer to meaningful results.

Knowledge applications make the world of the web a smaller place. They create a more narrow target and provide validated responses that are themselves personalized, date effective, targeted toward the person asking the question—be it an employee or customer service representative. Finally, knowledge applications allow organizations to speak to an audience of one—enabling the kind of high-touch, service results that employees seek in benefits communication.

| CHAPTER FOUR |

Leading and Managing People in a Networked World

Joseph H. Boyett PhD

Joseph H. Boyett PhD and Jimmie T. Boyett are co-founders of Boyett & Associates, an Atlanta-based consulting and research firm specializing in helping companies understand and implement state-of-the-art management and organizational practices. Dr. Boyett has worked with companies such as IBM, BP Oil, Merck & Company, EDS, and BellSouth on leading-edge strategies for securing competitive advantage. He is an internationally recognized expert, author, and speaker on such topics as change management, high performance work teams, and innovative compensation practices. He holds a PhD from the University of Georgia in Political Science. He can be reached at joe@jboyett.com.

Jimmie T. Boyett

Jimmie T. Boyett specializes in business systems re-engineering and the innovative use of information systems technology. Her research includes international systems and techniques for the radical redesign and re-engineering of business processes as well as the application of leading edge information systems technology. She is the co-author of six books and holds an MA in history from the University of Georgia. Ms. Boyett can be reached at jimmie@jboyett.com.

four : 1

Building a High-Performance Culture: Timeless Lessons from the World's Greatest Entrepreneurs

When we were conducting research for *The Guru Guide™ to Entrepreneurship* (Wiley, 2001), we studied the lives of seventy of the world's greatest entrepreneurs. They include such business titans as Sam Walton, Fred Smith, Bill Gates, Soichiro Honda, Body Shop founder Anita Roddick, Walt Disney, Michael Dell, Jeff Bezos, Sony co-founder Akio Morita, and over sixty others. One of the things we hoped to learn from the experiences of these business legends was how they were able to create strong and enduring cultures that enabled their companies to perform at peak levels in good economic times and bad. While there is probably no definitive list of what it takes to make a truly great company, we identified ten cultural imperatives from our study of the great entrepreneurs that undoubtedly represent an excellent starting point.

Culture Lesson #1: Commit to Nothing Less than Performance Excellence

This is perhaps the strongest and most important culture lesson we learned from the great entrepreneurs. The key to building a company that lasts is embedding an obsession with outstanding performance and precise execution within the very fabric of the business. The world's greatest entrepreneurs were obsessed with getting every detail of performance right and insisted that their employees do the same. They were tough and demanding bosses. In fact, company legends develop around instances of the founding entrepreneur's anger at shoddy work. For example, Howard Johnson had a problem with one of his franchisees not keeping his restaurant clean. Johnson had complained several times without results, so one day he went to the restaurant, called everyone outside, including the franchisee, and padlocked the door. He then pointed to the sign over the restaurant and said, "You see that sign up there, it says Howard Johnson and the way you're keeping this place says Howard Johnson is a slob. I'm not removing the lock until you clean up."[1]

Ray Kroc was so obsessed with getting every little thing right at McDonald's that he laid out elaborate guidelines for constructing the perfect hamburger. Hamburger patties were to weigh precisely 1.6 ounces and measure 3.875 inches in diameter—not four inches, but 3.875 inches. Each pound of meat was to make 10 hamburgers and the meat was to contain no lungs, hearts, or cereal and only 19 percent fat. The meat patty was to be place on a bun that had to be exactly 3½ inches wide and was to be topped with precisely one-fourth ounce of onions. Everything was to be kept fresh. French fries were to be thrown away if not sold within seven minutes. Hamburgers could be kept only ten minutes and coffee only thirty.[2]

And Then Some

A very successful businessman was once asked, "To what do you attribute your success?" "I can tell you in three words," he answered. "And then some." "What do you mean, 'and then some'?" he was questioned. "Do everything that's expected of you," he explained, "and then some."[3]

—*Mary Kay Ash*

This determination to accept nothing less than the highest standard of performance is a culture lesson taught by all of the great entrepreneurs. Their reasoning, says Steven Jobs, co-founder of Apple Computer, is that "people get far more excited about doing something as well as it can be done than about doing something adequately. If they are working in an environment where excellence is expected, then they will do excellent work without anything but self-motivation."[4]

> If you don't like to work hard and be intense and do your best, [Microsoft] is not the place to work.[5] —*Bill Gates*

The great entrepreneurs frequently carried their obsessions with perfection to extremes. For example, Dave Thomas recalls that Colonel Harland Sanders was a really nice man, but he had a mean temper. "If something wasn't right, he'd let loose with a string of cuss words that could make you feel two feet high."[6] Thomas said the Colonel didn't want to cuss and felt really bad about it. He even prayed to stop but couldn't.

Sochiro Honda had a similar fiery temper that could actually, on occasion, lead him to strike workers when their performance didn't live up to his expectations. Hideo Sugiura, an engineer who worked with Honda, recalled one of his scariest encounters with his boss as follows:

> On many occasions Honda struck me. One time, he hit me in front of twenty or thirty of my subordinates. Earlier that day, I was working in my office when an employee ran in with a panicked expression, saying that the president was asking for me. I ran out and asked Honda what was wrong. Without saying a word, he suddenly hit me.
>
> It turned out that the cause of his anger was a bolt that was supposed to stick out by a maximum of 2mm was but was protruding by 5mm. Honda screamed, "Who was in charge of such a ridiculous design? It was you!"
>
> Before I could say anything or apologize, wham! He hit me again. Frankly, I was seething with resentment. As the chief leader of a thousand employees at the research lab, I had my pride, too. Sure, what he was saying was true, but he didn't have to hit me in front of everyone.[7]

A former President of Honda recalls that the founder would also throw things at people who displeased him. "When he got mad, he blindly reached for anything lying around, and started throwing whatever was in reach randomly at people; it was dangerous! The desks in our office were covered with dents and scratches from the wrenches and hammers that the boss threw around."[8]

In spite of such tirades, Sochiro Honda was worshipped and respected by many, if not most, of his employees. How could that be true? Hideo Sugiura provides an explanation in the second half of his recollection of the hitting incident. Sugiura says he was standing there after being hit the second time and was thinking he couldn't take such abuse any more and was just going to quit right then. But, recalls Sugiura, when he raised his head to glare at Honda, he saw something that changed his mind.

> His eyes had welled up with tears. When I saw that, I couldn't say anything. I thought, he's serious. The boss just wanted to convey to me how important vehicle design was, and how rigorous we must be at every step. It was a small detail, but if we slacked off with even a small part, we could not make reliable products.
>
> That's the point he wanted to make. And to teach not just me, but all the engineers, he hit me.
>
> Believe me, I learned an important lesson that day.[9]

While hitting employees is definitely not something we would recommend, the incident illustrates just how serious the great entrepreneurs were about performance excellence and how determined they were to instill those values in all who worked for them.

> People . . . generally do what you expect them to do! If you expect them to perform well, they will; conversely, if you expect them to perform poorly, they'll probably oblige.[10] —*Mary Kay Ash*

Note: For an excellent discussion and summary of research that supports this cultural lesson about the importance of tough and demanding performance goals see Gary P. Latham, "Motivating Employee Performance through Goal-Setting" in Edwin A. Locke, editor, *The Blackwell Handbook of Principles of Organizational Behavior* (Malden, MA: Blackwell Publishers, Ltd., 2000), pp. 107–119.

Culture Lesson #2: Be Obsessed with Listening to Your Customers and Responding to Their Concerns

The great entrepreneurs understand that excellence today doesn't mean excellence tomorrow. Customers needs, desires, hopes, and expectations are constantly changing. The company that doesn't listen to its customers soon ends up with no customers to listen to at all. That's why the great entrepreneurs are obsessed with customer contact.

In fact, many of the great entrepreneurs saved their businesses because they were smart enough to listen to and learn from their customers. For example, Robert Greenberg, founder of LA Gear, originally opened a retail store on Melrose Avenue in Los Angeles to sell his own line of apparel, jeans, and footwear. Greenberg said that he wasn't sure at the start which part of the business would catch on, but he hoped that at least one would. When he observed that customers were buying a lot more shoes than they were apparel and jeans, he sold off the apparel business and announced that from then on he was in the shoe business.[11]

The great entrepreneurs understand that excellence today doesn't mean excellence tomorrow.

Other successful entrepreneurs have listened to their customers and found themselves totally rethinking their ideas. For example, Joshua Lionel Cowen originally marketed his Lionel train as a store window novelty meant to be used to display merchandise and attract customers.

It was only when the customers began insisting on buying the trains themselves that Cowen got the idea to market his device, not as a store display, but as a toy.[12] William Alle Burpee, founder of Burpee Seed, had a similar experience. He set out originally to sell purebred livestock and fowl by mail order. As an additional service, he began including several varieties of seeds to provide purchasers of his livestock and fowl with the proper feed for their animals. It wasn't until he noticed that his seed were outselling his animals that Burpee came to the conclusion that he was in the seed business, not the animal business.[13]

> Companies that are successful today—and, perhaps more importantly, companies that will be successful tomorrow—are those that can get closest to their customers' needs.[14] —*Michael Dell*

Michael Dell says that when he tells people he spends nearly 40 percent of his time with customers, the reaction he usually gets is, "Wow—that's a lot of time to spend with customers." His response? "I thought that was my job."[15]

Almost all of the entrepreneurs we cover in *The Guru Guide™ to Entrepreneurship* reported spending much of their time out of their offices, meeting with, and talking to customers. For example, Bernie Marcus and Arthur Blank donned orange aprons and worked in their Home Depot stores, waiting on customers, listening to complaints, and asking questions. Marcus says it was through those personal experiences that he and Blank found out what they were doing right and wrong during the early years of building the company. In the beginning, he reports, he would even chase down customers in the parking lot to find out what they needed.[16]

> A very important part of our philosophy . . . is letting the customers provide the yellow brick road to success . . . We have always felt that if we listen, they'll give us the answer we need.[17] —*Arthur Blank*

Richard Branson took a similar hands-on approach to listening to customers when he was starting Virgin Atlantic Airlines. Among other things, Branson would call Virgin reservations to see how his people were handling calls. He frequently boarded Virgin flights and spent the time aloft talking to the passengers and cabin crew. He insisted that every Virgin flight have a visitor's book where passengers could record their comments. Each month Branson picked fifty passengers at random who had written comments in the book and called them to apologize for the airline's mistake or comment on their idea. And, when station managers informed him that Virgin flights had been severely delayed, as they had standing orders to do, he would call the departure lounge and ask his staff to pass along his personal apologies for the delay. Customers were often astonished at Branson's personal involvement. Here was the chairman of Virgin Group on the telephone with an apology. Some were so surprised they refused to take the call or believe it was really Branson, thinking it was just a practical joke.[18]

> One of the most surprising things we learned early on from our customers was that they really valued being asked [their opinion.][19]
>
> —*Michael Dell*

The great entrepreneurs think that embedding customer listening into the very fabric of their companies is so important that most require their entire top management team to spend at least some time each year working directly with customers. Herb Kelleher, for example, requires each officer of Southwest Airlines to work in the field as a reservation agents, baggage handler, dispatcher, or in some similar position where they have hands-on contact with customers. The officers must report back to Kelleher on what they did, what they found, and the steps they took to improve the job they performed. Kelleher says that the exposure senior managers get to line operations can have enormous benefits. He credits the development and implementation of a major proprietary sales system to the experience one group of Southwest officers had while working a late night shift at the airport. This night there were an unusual number of weather-related problems and delays. The officers stood helpless as their employees shuffled through mounds of forms while the passengers became increasing irritated. They came away from the experience convinced that the system had to be changed, and it was.[20] And, Marcus and Blank required all new employees of Home Depot, including executives, to spend two weeks on the sales floor of a Home Depot store so they could get to know the company's customers.

Dell says the key to making your customer contact work for you is to really make an effort "to engage in a cooperative, mutually beneficial dialogue—not just talking at, or talking to, your customers, but talking with them—and really listening to what they have to say." "When you engage directly with customers," says Dell, "you begin to develop an intimate understanding of their likes, needs, and priorities. You find out what's working for them—and why. You can try out new ideas on them—ideas worth millions of R&D dollars and countless hours of your people's valuable time—and they'll tell you whether you're on track or not."[21]

Dell adds that listening to customers is a job that is not only redeeming and refreshing for employees but also highly lucrative. For example, he says lessons Dell executives learned during a visit with BP Oil led Dell to create Dell Plus, a multi-million dollar program of system integration services. But, what happens when your chain of businesses grows so big that you can't fly on every flight, chase down disenchanted customers in every parking lot, or personally visit every corporate customer's business? What do you do then? You create the infrastructure to keep listening, say the great entrepreneurs.

You create the infrastructure to keep listening, say the great entrepreneurs.

When Home Depot began to grow, Marcus and Blank decided they needed a more formal mechanism for listening to customers, so they created the position of director of consumer affairs and staffed it with the now-famous Ben Hill. They posted large signs and freestanding sandwich boards at the front of every store with a silhouetted profile of Ben and the words: "Are you satisfied? If not, contact the store manager, _______________, or call me, Ben Hill, director of consumer affairs, at 800-533-3199." Dissatisfied customers who called that number reached a main office switchboard at Home Depot's corporate headquarters in Atlanta. What they didn't know when they asked to speak to Ben Hill was that there was no such person. Ben Hill was fictitious. The words "Ben Hill," however, were a code-red signal to "expedite the call right now." And, who took those expedited calls? Bernie Marcus, Arthur Blank, or if they were not available for some reason, the highest ranking person in the company available to take the call. Whoever was available dropped whatever they were doing, even if it was signing a million-dollar deal, to take the call. It didn't take long, says Marcus, for word to get around Home Depot stores that if you let a customer leave unhappy, the next call you got might be from Marcus or Blank with a order something like this: "I just got a call from a customer on the Ben Hill line, and we're in trouble.... I would like you to run to one of our other stores, get the product the customer needs, drive it over to the customer's house, and apologize."[22] Marcus says the Ben Hill system worked extremely well, and Home Depot continues to monitor those calls very closely. Stores with the fewest Ben Hill calls get awards. Those with too many calls.... Well, as Marcus says, a store doesn't want too man Ben Hill calls.

Herb Kelleher says he came to the realization that Southwest Airlines needed a more formal structure for listening to the customer several years ago during a meeting between his maintenance department and ground operations personnel. Maintenance wanted to resolve a particular problem one way. Ground operations wanted to resolve it another. Suddenly, says Kelleher, it occurred to him that the only person who wasn't being heard from was the most important person of all—the customer. Kelleher immediately set up a consumer relations function in his own office through which he could personally monitor all customer complaints. Having customer relations reporting directly to him, says Kelleher, means that he can keep close tabs on what customers are actually saying about all facets of Southwest Airlines' operations. It also means that he can make phone calls when he thinks they are needed. "Hey, wait a second. Six letters have shown up in the last two months about inadequate baggage service in Albuquerque. What's wrong? What's changed?" or, "We never used to get a complaint on your ticket counter in Las Vegas. How come we suddenly had eight complaints in the past month?"

Note: For more about listening to customers including how to use technology to build and maintain customer relationships see Chapter 4: Customer Relationship Management in *The Guru Guide™ to the Knowledge Economy* (Wiley, 2001), pp. 164–231; and, Chapter 4: All You Need is a Customer Relationship, and Chapter 5: All You Need is Customer Equity in *The Guru Guide™ to Marketing* (Wiley, 2003), pp. 99–185.

Culture Lesson #3: Don't Perfume the Pig

Michael Dell refers to this cultural value as not "perfuming the pig." Bill Gates talks about it as making bad news travel fast. Both see it as a sometimes painful but always critical requirement of identifying problems, facing the disappointment, hunting down the bad news, and then doing something with that information to change things and make customers' experiences improve. Dell admits it is a hard thing to do. After all, he says, "it's human nature to shrink in the face of bad news or disappointments and to hope that something will just happen to make the situation better."[23] The problem, says Dell, is that things don't usually get better by themselves, and in the meantime, you have lost valuable time. It is a lot better to find out fast, when something isn't going right, and then get to work fixing it—fast.

> Don't tell me about the good things, tell me about the problems and I don't want any surprises.[24] —*Wayne Huizenga*

Bill Gates echoes Dell's sentiments.

> I have a natural instinct for hunting down grim news. If it's out there, I want to know about it. The people who work for me have figured this out. Sometimes I get an e-mail that begins, "In keeping with the dictum that bad news should travel faster than good news, here's a gem."
>
> A lot goes wrong in any organization, even a good one. A product flops. You're surprised by a customer's sudden defection to another

> vendor. A competitor comes out with a product that appeals to a broad new market. Losing market share is the kind of bad news that every organization can relate to.
>
> Other bad news may have to do with what's going on internally. Maybe a product is going to be late, or it's not going to do what you expected it to do, or you haven't been able to hire enough of the right kinds of people to deliver on your plans.
>
> An essential quality of a good manager is a determination to deal with any kind of bad news head on, to seek it out rather than deny it. An effective manager wants to hear about what's going wrong before he or she hears about what's going right. You can't react appropriately to disappointing news in any situation if it doesn't reach you soon enough.
>
> You focus on bad news in order to get cracking on the solution. As soon as you're aware of a problem, everybody in your organization has to be galvanized into action. You can evaluate a company by how quickly it engages all of its available intellect to deal with a serious problem.[25]

The problem, say Gates, Dell, and many others, is that bad news travels too slowly in most companies. People have to dig information out of paper files, find someone they can talk to who knows something about the problem, and then muster up the courage to telephone or meet with their boss to discuss it. By the time the boss finds out that a problem exists, it's already serious.

Culture Lesson #4: Hire Smarts and Attitude

Early in his company's history, Michael Dell tried very hard to hire just the right people for every job vacancy that came open. Looking back on the experience, he says that he found it both frustrating and futile. Even though his company was small, it was growing rapidly. Before he knew it, the people he had so carefully selected for specific jobs found themselves out of their league. Although they were talented, they were soon overwhelmed as the job for which they had been hired changed.

That early experience, says Dell, taught him a lesson about hiring that he still applies today—don't hire people for a specific job; hire them with the long-term in mind. Invite them to join your company and to grow with it. "If you hire them to grow far beyond their current position, you build depth and additional capacity into your organization."[26] The other great entrepreneurs echo these sentiments. Hire for potential, they say, don't just hire for the moment.

What does it mean to hire for potential? What should you be looking for in prospective candidates? Two things, say the great entrepreneurs—smarts and attitude.

> It's not enough to hire to fill a job. It's not even enough to hire on the basis of one's talents. You have to hire based upon a candidate's potential to grow and develop.[27] —*Michael Dell*

Hire Smarts

When hiring people for the long-term, Michael Dell first looks for "people who have the questioning nature of a student and are always ready to learn something new."[28] These are people who have an open and questioning mind, who have a healthy balance of experience and intellect, and who aren't afraid to make a mistake in the process of innovating. They are "people who expect change to be the norm and are liberated by the idea of looking at problems or situations from a different angle and coming up with unprecedented solutions."[29]

Bill Gates describes these ideal long-term candidates as simply being "smart." When asked in a 1994 interview to explain what he meant by "smart," Gates replied, "There's a certain sharpness, an ability to absorb new facts. To walk into a situation, have something explained to you and immediately say, 'Well, what about this?' To ask an insightful question. To absorb it in real time. A capacity to remember. To relate to domains that may not seem connected at first. A certain creativity that allows people to be effective."[30] Gates' bias for "smarts" over almost anything else is said to have led him to devalue previous programming experience, particularly mainframe experience, in favor of inexperienced young people with degrees in math, the sciences, and physics. His hiring theory was that candidates with backgrounds in math or the sciences had proved their intellectual mettle, by virtue of their degree, and could easily apply their "smarts" to computers. To reinforce his commitment to hiring "smarts," Gates insists that Microsoft managers hire fewer people than they need for a project—"n minus one"—reasoning that his managers will be forced always to hire only the smartest people, since they know they will never be able to hire as many people as they want.

Hire Attitude

In order to gauge the attitude of job candidates, Michael Dell makes a point of disagreeing with them during the course of their interview. "I want to know if they have strong opinions and are willing to defend them," he says. "At Dell, we need people who are confident enough of their abilities and strong in their convictions, not people who feel the need to give in the face of conflict."[31]

I want to know if they have strong opinions and are willing to defend them.

Like Michael Dell, Bill Gates frequently interjects tough questioning and disagreement into interviews with job candidates. In his 1996 book, *The Microsoft Way: The Real Story of How the Company Outsmarts its Competition*, Randall Stross describes one infamous exchange between Gates and an aspiring candidate for a Microsoft position this way, "Once, a senior vice-president of a leading computer company who was being interviewed for a position at Microsoft told Gates that she would have to research the answers to some of his questions. He is said to have demanded of her, 'Why don't you have an answer? Are you stupid?'"[32] Stross notes that the exchange was widely reported in the press, and when most people read about it, they just thought it provided another example of Microsoft's hostile "macho" culture. Yet, writes Stross, there was more to the "Are you stupid?" remark. "[The] remark obscures the real issue at the heart of Gates' displeasure, which was not lack of smarts, which hardly could be determined by Gates' question, but lack of another attribute that Gates sought: verbal facility.[33] Gates' combative posturing, writes Gross, could be taken as just a way of emphasizing that Microsoft wanted to hire people who were smart *and* "who were also pragmatically inclined, verbally agile, and able to respond deftly when challenged."[34] He was just putting the candidate to a test of attitude, according to Gross.

The great entrepreneurs say a candidate's attitude must match the company's culture. The "right" attitude might be "self-confidence" for one company, "combativeness" for another, and "arrogance" for still another. Every company is unique, so the key is to match the attitude to your unique culture. Take Southwest Airlines as an example. Herb Kelleher says he looks for a sense of humor coupled with the ability to work in a collegial environment and a need to excel.

> We look for people who are unselfish and altruistic and who enjoy life. The focus is on the intangibles, the spiritual qualities, not an individual's educational experience. We can train anybody to do a job from a technical standpoint. We're looking for an esprit de corps, an attitude. We try to hire and promote people who have a humane approach.[35]

Kelleher believes that a person's values are more important than their experience.

> We say, "OK, here's a guy with thirty years' experience in the field, a very distinguished record. The contender is someone with five years' experience in the field and doesn't have the laurels the other guy does." But what are their values? We'll take the one with less experience if he has the values we're looking for, and someone else can take the expert. We look for attitudes. We'll train you on whatever you need to do, but the one thing we can't do is change inherent attitudes in people.

> I've often said, if I could do that, if I could change attitudes, I'd be on Park Avenue making $5,000 an hour as a psychologist. But you can't. Once we've got people with the right attitudes, we can do almost anything we want thereafter.[36]

And, so can you, say the great entrepreneurs. Of course, it isn't going to be easy to hire people with both smarts *and* the right attitude. Ross Perot says that when he describes the kind of person he is trying to hire, recruiters insist that finding that person will be like looking for needles in a haystack. Wrong, Perot replies, I want "needles in a haystack with a red dot—very special people."[37]

Note: For an excellent summary of research that supports this cultural lesson about hiring smarts and attitude see Leatta M. Hough and Frederick L. Oswald, "Personnel Selection: Looking Toward the Future—Remembering the Past," *Annual Review of Psychology 2000*, Vol. 51, pp. 631–64; and, Linda S. Gottfredson, "Where and Why g Matters," *Human Performance*, 2002, Vol. 15, No. 1-2, pp. 25–46.

> Entrepreneurs need employees who are racehorses. We need chargers who can make things happen. We need people who are creative and innovative, and who don't know what it means to say something can't be done. It helps if they are workaholics with an excess of nervous energy, and even better if they never sleep. But, above all, they can't be the kind of people who like to follow "proper procedures," or who value security over the thrill of the chase.[38]—*Wilson Harrell (founder of over one hundred companies, columnist for* Success Magazine *and former publisher of* Inc. Magazine)

Culture Lesson #5: Build Cathedrals

If you want your business to prosper, say the entrepreneurs, then you must create a culture that inspires those you hire. Ricardo Semler, CEO of Semco S.A., likes to illustrate the difference between an employee who is simply hired and one that is inspired by recalling the parable of the stone cutters. It goes like this:

> Three stone cutters were asked about their jobs. The first said he was paid to cut stones. The second replied that he used special techniques to shape stones in an exceptional way, and proceeded to demonstrate his skills. The third stone cutter just smiled and said: "I build cathedrals."[39]

Sounds great, you say, but suppose you're not in the business of building cathedrals. Suppose, instead, you manufacture pumps or dishwashers like Semco, sell cosmetics like The Body Shop and Mary Kay, or make ice cream like Ben & Jerry. Suppose your product or service isn't inspirational in itself. Suppose it is just plain mundane. Can you still inspire your people? Can you turn your crew of stone cutters into energetic cathedral-builders? Yes, you can, say the great entrepreneurs. In fact, they say, you must, and you do it by making the workplace inspirational. When asked how she was able to inspire her employee to sell something as inconsequential as cosmetic cream, Anita Roddick responded:

> You do it by creating a sense of holism, of spiritual development, of feeling connected to the workplace, the environment and relationships with one another. It's how to make Monday to Friday a sense of being alive rather than slow death. How do you give people a chance to do a good job? By making them feel good about what they are doing. The spirit soars when you are satisfying your own basic material needs in such a way that you are also serving the needs of others honorably and humanely. Under these circumstances, I can even feel great about a moisturizer.[40]

Likewise at Mary Kay Cosmetics, the inspiration comes from the work environment and not necessarily the product line. As Mary Kay puts it, the thrill of Mary Kay Cosmetics comes from "teaching bumblebees to fly." She explains,

> Aerodynamics has proven that the bumblebee cannot fly. . . . The body is too heavy, and the wings are too weak. But the bumblebee doesn't know that, and so it goes right on flying. Without a doubt, my biggest thrill in this business is seeing women have their own personal dreams fulfilled in a career. So many women don't know how great they really are, that [like the bumblebee] they really can fly! They come to us all

> Vogue on the outside—and vague on the inside. In the beginning, many women just have no confidence at all . . .
>
> A woman usually comes into our organization as a tight little rosebud, sometimes appearing at my door too timid to even tell me who she is. Then I watch her after six months of praise and encouragement and she's hardly recognizable as the same person.[41]

The secret of inspiration, writes Howard Schultz, is to provide your employees with a larger purpose for their day-to-day activities. "If people relate to the company they work for," says Schultz, "if they will form an emotional tie to it, and buy into its dreams, they will pour their hearts into making it better."[42] "If people understand that the work they do produces more than just profits," write Ben & Jerry, "and they're in alignment with the values of the company, there's no end to what they can contribute."[43] You'll tap the discretionary beyond-the-call-of-duty effort everyone is capable of giving if they are inspired to do so. The secret of a great culture, say the great entrepreneurs, is to create an environment in which your stone cutters don't just shape stones. They build cathedrals.

If people understand that the work they do produces more than just profits . . . they're in alignment with the values of the company.

Culture Lesson #6: Create a Partnership

If you want superior performance the great entrepreneurs say you must create a culture in which employees and managers work together as equal partners. Among other things that means freely sharing information and eliminating the trappings of power.

Share Information with Employees

If you are going to hold people to high standards of performance, they must be told what those standards are and how well they are performing in respect to them. In short, says Herb Kelleher, "if you want your employees to do their best for the company, then you have to give them the necessary information ..."[44] That means you have to share information about your company's performance openly and freely. That's not something most companies do. The arguments against sharing information are endless: Employees will use the numbers to argue for higher raises, sensitive information will be improperly disclosed to competitors, bad news will frighten employees. Well maybe, say the great entrepreneurs, but the advantages of being open and candid with employees far outweigh the potential disadvantages.

In reality, the more an employee knows about the operations of a company, the better prepared he or she is to serve the company's and customers' interests. Herb Kelleher notes that Southwest Airlines is known for saturating its employees with information about the company, its customers, and its competition. Such openness, says Kelleher, leads directly to better customer service.

> Access to critical information grants customer-contact people the knowledge and understanding they need to take ownership and responsibility for doing the right thing. For example, a Southwest customer service agent who understands how the company makes its money, where profits come from and what they mean to the company, is in a better position to serve a customer who is making a special request. An agent who doesn't have access to this knowledge is limited by the company's rules and regulations.
>
> Customers who deal with Southwest employees rarely get the runaround. Instead, they are likely to deal with a person who is well informed, makes sound decisions, and has a flexible, creative problem-solving approach. Their solid knowledge of the company gives the people of Southwest Airlines the confidence and power to truly make a difference in the lives of their customers.[45]

What kind of information should employees be seeing on a regular basis? Just about anything and everything. For example, every month at Semco each employee gets a balance sheet, a profit-and-loss analysis, and a cash-flow statement for his or her division which they are taught how to read.[46] At Wal-Mart, employees (associates) receive regular reports on their store's purchases, sales, profits, and markdowns.[47] If you get the information, say the great entrepreneurs, your employees probably should get it also.

> There are really just two ways to go on the question of information-sharing: Tell employees everything or tell them nothing. Otherwise, each time you choose to withhold information, they have reason to think you're up to something. We prefer to tell employees everything. We hold back nothing.[48]
>
> —*Ken Iverson*

Get Rid of Executive Limos and Executive Parking Spaces

Ken Iverson says that when Nucor acquired a new plant several years ago one of his first actions was to sell off the company limousine and eliminate the executive parking spaces. Soon afterward, he was greeting his new employees outside the plant one morning when he was approached by a young man who pointed back toward the parking lot and said, "Look where I'm parked. That's the *boss'* spot."

"You mean, that *was* the boss' spot," replied Iverson.

"Yeah, I guess so," responded the young man. Then, turning serious, he continued, "You know, that makes me feel a whole lot better about working here."[49]

If you are having difficulty with the idea of giving up your reserved spot, just pause for a moment, says Iverson, and think how your employees will feel on a rainy day when they have to park all the way across the parking lot and walk past your reserved space as it sits empty because you are out of town on business.[50] Keep in mind that these rain-soaked workers are the same ones you are depending upon to make products, respond to customers, and generally make your company succeed.

> Respect is not a function of the distance from car door to plant door.[51]
>
> —*Richard Semler*

Eliminate Executive Dining Rooms, Executive Bathrooms, and Exclusive Executive Offices

Ross Perot recalls that an executive from a big company who was visiting him at EDS was shocked to learn that there was no executive dining room. "I can't believe you eat in the cafeteria," said the executive. "It's the only place to eat," replied Perot. Later as the executive and Perot went through the cafeteria line, the visitor tapped him on the shoulder and whispered, "I can't believe you stand in line." "Well," said Perot, "these guys are bigger than I am. I have to." Later as they sat eating, the executive remarked on how good the food was. "What do you do to make the food so good in your cafeteria?" he asked. "I eat here," replied Perot.[52]

Don't Employ Receptionists, Executive Secretaries, Personal Assistants, and Other Support Staff

This is one of the most controversial suggestions but it is one which Richard Semler particularly favors as a way to create a culture of partnership. Semler recalls that the idea to eliminate, or at least significantly reduce, so-called support staff came to him one day when he heard about an assistant cashier who had applied for work at Semco. When asked to describe the job she was leaving, the clerk responded: "I stamp the pink copies and hand them to another girl." Pressed to describe her work in greater detail, the clerk couldn't. The only thing she seemed to know was that she was paid to stamp the pink forms, but she had no idea what the forms were for or what happened to them once they left her desk. As he thought about the hapless clerk several questions came to Semler's mind.

> Can people truly be inspired by purely repetitive clerical work performed without any sense of context? How much of it is really necessary? What if we could eliminate all those dead-end jobs and keep only positions with the potential for making people feel gratified?

> Could we run our company without secretaries, receptionists, and personal assistants?[53]

Determined to seek answers, Semler says he decided to try an experiment. He would employ his support staff to send a copy of a ten-page *Harvard Business Review* article to a fellow executive whose office happened to be on the same floor and, coincidentally, right next door to his own. Semler calculated that the article would have to travel a grand total of ten feet. The question was, how long would it take for the article to make the trip?

> First, I gave the article to Irene Tubertini, one of my secretaries, and asked her to have it copied, then to bring it back to me so I could write a short comment on it, then to send it on to Clovis [the executive next door]. But because the article was long, it first had to go to our central mailroom to be copied by a clerk who handled long documents. The mail is only picked up twice a day—between nine and ten in the morning and four and five in the afternoon. Since my test began at 11 A.M., the article sat in Irene's outbasket for most of the first day. By the time it got to the mailroom, the clerk had left for the day, so it wasn't copied until the next morning. By then it missed the morning pickup and sat in the mailroom for most of that day.[54]

In total, it took twenty-two hours for the article to travel ten feet—a rate of some 2.2 hours per foot. Armed with the results of his research, Semler announced his decision to phase out most receptionist and secretarial positions over a period of two years. Existing receptionists and secretaries would be offered different jobs in marketing, sales, or other parts of the firm.

As you might expect, Semler's proposal was met with opposition from most receptionists and secretaries and from almost all of Semco's managers. Still, Semler persisted. As a result, most clerical positions were eventually eliminated and managers learned to fetch their own guests, make their own photocopies, send their own faxes, type their own letters, dial their own phones and even do their own filing. Semco not only saved the cost of all the previous clerical help, but there were other side benefits. Forced to file his own papers, Semler found to his amazement that fewer papers needed filing. He went from filing fifty or sixty documents per week to filing just two or three. Other managers did the same. As a consequence, Semco was able to cancel an order for $50,000 worth of new filing cabinets and even sold off some they no longer needed.

> I do not like to have my managers think they are a special breed of people elected by God to lead stupid people to do miraculous things.[55]
>
> —*Akio Morita*

Culture Lesson #7: Fly in a "V" Formation

A side benefit of stripping away the unnecessary perks and privileges of management and treating people equally is that you begin to build genuine team culture which the great entrepreneurs consider crucial to success. The ultimate team-spirited company, Southwest Airlines, published the following based upon naturalist Milton Olsen's description of the behavior of geese in their employee newsletter, LUV Lines, to emphasize the importance of teamwork.

> This spring when you see geese heading back north for the summer flying along in "V" formation, you might be interested in knowing what scientists have discovered about why they fly that way. It has been learned that as each bird flaps its wings, it creates an uplift for the bird immediately following.
>
> By flying in "V" formation, the whole flock adds at least 71 percent greater flying range than if each bird flew on its own.
>
> **Basic Truth No. 1:** People who share a common direction and sense of community can get where they are going quicker and easier because they are traveling on the thrust of one another.
>
> Whenever a goose falls out of formation it suddenly feels the drag and resistance of trying to go it alone and quickly gets back into formation to take advantage of the lifting power of the bird immediately in front.

ulture Lesson #8: Empower People to Do the Right Thing

r Blank says the best way is to think of empowerment is in terms "three bundles"—an idea he credits to GE Chairman Jack Welch.

ındle 1: This is the nonnegotiable bundle. There are very few of em in Home Depot; those are the things we do the same across the mpany. Many of these are operational in nature, areas where invest-ent in systems dictates a more uniform compliance. They are usually nsparent to the customer, things that have to be done to maintain y consistencies between the stores.

ndle 2: This is the entrepreneurial bundle. Entrepreneurship comes o play here because this involves challenges in which the company ovides only a minimum standard. If a store can extend that standard, at! We say, "Your store will carry such-and-such product lines. How ı sell or display them is up to you." As a result, we get the benefit of ne extraordinary creativity in this bundle; many of these ideas get tributed company wide as part of the "Best Practices" program.

e entrepreneurship bundle works at every level of the company. We n use it to further our community programs by giving the stores a dget for spending in their own communities. We don't tell them ctly how to spend the money. Instead, they find causes and become ched to those causes, emotionally and financially. The empower-nt is great.

ndle 3: This is when we give associates complete autonomy to ke their own decisions in the way they operate their store. They 't make the decision about the assortment in the store, although do talk to the merchants about what their customers are looking so in a sense they're responsible for the fine-tuning of the assort-t. But they're totally responsible for the amount of merchandise we have in stock. They're responsible for being sure our pricing is t in the stores, for building the displays, for signing, hiring, and ning. And they're responsible for paying people what they're th, which is the backbone of our entire organization. The people in stores are responsible for moving people along in the company

> **Basic Truth No. 2:** There is strength and power (safety, too) in numbers when traveling in the same direction as others with whom we share a common goal.
>
> When the lead goose gets tired, he rotates back in the wing and another goose flies point.
>
> **Basic Truth No. 3:** It pays to take turns doing hard jobs—with people or with geese flying north.
>
> These geese honk from behind to encourage those up front to keep up their speed.
>
> **Basic Truth No. 4:** Those who are exercising leadership need to be remembered with our active support and praise.
>
> Finally, when a goose gets sick or is wounded by gunshot and falls out, two geese fall out of formation and follow him down to help and protect him. They stay with him until he is either able to fly or until he is dead, and then they launch out on their own or with another formation to catch up with their group.
>
> **Basic Truth No. 5:** We must stand by those among us in their times of need.[56]

So, how do you go about cementing a team spirit and getting all of your geese flying in formation? Here are some of the team-building tips and techniques the great entrepreneurs have employed.

Parties, Retreats, and Other Fun Activities

In his book, *Virgin King*, Tim Jackson reports that one of the primary vehicles Richard Branson used to cement a team spirit during the early days of Virgin Records was to hold weekend retreats.

> Starting on a Friday and ending on a Sunday night, the entire staff of the record company, publishing company, and studio management team would decamp to a country house hotel. Attendance was in theory optional, but those who did not come were told jokingly that they were expected to spend the week-end working in the office. At the

> hotel, other record companies might fill the days with talk of sales targets or new products. At Virgin, business was banned. Instead, the guests would spend the weekend playing tennis or golf, swimming and sunning themselves, eating and drinking with great gusto . . .[57]

Similarly, Arthur Blank recalls some festive weekends during the early days of Home Depot. Once the last customer went home and the doors were closed, employees would crank up the music on the PA system and haul out stacks of pizza and six-packs of beer to celebrate the week's sales.[58]

Singing Songs

Mary Kay Ash is such a fan of songs as a way to build *esprit de corps* that she initiated a song contest when she started her company. Employees are invited to write their own words to well-known tunes and submit them for consideration. The best are sung at company gatherings. One of the most popular Mary Kay songs is said to be entitled, "I've Got That Mary Kay Enthusiasm." Another is "If You Want to be a Director, Clap Your Hands," which ends with the line, "If you want to be a Director, you've got to be a 'perfecter,' so do all three, clap your hands, stomp your feet, and yell *hooray*."[59] Mary Kay says that guests who have never attended her company's gatherings sometimes find the singing a bit strange. Eventually, however, even they are caught up in the enthusiasm and join in the singing.

A Company Cheer

One of Sam Walton's favorite methods for kicking off company meetings was to do the University of Arkansas Razorback cheer.

> Whoooooooooooooooooooo Pig. Sooey!
> Whoooooooooooooooooooooooooo Pig. Sooey!
> Whoooooooooooooooooooooooooooooo Pig. Sooey!
> RAZORBACKS!!!!!

He would then follow-up with the official Wal-

> Give Me a W!
> Give Me an A!
> Give Me an L!
> Give Me a Squiggly! (Here, everybody sort of do
> Give Me an M!
> Give Me an A!
> Give Me an R!
> Give Me a T!
> What's that spell?
> Wal-Mart!
> What's that spell?
> Wal-Mart!
> Who's number one?
> THE CUSTOMER!

Walton admitted that guests at company event cheers—well, unusual. For example, during Arkansas, Wal-Mart's headquarters, President were treated a rousing rendition of the hog c Wal-Mart cheer. Walton said he could tell by t faces that weren't used to witnessing such enthu

> Remember: You'll be left with an empty feeling if alone. When you run a race as a team, though much of the reward comes from hitting the tape be surrounded not just by cheering onlookers bu ners, celebrating as one.
>
> Victory is much more meaningful when it com efforts of one person, but from the joint achiev euphoria is lasting when all participants lead w ning not just for themselves but for one another.
>
> Success is sweetest when it's shared.[60]

> **Basic Truth No. 2:** There is strength and power (safety, too) in numbers when traveling in the same direction as others with whom we share a common goal.
>
> When the lead goose gets tired, he rotates back in the wing and another goose flies point.
>
> **Basic Truth No. 3:** It pays to take turns doing hard jobs—with people or with geese flying north.
>
> These geese honk from behind to encourage those up front to keep up their speed.
>
> **Basic Truth No. 4:** Those who are exercising leadership need to be remembered with our active support and praise.
>
> Finally, when a goose gets sick or is wounded by gunshot and falls out, two geese fall out of formation and follow him down to help and protect him. They stay with him until he is either able to fly or until he is dead, and then they launch out on their own or with another formation to catch up with their group.
>
> **Basic Truth No. 5:** We must stand by those among us in their times of need.[56]

So, how do you go about cementing a team spirit and getting all of your geese flying in formation? Here are some of the team-building tips and techniques the great entrepreneurs have employed.

Parties, Retreats, and Other Fun Activities

In his book, *Virgin King*, Tim Jackson reports that one of the primary vehicles Richard Branson used to cement a team spirit during the early days of Virgin Records was to hold weekend retreats.

> Starting on a Friday and ending on a Sunday night, the entire staff of the record company, publishing company, and studio management team would decamp to a country house hotel. Attendance was in theory optional, but those who did not come were told jokingly that they were expected to spend the week-end working in the office. At the

> hotel, other record companies might fill the days with talk of sales targets or new products. At Virgin, business was banned. Instead, the guests would spend the weekend playing tennis or golf, swimming and sunning themselves, eating and drinking with great gusto . . .[57]

Similarly, Arthur Blank recalls some festive weekends during the early days of Home Depot. Once the last customer went home and the doors were closed, employees would crank up the music on the PA system and haul out stacks of pizza and six-packs of beer to celebrate the week's sales.[58]

Singing Songs

Mary Kay Ash is such a fan of songs as a way to build *esprit de corps* that she initiated a song contest when she started her company. Employees are invited to write their own words to well-known tunes and submit them for consideration. The best are sung at company gatherings. One of the most popular Mary Kay songs is said to be entitled, "I've Got That Mary Kay Enthusiasm." Another is "If You Want to be a Director, Clap Your Hands," which ends with the line, "If you want to be a Director, you've got to be a 'perfecter,' so do all three, clap your hands, stomp your feet, and yell *hooray*."[59] Mary Kay says that guests who have never attended her company's gatherings sometimes find the singing a bit strange. Eventually, however, even they are caught up in the enthusiasm and join in the singing.

A Company Cheer

One of Sam Walton's favorite methods for kicking off company meetings was to do the University of Arkansas Razorback cheer.

> Whoooooooooooooooooooo Pig. Sooey!
> Whoooooooooooooooooooooooooo Pig. Sooey!
> Whoooooooooooooooooooooooooooooo Pig. Sooey!
> RAZORBACKS!!!!!

He would then follow-up with the official Wal-Mart cheer:

Give Me a W!
Give Me an A!
Give Me an L!
Give Me a Squiggly! (Here, everybody sort of does the twist.)
Give Me an M!
Give Me an A!
Give Me an R!
Give Me a T!
What's that spell?
Wal-Mart!
What's that spell?
Wal-Mart!
Who's number one?
THE CUSTOMER!

Walton admitted that guests at company events sometimes found the cheers—well, unusual. For example, during a visit to Bentonville, Arkansas, Wal-Mart's headquarters, President and Mrs. George Bush were treated a rousing rendition of the hog calling followed by the Wal-Mart cheer. Walton said he could tell by the expression on their faces that weren't used to witnessing such enthusiasm.

Remember: You'll be left with an empty feeling if you hit the finish line alone. When you run a race as a team, though, you'll discover that much of the reward comes from hitting the tape together. You want to be surrounded not just by cheering onlookers but by a crowd of winners, celebrating as one.

Victory is much more meaningful when it comes not just from the efforts of one person, but from the joint achievements of many. The euphoria is lasting when all participants lead with their hearts, winning not just for themselves but for one another.

Success is sweetest when it's shared.[60] —*Howard Schultz*

Culture Lesson #8: Empower People to Do the Right Thing

Arthur Blank says the best way is to think of empowerment is in terms of the "three bundles"—an idea he credits to GE Chairman Jack Welch.

> **Bundle 1:** This is the nonnegotiable bundle. There are very few of them in Home Depot; those are the things we do the same across the company. Many of these are operational in nature, areas where investment in systems dictates a more uniform compliance. They are usually transparent to the customer, things that have to be done to maintain key consistencies between the stores.
>
> **Bundle 2:** This is the entrepreneurial bundle. Entrepreneurship comes into play here because this involves challenges in which the company provides only a minimum standard. If a store can extend that standard, great! We say, "Your store will carry such-and-such product lines. How you sell or display them is up to you." As a result, we get the benefit of some extraordinary creativity in this bundle; many of these ideas get distributed company wide as part of the "Best Practices" program.
>
> The entrepreneurship bundle works at every level of the company. We even use it to further our community programs by giving the stores a budget for spending in their own communities. We don't tell them exactly how to spend the money. Instead, they find causes and become attached to those causes, emotionally and financially. The empowerment is great.
>
> **Bundle 3:** This is when we give associates complete autonomy to make their own decisions in the way they operate their store. They don't make the decision about the assortment in the store, although they do talk to the merchants about what their customers are looking for, so in a sense they're responsible for the fine-tuning of the assortment. But they're totally responsible for the amount of merchandise that we have in stock. They're responsible for being sure our pricing is right in the stores, for building the displays, for signing, hiring, and training. And they're responsible for paying people what they're worth, which is the backbone of our entire organization. The people in our stores are responsible for moving people along in the company

> and for deciding who doesn't move along. All of those things come from the individuals making those decisions in their stores.[61]

Ultimately, the great entrepreneurs say, a high-performance culture is one of high trust. It is the firm belief that, as Arthur Blank writes, "with the right value system and the right knowledge to do their job people can be trusted to make the right decisions." "If you can operate with that kind of trust," he goes on, "you don't have to micromanage. And people will do more good for the company than anyone could ever dictate."[62]

Lack of trust between managers and employees, the entrepreneurs warn, causes all kinds of problems. David Packard says that was brought home to him early in his career.

> In the late 1930s, when I was working for General Electric in Schenectady, the company was making a big thing of plant security. I'm sure others were, too. GE was especially zealous about guarding its tool and parts bins to make sure employees didn't steal anything. Faced with this obvious display of distrust, many employees set out to prove it justified, walking off with tools or parts whenever they could. Eventually, GE tools and parts were scattered all around town, including the attic of the house in which a number of us were living. In fact, we had so much equipment up there that when we threw the switch, the lights on the entire street would dim.
>
> The irony in all of this is that many of the tools and parts were being used by their GE "owners" to work on either job-related projects or skill-enhancing hobby activities that would likely improve their performance on the job.[63]

When Packard started HP with Bill Hewlett, the memories of GE were still strong, and he was determined that parts bins and storerooms at HP would be kept open. From a practical standpoint keeping the parts bins and storerooms open made it easier for product designers to get access to the parts and tools they needed to work on new ideas at home and on the weekends. More importantly, says Packard, the open bins and storerooms were symbols of trust.

Perhaps the most publicized example of trust at HP occurred in the 1960s when HP became the first company in the United States to implement flextime. Workers were allowed to come to work early in the morning or as late as 9:00 A.M. "To my mind," writes Packard, "flextime is the essence of respect for and trust in people. It says that we both appreciate that our people have busy personal lives and that we trust them to devise, with their supervisor and work group, a schedule that is personally convenient yet fair to others."[64] That trust, says Packard, has paid off and HP has rarely had a problem with work schedules.

Ricardo Semler reports similar results from flextime at his company. At Semco factory workers are allowed to arrive anytime between 7 A.M. and 9 A.M. When the system was first initiated a number of people expressed concern that workers wouldn't coordinate their schedules and production would suffer. Consequently, the company set up a task force to mediate any scheduling conflicts. But, the task force never met. "Our workers knew that production would suffer if they didn't coordinate their schedules," writes Semler, "so that's what they did."[65]

Culture Lesson #9: Praise People to Success

Mary Kay Ash admits that when she promotes praise as a corporate culture imperative, she often encounters skeptics. "Come on, now, Mary Kay," they say, "it may work for you to award ribbons, honor sales leaders on stage before large audiences, and name top achievers in your publications, but this kind of thing doesn't work with men." When Ash hears such remarks, she just smiles and asks, "Did you ever notice the stars on a six-foot-seven-inch, 275-pound linebacker's helmet? Or the medals on a soldier's uniform? Men are willing to risk bodily injury and even their lives for praise and recognition!"[66]

The entrepreneurs add that the tricks to making praise work are being sincere—don't say it unless you mean it—delivering the praise in public, and making the praise or reward fit the recipient. Ash relates the story of how the importance of making praise public came home to her several years ago when she was attending a sales convention for a multi-billion-dollar corporation.

> I noticed several of the salesmen wearing green sports jackets. I could tell the coats were brand-new because many of the men's sleeves were too long or too short, or their jackets simply needed some tailoring.
>
> "What are all these green jackets for?" I asked one of the company's vice presidents.
>
> "This year's top salesmen received the jackets as a gift."
>
> "When was the ceremony where the jackets were awarded?" I asked.
>
> "Oh, there was no ceremony," he explained. "The jackets were just sent to their rooms."
>
> That evening, at the convention's main banquet, I eagerly waited for the big moment when the company would recognize its top salesmen. Finally, at the end of the meal, hundreds of balloons fell from the ceiling, and I thought, "Oh, good opening. Now the awards are going to be presented." But much to my surprise, the evening ended there. Not a mention of achievement was made. No applause, no recognition, nothing!
>
> As a guest, I couldn't say anything, but I thought, "This company missed a golden opportunity to proudly award the jackets to their star performers in the presence of their peers!" I was certain the salespeople would have valued the recognition much more than the actual green jackets.[67]

The final trick to making praise effective is to make sure the praise or tangible reward you bestow fits the person being honored. Early in her career Mary Kay worked very hard to win a sales contest and was excited to discover that she had won. When her sales manager, an avid fisherman, presented her with her prize, she accepted it gracefully, though she later admitted that she had no idea what it was. Then someone explained it was a flounder light and that it would come in handy the next time she tried to gig fish while wading into water wearing hip boots. Ash was proud of winning the sales contest but had to admit that a flounder light was somewhere near the bottom of her list of preferred prizes.[68]

Culture Lesson #10: Sharing the Financial Rewards

Admittedly, a flounder light probably isn't right for everyone, but the great entrepreneurs generally agree that there is one prize that is on just about everyone's approved list—money. They learned—many of them the hard way—that some form of group incentive, bonus, profit sharing, and/or stock ownership plan is the best way to reward employees and build a culture of excellence. Sam Walton, for example, admits that in the early days of Wal-Mart, he was far from generous when it came to sharing the financial rewards.

> We didn't pay [our employees] much. It wasn't that I was intentionally heartless. I wanted everybody to do well for themselves. It's just that in my very early days in the business, I was so doggoned competitive, and so determined to do well, that I was blinded to the most basic truth, really the principle that later became the foundation of Wal-Mart's success. You see, no matter how you slice it in the retail business, payroll is one of the most important parts of overhead, and overhead is one of the most crucial things you have to fight to maintain your profit margin. That was true then, and it's still true today. Back then, though, I was so obsessed with turning in a profit margin of 6 percent or higher that I ignored some of the basic needs of our people, and I feel bad about it.
>
> The larger truth that I failed to see turned out to be another of those paradoxes like the discounters' principle of the less you charge, the more you'll earn. And here it is: The more you share profits with your associates—whether it's in salaries or incentives or bonuses or stock discounts—the more profit will accrue to the company. Why? Because the way management treats the associates is exactly how the associates will then treat the customers.[69]

Walton admitted that one of his biggest single regrets in his whole business career was that he didn't include his employees in the initial, managers-only profit-sharing plan that his company put in place in 1970. That is a mistake other gurus, like Bill Gates, didn't make. Microsoft offered stock purchases at a 15 percent discount and has long used stock options as a recruiting and retention tool early on. In the late 1980s, for example, Microsoft was offering options for up to 3,000 shares of Microsoft stock to programmers who joined the company right out of college. While the details of stock purchase and options packages have changed over time, stock ownership by Microsoft employees has been called one of the most important employee benefits the company has ever offered. It's a benefit that has made Microsoft a financially lucrative place to work. It is, says Gates, one of the key things that tie Microsoft employees together and create a common bond. It has also made many of Gates' employees millionaires.

A Culture of Excellence

Building a company that lasts isn't an easy task. In fact, most of the great entrepreneurs we studied failed more than once. Some failed dozens of times before they finally succeeded. What made the great entrepreneurs different is that they learned from their failures and some of the most important things they learned had to do with what it takes to create a high-performance culture. Truly great companies have to get a lot of things right to become great but one of the most important things they must get right is their culture. Some of the world's greatest business minds say getting your culture right means doing most, if not all, of the following:

1. Committing to performance excellence
2. Being obsessed with listening to customers
3. Not perfuming the pigs
4. Hiring smarts and attitude
5. Building cathedrals
6. Creating a partnership
7. Flying in a "V" formation
8. Empowering people

9. Praising people to success
10. Sharing the financial rewards

These are ideas about culture-building that are well worth heeding.

Endnotes

1. Timothy Patrick Cahill, *Profiles in the American Dream: The Real-Life Stories of the Struggles of American Entrepreneurs*, Hanover, MA: Christopher Publishing House, 1994), p. iii.
2. Maxwell Boas and Steve Chase, *Big Mac: The Unauthorized Story of McDonald's*, New York: Dutton, 1976, pp. 26–27.
3. Mary Kay Ash, *Mary Kay You Can Have It All: Lifetime Wisdom from America's Foremost Woman Entrepreneur*, Rocklin, CA: Prima, 1995, pp. 213–214.
4. G. Gendron and B. Burlingham, "The Entrepreneur of the Decade," *Inc.*, April 1989, p. 119.
5. Daniel Ichbiah and Susan L. Knepper, *The Making of Microsoft: How Bill Gates and His Team Created the World's Most Successful Software Company*, Rocklin, CA: Prima Publishing, 1991, p. 226.
6. R. David Thomas, *Dave's Way*, New York: Berkeley Books, 1992, p. 64.
7. Satoru Otsuki, *Good Mileage: The High-Performance Business Philosophy of Soichiro Honda*, Japan: NHK Publishing, 1996, p. 39.
8. Ibid., p. 40.
9. Ibid., pp. 39–40.
10. Mary Kay Ash, *Mary Kay on People Management*, New York: Warner Books, 1984, p. 17.
11. Craig E. Aronogg and John L. Ward, *Contemporary Entrepreneurs: Profiles of Entrepreneurs and the Businesses They Started, Representing 74 Companies in 30 Industries*, Detroit: MI: Omnigraphics, 1992, p. 182.
12. Joseph J. Fucini and Suzy Fucini, *Enterpreneurs: The Men and Women Behind Famous Brand Names and How They Made It*, Boston: G. K. Hill & Co., 1985, p. 4.
13. Ibid., pp. 6–7.
14. Michael Dell and Catherine Fredman, *Direct from Dell: Strategies That Revolutionized an Industry*, New York: HarperBusiness, 1999, Direct from Dell, p. 200.
15. Ibid., pp. 167–168.
16. Bernie Marcus and Arthur Blank, *Built from Scratch: How a Couple of Regular Guys Grew the Home Depot from Nothing to $30 Million*, New York: Random House, 1999, pp. 133–134.

17. David Roush, *Inside Home Depot: How One Company Revolutionized an Industry through the Relentless Pursuit of Growth*, New York: McGraw-Hill, 1999, p. 82.

18. Tim Jackson, *Richard Branson, Virgin King: Inside Richard Branson's Business Empire*, London: HarperCollins, 1995, pp. 247–248.

19. Dell and Fredman, Direct from Dell, p. 144.

20. Herb Kelleher, "Customer Service: It Starts at Home," *Secured Lender*, May/June 1998, p. 69.

21. Ibid., p. 140.

22. Marcus and Blank, *Built from Scratch*, p. 142–143.

23. Dell and Fredman, *Direct from Dell*, p. 130.

24. Gail Degeorge, *The Making of a Blockbuster: How Wayne Huizenga Built a Sports and Entertainment Empire from Trash, Grit, and Videotape*, New York: John Wiley & Sons, 1996, p. 136.

25. Bill Gates with Collins Hemingway, *Business @ The Speed of Thought: Using a Digital Nervous System*, New York: Warner Books, 1999, pp. 159–160.

26. Dell and Fredman. *Direct from Dell*, p. 110.

27. Ibid., p. 109.

28. Ibid., p. 110.

29. Ibid.

30. Michael A. Cusumano and Richard W. Selby, *Microsoft Secrets: How the World's Most Powerful Software Company Creates Technology, Shapes Markets, and Manages People*, New York: Free Press, 1995, p. 58.

31. Ibid.

32. Randall E. Stross, *The Microsoft Way: The Real Story of How the Company Outsmarts Its Competition, Reading*, MA: Addison-Wesley, 1996, p. 37.

33. Ibid.

34. Ibid.

35. Michael A. Verespeg, "Flying His Own Course" *Industry Week*, November 20, 1995, pp. 22–23.

36. William G. Lee, "A Conversation with Herb Kelleher," *Organizational Dynamics*, Autumn 1994, 72.

37. Ross Perot, "Change is Fun," *Executive Excellence*, September 1996, 10–11.

38. Wilson Harrell, *For Entrepreneurs Only*, Hawthorne, NJ: Career Press, 1994, p. 79.

39. Ricardo Semler, *Maverick: The Success Story Behind the World's Most Unusual Workplace*, London: Century Press, 1993, p. 42.

40. Anita Roddick and Irene Prokop, *Body and Soul: Profits with Principles—The Amazing Success Story of Anita Roddick and the Body Shop*, New York: Crown, 1991, pp. 22–23.

41. Robert L. Shook, *The Entrepreneurs: Twelve Who Took Risks and Succeeded*, New York: Harper & Row, 1980, p. 106.
42. Liz Harman, "Starbuck's Schultz Reveals How Firm Keeps Perking," *San Diego Business Journal*, September 29, 1997, p. 4.
43. Ben Cohen, Jerry Greenfield and Meredith Maran, *Ben & Jerry's Double-Dip: How to Run a Values-Led Business and Make Money Too*, New York: Simon & Schuster, 1997, p. 165.
44. Ronald B. Lieber, "Why Employees Love These Companies," *Fortune*, January 12, 1998, p. 72.
45. Kevin Freiberg, Jackie Freiberg, and Tom Peters, *Nuts! Southwest Airlines' Crazy Recipe for Business and Personal Success*, New York: Broadway Books, p. 285.
46. Ricardo Semler, "Managing without Managers," H*arvard Business Review*, September/October 1989, p. 81.
47. Sam Walton and John Huey, *Sam Walton: Made in America—My Story*, New York: Bantam Books, 1993, p. 177.
48. Ken Iverson and Tom Varian, *Plain Talk: Lessons from a Business Maverick*, New York: John Wiley & Sons, 1998, p. 67.
49. Ibid., pp. 58–59.
50. Ibid., p. 59.
51. Ricardo Semler, *Maverick: The Success Story Behind the World's Most Unusual Workplace*, London: Century Press, 1993, p. 58.
52. Ross Perot, "Caring Leaders," *Executive Excellence*, April 1996, p. 6.
53. Semler, *Maverick*, p. 114.
54. Ibid.
55. Akio Morita with Edwin M. Reingold and Mitsuko Shimomura, *Made in Japan: Akio Morita and Sony*, New York: E.P. Dutton, 1986, p. 154.
56. Freiberg, Freiberg, and Peters, *Nuts!* pp. 118–119.
57. Jackson, Richard Branson, *Virgin King*, p. 51.
58. Marcus and Blank, *Built from Scratch*, p. 126.
59. Mary Kay Ash, *Mary Kay*, New York: Harper & Row, 1981, p. 40.
60. Howard Schultz and Dori Jones Yang, *Pour Your Heart Into It: How Starbucks Built a Company One Cup at a Time*, New York: Hyperion, 1997, pp. 337–338.
61. Marcus and Blank, *Built from Scratch*, pp. 242–243.
62. Marcus and Blank, *Built from Scratch*, p. 107.
63. David Packard, *The HP Way*, New York: HarperBusiness, 1995, pp. 135–136.
64. Ibid., p. 137.
65. Semler, *Maverick*, p. 5.
66. Ash, *Mary Kay on People Management*, p. 27.

67. Mary Kay Ash, *Mary Kay You Can Have It All*, pp. 200–201.

68. Ibid., p. 201.

69. Walton and Huey, *Sam Walton*, pp. 162–163.

Note: *This article was adapted from* The Guru Guide™ to Entrepreneurship *by Joseph H. Boyett and Jimmie T. Boyett (John Wiley & Sons, 2001).*

Libby Sartain

Libby Sartain is Senior Vice President, Human Resources and Chief People Yahoo at Yahoo! Inc. and former Vice President, People, for Southwest Airlines. With more than twenty years of experience in human resource management, Ms. Sartain is considered an industry expert in global human resources and human resources team building. She focuses on attracting, retaining, and developing employees who promote and strengthen a company culture, as well as on developing employment brand strategy. Ms. Sartain has served as chairman of the Society for Human Resource Management and was fellow of the National Academy of Human Resources. She holds a BA degree in business administration at Southern Methodist University and an MBA from the University of North Texas. Ms. Sartain can be reached at libby@yahoo-inc.com.

four : **2**

HR's Role in Driving a High-Performance Culture

"Proceed With Caution"

The global positioning system in my car has a robotic voice that lets me know when I have arrived at my destination. I find that when I hear those words, I already know I am there, or I have no idea where I am at all. In a way, that's where we are in HR right now.

Over the past few years, the HR profession has been on the receiving end of criticism and outright bashing that caused us to find metrics and measurements to justify our existence, to reposition HR departments as a profit center, to establish employee self-service centers, use technology and outsourcing to reduce costs, and to re-brand the function as strategic versus tactical. Many CEO's now rank HR as one of the functions that adds the most value to their organization. And people issues, such as finding and keeping the right talent and building a high-performance culture, are at the top of the corporate strategic agenda as keys to sustainable competitive advantage. When HR can be sure the right talent is available and ready at the right time, and be part of driving a culture that leads to high performance, the consequential relationship with the organization and senior leaders is one of importance. More and more executives are saying, "I can't function without my HR person." We need to get past the criticism so we can be actively involved in helping our organizations shape their future and strategy, and be recognized for the value that we bring to our organizations. So why does it still seem like a losing battle to earn the respect we know we deserve? Because some of us have arrived, and some aren't there yet. And because the destination is reset again and again as our organizations grow and change. HR as a profession must elevate itself from being a necessary administrative function to a performance driven contributor who can execute for results. But that can only be done one HR professional at a time, one career at a time, and one company at a time. It's amazing, though, what a difference critical mass can make!

HR as a profession must elevate itself from being a necessary administrative function to performance driven contributor who can execute for results.

A proven method for elevating the HR role is for HR to become the change agent for creating a high-performance culture. Under this scenario, the HR agenda is crafted to build organizational capability and to drive business performance leading to results. The outcome of this approach is a new way of looking at HR programming and people practices. Organizations that have adopted this approach have adopted balanced scorecards or other metrics to assure that managers are more involved in performance management and accountable for productivity. HR provides the tools that focus on measuring and rewarding the desired outcomes. Performance, execution, and delivering results permeate the organization. There are clear rewards for high levels of performance, and consequences if results are not delivered. HR takes on a high impact role in the organization, because it is viewed as the driver of the high-performance culture and has a visible impact on overall capability of the people in the organization. HR's primary focus in this environment is talent and leadership acquisition and development. Clear expectations are set for excellence in the leadership team and a consistency in how leaders function and take responsibility for results that transcend all lines of business. HR is part of the leadership team at all levels, focusing on business priorities, rather than just people issues. When this is working, the entire enterprise sees the importance of people and leadership and HR becomes a contributor at a much higher level and with much more influence.

Before you decide to undertake the challenge of becoming the change agent who drives a cultural change leading to a high-performance organization, I have some advice: "Proceed with caution!" I think it is a mistake to look to HR as the sole source or owner of corporate culture. While culture is primarily about people, it is not necessarily just HR's domain. Beware of falling into a culture trap. Many corporate leaders don't want to be bothered with such an esoteric, hard to define outcome as culture, so they delegate it to HR. If it doesn't occupy the top of the business agenda, everyone thinks it's HR's problem.

Very few high-performance cultures are created or owned by HR. In fact, HR is rarely at the table at the inception of such a culture. Usually the company's culture begins from those very first hours when a dream of a new business idea started taking shape. Each business founder has his or her own personal set of values, beliefs, and behaviors that shapes the initial work environment. More likely than not, the first group of employees are driven to succeed by their sense of mission, passion, and shared values and culture began to evolve, rather than being deliberately created. Certain values, behaviors, work ethics, and communications channels become core to the how things get done. If the venture survives and grows, leaders emerge in true entrepreneurial style, reflecting the core cultural attributes. Few start-ups have the foresight to invest in HR, yet start-ups are often praised for their culture. Somehow culture happens without the presence of HR.

HR usually arrives on the scene as the enterprise reaches the stage where HR administration is needed. An organization's first HR leader is often focused on getting the basics in place and finding a way to compete for talent, create a good working environment, help the workforce develop new skills, formalize rewards systems, and comply with applicable regulations. These key activities allow HR to lead, and drive cultural development, but not to create it. Somewhere along the evolutional path, the best companies recognize the importance of a sustaining a high-performance culture as a competitive advantage. HR plays an important role in creating an overall employee experience in alignment and every employee becomes a "keeper of the culture."

While many in HR talk about the need to transform their cultures, fewer have actually succeeded because it requires changing behavior of the entire workforce. This is most easily done when a new CEO or leadership team is called in because change is needed to survive. Without a true burning platform, or commitment from the top, cultural change initiatives are doomed. To affect true cultural transformation, the structure, and every system and process must reinforce the desired culture. And worse, all leaders must embrace new attitudes and conduct their activities in new and different ways. HR leaders cannot go it alone in these endeavors. Changing the culture requires the efforts of everyone in the enterprise. It is sometimes better to work to shape the culture in a natural evolution, rather than to try to change deeply ingrained working styles and behavioral norms.

With support of the senior team, HR can begin to define what the current cultural state and how it adds or detracts from the company's objectives. We can determine whether or not the culture attracts, retains, and engages the right talent. We can identify the best parts of the culture, and the undesirable aspects can be discussed. This work leads to identifying what aspects of your culture are actually cultural imperatives. (Collins and Porras call this "core ideology" in *Built to Last.*) Within most organizatins there are non-negotiables that would immediately spit out people who somehow don't fit. At Southwest, for example, our culture was zany, fun, but very disciplined. At Yahoo!, one has to hit quickly and learn how to navigate a complex labyrinth of businesses and personalities to determine how to get things done.

Where HR Can Add the Most Value

Start the culture conversation at all levels: One way to accomplish this is to conduct a cultural assessment or audit of your organization through employee surveys, focus groups, or interviews. Review your organizational history, leadership styles, HR programming, and industry practices to determine what currently drives and reinforces the culture. Finally, what is your customer experience? What cultural elements are obvious to customers? Is culture aligned with business strategy? Where are the disconnects? What needs to change? This can be the basis for healthy discussion at team meetings and employee chat sessions.

Develop a business case for cultural change: Why is the change needed? How will desired changes in culture support the business strategy?

Work with the senior leadership team to determine the desired culture: Core values, desired behaviors, and shared vision are essential for a positive culture change effort to succeed. Every leader must embrace the need to change, or it won't happen. Senior leaders must make new behaviors their way of life to reinforce desired change.

Develop an agenda or action plan for enhancing the culture or bringing about change: Start with the highest priorities and work on the toughest issues. For your culture to become self replicating, the way things are done will have to reinforce the core values and the culture.

Communicate what needs to change and why: Solicit input from people. Once the needed changes and process for change is defined, tell people what is expected. What are the rewards for changing, and the consequences for more of the same.

Change the organizational structure to enable change: Find new ways to accomplish work tasks. Use teams for one-time projects. Broaden roles and responsibilities.

Acquire talent based on cultural fit: Identify the characteristics of people who exhibit those behaviors that you've identified as desirable. The people who fit and thrive in your culture will perpetuate that culture in everything they do. If you have to choose between the candidate who has better skills or knowledge but doesn't fit, and a candidate who is slightly less qualified but fits culturally, choose the slightly less qualified person and provide the necessary training or on-the-job experience. Get rid of those who don't fit in the culture.

Redesign your on-boarding process: Make sure that every new hire knows what it will take to fit in, and understands the cultural imperatives. Talk about the ways of working that lead to success and those that are, will derail careers. Create legendary stories of successes and failures.

Create cultural messages: Be sure that every meeting, every training program, every communication to people includes cultural messaging and reinforces the values, mission, traditions, and practices.

Involve Everyone: Southwest Airlines has a culture committee, but there are many ways to get people involved. Try focus groups around topics. Form cross functional teams. Call random groups of employees together for monthly breakfast or lunch meetings. Engage the help and support of a group of passionate, committed people to identify cultural disconnects and recommend remedies.

Build an internal brand that supports the external brand: Make a promise to deliver a consistent employee experience. Be sure that your employees know the differentiating elements in their experience in the organization that will enhance their work lives and careers. Begin to create an employer of choice reputation internally and externally.

Recognize and reward results: Your recognition and rewards should support the culture that you are working to reinforce.

Cultivate leaders who promote your culture: Develop excellent leaders who will propel the culture down the ranks. Identify high potential leaders and promote them. Invest in leadership development programs. Be sure content reinforces cultural messages. Keep the good ones, and get rid of those who are unable to pass the culture on.

Make it interesting and fun: Create contests, activities that enhance the culture. Decorate the office in inspiring ways. Celebrations and events can reinforce the message.

Use HR tools: Something as mundane as the annual benefits enrollment can be a source of key cultural messages. Every training class should reinforce the basic behaviors and values that reinforce the culture. Performance review forms should measure cultural fit, as well as, job performance.

No one should be locked out of the efforts to build a high-performance culture. Culture has to become the DNA that forms the building blocks over everything else. So the entire organization must have a role in keeping it alive. Work with corporate communications, advertising, and marketing to capture the culture messages and tout these internally and externally. Let Product Management see that new product development manifests the cultural values in the way it responds to the marketplace demand for quality and service. Work with your legal department to demonstrate the company culture by developing ethical standards and a code of conduct that is not just in compliance but also the right thing to do.

And remember that no one department can force corporate culture on to the rest of the company. You must achieve buy-in from everyone, from the CEO all the way down. This way you play it safe and also to win!

This article is based on the principles of Ms. Sartain's book HR from the Heart: Inspiring Stories and Strategies For Building the People Side of Great Business *which she wrote with Martha I. Finney.*

Robert Sutton PhD

Robert Sutton PhD is Professor of Management Science and Engineering in the Stanford Engineering School, where he is Co-Director of the Center for Work, Technology, and Organization and an active researcher in the Stanford Technology Ventures Program. He is co-author of *The Knowing-Doing Gap: How Smart Firms Turn Knowledge Into Action*, and author of *Weird Ideas That Work: 11½ Practices for Promoting, Managing, and Sustaining Innovation*. Dr. Sutton's research and opinions are often described in the business press, including stories in *Business Week*, *The New York Times*, *Fast Company*, *The Boston Globe*, *Upside*, *Red Herring*, *Industry Standard*, *Investor's Business Daily*, *Computer World*, *Wired*, *San Jose Mercury*, and *The San Francisco Chronicle*. Dr. Sutton can be reached at Sutton_bob@gsb.stanford.edu.

four : **3**

Forgive and Remember

> The best managers follow the mantra "forgive and remember" rather than "forgive and forget" or worse, "blame, remember who screwed up, and hold a grudge."

This is a trick question. Imagine that you have just had a major operation, and you are given the choice: Would you rather be put in a nursing unit that administers the wrong drug or the wrong amount, or forgets to give the right drug, only about once out every 500 "patient days," or would you rather be in a unit that blunders ten times as often, where the odds against you are 1 in 50 rather than 1 in 500?

Amy Edmondson, Associate Professor of Management at the Harvard Business School, was tricked, too. In the mid-1990s, Edmondson was doing what she thought was a straightforward study of how leadership and co-worker relationships influenced drug treatment errors in eight nursing units. Edmondson, along with the Harvard Medical School physicians who were funding her research, were stunned when questionnaires completed by these nurses showed that the units with superior leadership and relationships between coworkers reported making far more errors. The best units appeared to be making more than ten times more errors than the worst!

Puzzled, but undaunted, Edmondson brought in another researcher, who used anthropological methods to interview people at these eight units and to observe them at work. Edmondson also was careful not to tell this second researcher about her findings or hypotheses, so he wasn't biased by what had already been discovered.

When Edmondson pieced together what this independent researcher found with her own research, and talked to the physicians who were supporting her research, she realized: The better units reported more errors because people felt psychologically safe to do so. In the two units that reported the most mistakes, nurses said reported that "mistakes were natural and normal to document" and that "mistakes are serious because of the toxicity of the drugs, so you are never afraid to tell the nurse manager."

The better units reported more errors because people felt psychologically safe to do so.

Now, consider the two units where errors where hardly ever reported. There, the story was completely different: Nurses' view of errors, Edmondson found, was that nurses said things like, "the environment is unforgiving, heads will roll," "you get put on trial," and that the nurse manager "treats you as guilty if you make a mistake" and "treats you like a two-year old."

Edmondson's research is helping to change the meaning and interpretation of reported medical errors. The physician's who sponsored her research have changed their views 180 degrees, no longer viewing errors as objective evidence at all, but as something that reflects whether people are trying to learn from mistakes or trying to avoid getting blamed for them.

A recent best-selling book by experienced surgeon Atul Gawande, *Complications: A Surgeon's Notes on an Imperfect Science*, makes much the same point. Gawande cites his extensive clinical experience (and also mentions Edmondson's research), as evidence that mistakes are inevitable at even the best hospitals, and that the difference between good and bad surgeons (and good and bad hospitals) is that the good ones admit and learn from mistakes, while the bad ones deny making mistakes, focusing their energies on pointing the finger at others rather than on what they can learn.

The implications of Edmondson's perspective on learning from errors go far beyond the medical arena. Related research including recent studies in the airline industry and manufacturing plants reinforce her perspective, and add important nuances. One of the most crucial lessons from these studies is that companies and groups that focus on how and why the system causes mistakes rather than which people *and* groups are to blame for mistakes not only encourage people to talk more openly about mistakes, they result in changes that actually reduce errors.

Jody Hoffer Gittell, Assistant Professor at Brandeis University, spent eight years studying the airline industry. She describes this research in her wonderful new book, *The Southwest Airlines Way*. I was especially struck by her comparison between how Southwest Airlines and American Airlines handled delayed planes. At American, at least in the mid-1990s, employees repeatedly told her things like, "Unfortunately, in this company when things go wrong, they need to pin it on someone. You should hear them fight over whose departments get charged for the delay." In contrast, at Southwest, the view was that when a plane was late, everyone needed to work together to figure out how the system could be changed so it wouldn't happen again. As one Southwest station manager told Gittell, "If I'm screaming, I won't know why it was late... If we ask 'Hey, what happened?' then the next day the problem is taken care of.... We all succeed together—and all fail together."

Certainly, there are many other reasons that American Airlines has lost billions of dollars in recent years, and Southwest continues to be profitable despite the horrible conditions for the airline industry, but Gittell makes a powerful case that Southwest's focus on repairing systemic problems rather than placing blame is an important part of the story.

Gittell's research suggests that having both psychological safety and a focus on trying to fix the system is important.

...focus on repairing systemic problems rather than placing blame is an important part of the story.

Indeed, focusing on the fix more than where the fault lies may feel counterintuitive and be tough to get any organization to do: There is a well-documented tendency in countries like the US that glorify rugged individualism to give excessive credit to individual heroes and to place excessive blame on individual scapegoats when things go wrong. Research on two process improvement efforts by MIT Professors Nelson Repenning and John Sternman examined how this tendency to over attribute success and failure to individuals undermines organizational change efforts, and explores how this tendency can be overcome. The two professors contrasted a successful and a failed change effort. In the unsuccessful one, (which focused on speeding product development) managers continually attributed good and bad performance to individual skills and effort, rather than systemic issues. Heroes and scapegoats were constantly produced, but little meaningful learning and change actually occurred.

In the successful effort (which focused on improving manufacturing cycle time), managers consciously fought their natural tendency to identify who deserved credit and blame, and instead, focused on how to strengthen the system. A supervisor explained their success this way: "There are two theories. One says 'there is a problem, let's fix it.' The other says 'we've got a problem, someone is screwing up, let's go beat them up.' To make improvement, we could no longer embrace the second theory, we had to use the first."

Clearly, CIOs and just about anyone else who manages a complex system face similar pressures to find and fix the causes of mistakes, and to create conditions where the system keeps getting better and better. The emerging research on this challenge suggests three key guidelines. First, when mistakes happen, begin by assuming that the system rather than the people are at fault. Second, forgive people who make mistakes, and encourage them to talk about what they have learned openly. The best managers follow the mantra "forgive and remember" rather than or "forgive and forget" or, worse yet, "blame, remember who screwed-up, and hold a grudge against them." Third, and finally, there are still times when people lack the training and skills to do a job well, and the system is not really to blame. When people keep making the same mistakes over and over again, even when people with similar training in similar positions don't make such mistakes, it is a sign that someone else ought to be doing the job.

To put it another way, my Stanford colleague and close friend Jeffrey Pfeffer jokes that some jobs come with a "brain vacuum" where one perfectly smart person after another takes the job, and almost immediately, they lose all common sense and skill. If you have a job, or a lot of jobs, like that in your company, it is probably time to stop blaming the people, and to start trying to change the system.

Edward E. Lawler PhD

Edward E. Lawler, PhD is a world authority in human resources strategy and systems, and an authority on creating tomorrow's organization. Professor of management and organization at the University of Southern California Marshall School of Business, Dr. Lawler is a founding director of USC's Center for Effective Organizations and has been on the faculty at Yale University and University of Michigan. He is the author and co-author of over 200 articles and twenty-five books, and major contributor to theory, research and practice in the fields of human resources management, compensation, organizational development, and organizational effectiveness. Dr. Lawler holds a BA from Brown University and received his doctorate from the University of California at Berkeley. He can be reached at elawler@marshall.usc.edu.

Susan A. Mohrman PhD

Susan A. Mohrman PhD is a Senior Research Scientist at the Center for Effective Organizations in the Marshall School of Business at the University of Southern California. She received her PhD in Organizational Behavior from Northwestern University and has served on the faculty of the Management and Organization department in the business school at the University of Southern California. Dr. Mohrman is active in the Organization Development and Change Division of the Academy of Management and serves on the review and editorial boards of several management journals. Dr. Mohrman can be reached at smohrman@marshall.usc.edu.

four : **4**

Beyond the Vision:
What Makes HR Effective?

Corporations are undergoing dramatic changes that have significant implications for how their human resources are managed and for how the human resource function is best organized and managed. The forces driving change include the rapid deployment of information technology, globalization of the economy, and the increasingly competitive dynamic business environments that corporations face. There is a growing consensus that effective human capital is critical to an organization's success and that the human resources function's focus must be more strategic. But, how can the HR function get beyond the rhetoric of wanting to be a strategic business partnership and make it a reality? How should the HR function itself be organized and managed to help corporations deal with and succeed in this new era? This article reports the results the second Human Resource Planning Society (HRPS) sponsored Center for Effective Organizations (CEO) study of HR in large corporations. The major focus of the study is on the practices, structures, and activities that determine the effectiveness of

HR organizations with particular attention to the development of a business partner relationship and the use of information technology.

Staff functions, in general, are under fire in organizations because they are frequently perceived as controlling rather than adding value, and as not responding to the demands for change that operating units need to make. They are being asked to change to provide expert support to the strategic initiatives of the company, and to take advantage of technology and other approaches to deliver more efficient and responsive services. Despite compelling arguments supporting the view that human resources management is the key strategic issue in most organizations, human resources executives historically have not been strategic partners (Lawler, 1995; Brockbank, 1999). The human resources function has been an administrative function headed by individuals whose roles are largely focused on cost control and administrative activities (Ulrich, 1997).

One study of large corporations and another study that focused on a cross-section of firms found that the major focus of most human resources functions is on controlling costs and on a host of administrative issues (Lawler, Cohen, and Chang, 1993; BNA, 1994). Missing almost entirely from the list of HR focuses were key organizational challenges such as improving productivity, increasing quality, facilitating mergers and acquisitions, and improving the ability of the organization to bring new products to market. Since it is likely that these are critical business concerns, we must ask why they were not the most important focuses for the human resources executives. Most likely, the executives in these firms simply felt that the human resources function could not have an impact in these areas. This view is supported by studies that have found that HR is seen as most successful by HR executives when it comes to administration (Csoka and Hackett, 1998).

This situation is changing, and the human resources function is beginning to redefine its role (Wright, Dyer and Takla, 1999). A number of studies have investigated the changing directions needed for the human resources function (e.g., Conference Board Study by Csoka and Hackett, 1998; the Human Resource Planning Society [HRPS] study by Eichinger and Ulrich, 1995; American Productivity and Quality Center study by Smith and Riley, 1994; Becker and Huselid, 1998, 1999). There is a growing body of evidence that HR can be a value-added function in organizations. The most important work on the relationship between firm performance and HR practices has been conducted by Becker and Huselid (1998). In their study of 740 corporations, they found that firms with the greatest intensity of HR practices that reinforce performance had the highest market value per employee. They go on to argue that HR practices are critical in determining the market value of a corporation and that improvements in HR practices can lead to significant increases in the market value of corporations. They conclude that the best firms are able to achieve both operational and strategic excellence in their HR systems.

Ulrich has championed the argument that the HR function needs to be redesigned to operate as a business partner (Ulrich, 1997; Ulrich, Losey and Lake, 1997). Brockbank (1999) has argued that the HR function needs to become "strategically proactive." A recent HRPS sponsored five-year study of the critical issues in the changing business has found that business challenges of growth, globalization, and rapid change have intensified, and that there is now broad consensus around the need for HR to go beyond its administrative expertise and be expert at strategic business partnering, change management, and employee advocacy (Wright, Dyer and Takla, 1999). The researchers conclude that it is imperative to go beyond talk about what the role should be and get on with executing it. Another study has found broad agreement on the competencies required for human resource leaders and managers (Walker and Reif, 1999), confirming the primary importance of the business partner roles. Yet, in this same study, both line managers and human resources leaders identify the most critical HR capability gaps in such business oriented areas as strategic assessment, organizational design, development and learning, strategic staffing, and envisioning the organization of the future.

Given the amount of attention during the past decade to the importance of HR becoming a business partner and the apparent slowness of actual progress in this direction, it is clear that describing the new human resources role and associated competencies constitutes only the first step in transitioning HR to this new role. A second step is needed. The human resources function has been organized to carry out an administrative function; enacting a new role requires organizing the HR function to carry out its new role.

A forward-looking view of the human resources function was presented in the Corporate Leadership Council's *Vision of the Future* (1995). It projected a gutting of the human resources function as we know it today; the transfer of many HR functions to the line, outside vendors, and high-efficiency processing centers; and an almost exclusive focus on business consulting and the management of the organization's core competencies. Certainly changing HR's role will require a different mix of activities and may necessitate reconfiguring the HR function to support changing business strategies and organization designs (Mohrman and Lawler, 1993). It also will require that the HR function make much greater use of information technology. Automating the transactional aspects of HR may free up resources to take on the new business partner activities and, just as importantly, changes the relationship of HR to employees by empowering employees to do things that HR used to do for them. A move toward e-HR also offers the potential for a personalized interface with individual employees. Additionally, HR can take advantage of data bases and powerful analytical tools to track trends and data useful in determining strategic HR policies and practices and ensuring that the organization maintains its needed talent pool.

Are HR functions implementing the changes in their own organizations that are required to support the new roles and capabilities that their businesses need? One study found that 64 percent of the companies examined report that they are transforming their human resources organization (Csoka and Hackett, 1998). In 1995, our first wave of this CEO-HRPS study of the HR organization found some evidence of change in HR activities, structures, and practices, but noted that there may be more discussion of change than actual organizational change (Mohrman, Lawler, and McMahan, 1996). In 1998 we once again examined whether the strategically oriented changes that have been predicted for human resources organizations are actually occurring, and what difference they make for HR effectiveness.

Methodology

Surveys were mailed to medium and large companies that are either sponsors of the Center for Effective Organizations at the University of Southern California or members of the Human Resource Planning Society, or both. The surveys were filled out by HR leaders who are in a director-level or above position with corporatewide visibility to the human resources function. In 1998, one hundred and nineteen usable surveys were received (17.9 percent response rate). In 1995 we had a slightly higher response rate and a sample of 130 companies. One hundred and fifteen companies responded to both surveys; thus, this second study offers a good picture of the amount of change in the HR function in this sample of companies. The surveys were generally filled out by large companies from a variety of industries. The average organizational size in 1998 was 34,948. Therefore, these findings must be considered as characterizing large companies.

The 1998 survey was an expanded version of the 1995 survey.[1] It covered nine general areas.

1. General descriptive information about the demographics of the firm and the human resources function.

2. The organizational context that the human resources function serves, including its broad organizational form and the amount and kinds of strategic change and organizational initiatives being carried out by the company.

3. The changing focus of the human resources function measured in terms of how much time it is spending in different kinds of roles compared with five to seven years ago.

4. The extent of emphasis that a number of human resources activities are receiving.

5. Human resources' use of various organizational practices to increase efficiency and business responsiveness and the extent to which human resources is investing in a number of strategic initiatives to support strategic change.

6. The use of shared service units and their effectiveness (new in 1998).
7. The use of outsourcing and the problems that have been encountered (new in 1998).
8. The use of information technology and its effectiveness (new in 1998).
9. The changing skill requirements for employees in the HR function and satisfaction with current skills.

Staffing of the Human Resources Function

In the firms studied, the average number of employees in the human resources function was 402, a slight increase from the 377 number in 1995. The ratio of human resources employees to all employees was 1 to 87. This ratio is slightly lower than the median 1 to 100 ratio reported in the Conference Board Study (Csoka, 1995) and lower than the 1 to 92 ratio we found in our 1995 survey, thus suggesting growth in the HR function of large organizations. A similar result is reported in the SHRM-BNA survey of human resources functions that shows a slight growth in both staff and budget from 1997 to 1998 (BNA, 1998). Thus, as of 1998, there was no evidence of a shrinkage of the HR function.

Demographic information on the staffing of the HR function for the firms responding to the study is portrayed in Table 1. Of the total human resources staff in these organizations, 59 percent were characterized as professional/managerial and 46 percent were described as generalists. The percentage of the human resources professional/managerial staff that are part of a centralized corporate staff function is 43 percent. Overall, there was no significant change in staffing of HR functions from 1995 to 1998.

Companies in the survey typically operated in several countries; 63.3 percent had more than 5 percent of their revenue come from outside the United States. In the companies that operated internationally, 17 percent of their HR professionals were located outside the United States, whereas 21.5 percent of their employees were outside the United

Human Resources Generalists and Specialists		
Percentage of human resources employees	**1995**	**1998**
• Professional/managerial	57	59
• HR generalist	46	46
• Corporate staff	44	43

Table 1.

States. This suggests that to some degree there is less staffing of the HR function outside of the United States than inside the United States. Undoubtedly this is because some corporate services from the United States are provided to employees in other countries. The locations outside the United States were typically staffed by local nationals. Seventy percent of the companies reported that they use only local nationals outside the United States. No company had most of their international HR staff come from the United States.

Seventy-five percent of the top human resources executives came up through the human resources function. In the other 25 percent of cases, these executives came from functions such as operations, sales and marketing, and legal. This number is slightly higher than the 21 percent we found in 1995. Hence, a substantial number of firms continue to place executives over the human resources function who are not trained as human resources executives.

Change in the Human Resources Organization and Activities

In order to become a business and strategic partner the HR function must go beyond developing administrative systems and practices and delivering HR services to ensuring that the company's human resources have the needed competencies and are motivated to perform effectively. It also must help the organization transform and develop itself to accomplish its strategy and be successful. Thus, the human resources function should be positioned and designed as a strategic business partner that participates in both strategy formulation and implementation.

When asked to look retrospectively, HR leaders in both 1995 and 1998 reported that during the last five to seven years there has been a significant decrease in the amount of HR time devoted to maintaining records, and auditing/controlling the HR practices of the organization. They also report that there has been a significant increase in time spent on the development of HR systems and practices and on being a strategic business partner. In 1995 they reported a decrease in time spent delivering HR services, but in 1998 they report that there has been no change in this area. When asked to estimate the percentage of time currently spent in these areas, the only significant change between 1995 and 1998 is a reported increase in the percentage of time spent on service delivery—the implementation and administration of HR practices. There is no decrease in the time spent on record keeping, control and audit, and no increase in the development of systems and processes or strategic business partnering activities (see Table 2). Thus, although HR leaders may have the impression of a shift in the way their function

Percent of Time Spent on Various Human Resources Roles	**MEANS**	
	1995	**1998**
Maintaining records Collect, track, and maintain data on employees	15.4	16.1
Auditing/controlling Insure compliance to internal operations, regulations, legal, and union requirements	12.2	11.2
Human resources service provider Assist with implementation and administration of HR practices	31.3	35.0*
Development of human resources systems and practices	18.6	19.3
Strategic business partner Member of the management team. Involved with strategic HR planning, organization design, and strategic change	21.9	20.0

N = 119

* The change is significant in all companies. The percent of change is significantly higher in companies with several groups or sectors of businesses.

Table 2.

is allocating its time, there does not appear to be much of a shift in the time spent in these broad categories of activities.

It is possible that the perceived increase in service delivery in 1998 reflects an expansion of HR services so that more of the services are strategically focused. Indeed, when asked about the focus of HR on specific activities (see Table 3), the respondents see an increase in focus on such strategic and business support areas as strategic and HR planning and on organization design and development, as well as on talent and performance oriented issues such as employee development, compensation, performance management, benefits, and recruitment and selection. HRIS also has increased in focus, no doubt reflecting the shift to automated systems. There has been no change in the focus on traditional HR areas of control, audit, and care of employees, such as legal affairs, affirmative action, and employee assistance and union relations. A very slight decrease in focus on record keeping is reported.

Change in Focus on HR Activities

Significant increase	No change
HR planning	Employee record keeping
Organizational development	Legal affairs
Organization design	Affirmative action
Strategic planning	Employee assistance
Employee development	Union Relations*
Management development	
Career planning	
Compensation	
Performance appraisal	
Benefits	
HRIS	*very slight decrease

Table 3.

A number of changes in structure and process have been advocated in order to increase business responsiveness of staff functions (Lawler and Galbraith, 1993; Mohrman, Galbraith, and Lawler, 1998). Table 4 shows the relative extent of use of them. Business support oriented practices that are frequently applied in these firms include decentralizing HR generalist support to operating units, the use of HR teams to support the business, and the use of joint HR/Line task teams to develop HR systems and policies. Additionally, these companies are employing corporate centers of excellence, and the centralization of administrative processing. Interestingly, this pattern of organization shows a blend of centralization and decentralization that may explain why the percentage of HR employees that are at the corporate level has not gone down, despite the fact that companies also say they are to some extent trying to maintain a very small corporate staff. Practices that have been advocated to increase the business orientation and responsiveness of HR but that are currently less widely used include outsourcing, providing employees and managers with the HR self-service, rotation of people within and in and out of HR, and self-funding for HR services. It is instructive to note that the infrequently utilized approaches are more radical in the sense that they blur the boundaries of the HR organization and change its relationship to the business.

Change in Application of Organizational Approaches

Low overall use	Higher overall use
Rotation into & out of HR	Corporate centers of excellence*
Rotation within HR	Decentralizing HR generalists*
Self-service	HR teams to support the business*
Outsourcing	Centralizing administrative processing
Allowing HR Practices to vary**	Small corporate staff
Self-funding for HR services	Joint HR / line task teams to develop HR systems

*Increased in use from 1995 to 1998 **Declined in use from 1995 to 1998

Table 4.

Determinants of HR Effectiveness

A basic premise underpinning the discussion of the appropriate HR role is that being a business partner is essential to HR effectiveness. Table 5 shows the relationship between the type of business partnership that the HR organization has and its rated effectiveness in a number of areas. For this analysis, each HR function was characterized as either a full business partner or not a full business partner based on the companies' answers to the questionnaire. The results for these two groups are significantly different on most of the measures of effectiveness. They clearly establish that HR rated itself as more effective when it is a full business partner. There are a few exceptions. Business partnership doesn't impact the effectiveness of managing outsourcing, shared services and centers of excellence, activities which for the most part transfer the traditional transactional, and the expert functional roles of HR into new units. These results suggest that making HR a business partner can enable HR staff to deliver business-oriented services more effectively. This makes sense since if HR executives understand the business strategy, they can do a better job supporting the business strategy and may even influence the business strategy so that it is more realistic in terms of the kind of support HR can offer.

Relationship of Type of Business Partner to Effectiveness	**MEANS**	
	NOT PARTNER (N=84)	**FULL PARTNER (N=35)**
Performance Effectiveness[1]	6.0	7.0*
Providing HR services	6.9	7.3
Providing change consulting services	5.3	6.0*
Being a business partner	6.1	7.5*
Developing organizational skills and capabilities	5.5	6.1*
Tailoring human resource practices to fit business needs	6.6	7.5*
Helping shape a viable employment relationship for the future	5.4	6.6*
Helping develop business strategies	5.6	7.6*
Being an employee advocate	6.5	7.5*
Overall performance	6.4	7.3*
Managing Outsourcing of Transactional Services (e.g., Benefits)	**6.4**	**6.9**
Managing Outsourcing of HR Expertise (e.g., Compensation Design)	**6.1**	**6.4**
Operating Centers of Excellence	**5.4**	**5.8**
Operating Shared-Service Units	**5.7**	**5.7**

Significant difference ($p \leq .05$) between the two categories.
Scale response: 1 = Not meeting needs, 10 = All needs met
[1]Scale score for 9 items that follow

Table 5.

It is important to point out that this is simply a statistical relationship, and it is possible that the causal direction between effectiveness and being a business partner operates in the reverse direction. That is, it may be that HR effectiveness is the price an HR organization has to pay in order to be regarded as a full business partner. Our estimate is that the influence is predominately from business partner to effectiveness, but both directions of causation may be operating.

Table 6 shows the relationship between how time is spent by the HR organization and the effectiveness of the HR organization. The table shows a negative relationship between the amount of time spent on records, auditing, and providing services and effectiveness. On the other hand, it shows a strong positive relationship between the degree to which a HR organization spends its time as a strategic business partner and its perceived effectiveness.

The results strongly support the idea that in order to be effective, the HR organization needs to decrease the amount of time it spends maintaining records and doing auditing and controlling, and increase the amount of time it spends as a strategic business partner. This conclusion is reinforced by the areas of human resource performance where effectiveness is most strongly related to being a strategic business partner. The correlation is highest for helping develop business strategies, providing change consulting services, and being a business partner. This suggests that being an effective business partner leads to the view that the HR organization is effective. It is also consistent with the work of Brockbank (1999), which finds that performance is higher when HR departments focus more on strategy.

Table 7 shows the relationship between effectiveness and how much HR organizations have increased their attention to certain activities. There are highly significant positive relationships between effectiveness and increased attention to organizational design and development. In particular, increasing the amount of activity in the area of strategic planning, organizational design, organizational development, and HR planning are all significantly related to high ratings on effectiveness. It is interesting that spending more time in other areas of activity with the exception of recruitment, a hot topic, is not significantly related to

Relationship of Human Resources Role to Effectiveness

	Activity Areas				
	MAINTAINING RECORDS	AUDITING/ CONTROLLING	PROVIDING HR SERVICES	DEVELOPING HR SYSTEMS	STRATEGIC BUSINESS PARTNERING
Effectiveness[1]	**-.35*****	**-.20***	**-.19***	**.15**	**.44*****
Providing HR services	-.19[t]	-.07	.00	-.02	.17[t]
Providing change consulting services	-.32***	-.12	-.21*	.19*	.46***
Being a business partner	-.39***	-.12	-.25**	.12	.53***
Developing organizational skills and capabilities	-.32***	-.10	-.05	.12	.24*
Tailoring human resource practices to fit business needs	-.15	-.05	-.17[t]	.01	.29*
Helping shape a viable employment relationship for the future	-.17[t]	-.14	-.15	.12	.24*
Helping to develop business strategies	-.25**	-.15	-.23*	.07	.46***
Being an employee advocate	-.14	-.19[t]	.03	-.01	.18[t]
Overall performance	-.25**	-.16[t]	-.13	.10	.32***
Managing Outsourcing of Transactional Services (e.g., Benefits)	**-.25***	**.08**	**-.09**	**.10**	**.14**
Managing Outsourcing of HR Expertise (e.g., Compensation Design)	**-.06**	**.00**	**-.14**	**-.02**	**-.01**
Operating Centers of Excellence	**-.22***	**-.08**	**-.03**	**.08**	**.16**
Operating Shared-Service Units	**-.16**	**-.12**	**-.01**	**.01**	**.11**

Zero order correlation: [t] $p \leq 0.10$ * $p \leq 0.05$ ** $p \leq 0.01$ *** $p \leq 0.001$
N = 119
[1]Scale score for 9 items that follow

Table 6.

Relationship of Human Resource Activity Increases to Effectiveness

	EFFECTIVENESS
Design & Organizational Development[1]	**.46*****
HR planning	.30***
Organizational development	.33***
Organizational design	.43***
Strategic planning	.40***
Employee Care [2]	**-.09**
Benefits	-.03
Employee record keeping	-.11
Legal affairs	.03
Affirmative action	-.13
Employee assistance	-.05
Employee & Management Development[3]	**.16t**
Employee training/education	.17t
Management development	.13
Recruitment & Selection[3]	**.17t**
Recruitment	.18*
Selection	.13
Compensation	**.07**
HR Information Systems	**.11**
Performance Appraisal	**.10**
Career Planning	**.07**
Union Relations	**-.14**

Zero order correlation: t $p \leq 0.10$ * $p \leq 0.05$ ** $p \leq 0.01$ *** $p \leq 0.001$
N = 119
[1]Scale score for 4 Items [2]Scale score for 5 Items [3]Scale score for 2 Items

Table 7.

effectiveness. Even an increased focus on such core areas as compensation, performance management, and employee and management development are not related to HR executives' own ratings of their function's performance effectiveness. Surely this represents a sea of change from the era when purely functional excellence was the standard by which HR was judged.

We have argued that HR must not only help the business with its organizational design, but that in order to develop new capabilities and perform differently, it must pay more attention to its own organizational

Relationship of Human Resources Organization to HR Effectiveness

	EFFECTIVENESS
Shared Services[1]	**.21***
Administrative processing is centralized	.08
Corporate centers of excellence	.26**
Deployment of HR Resources to Business Units[1]	**.24***
Decentralized HR generalist's support business units	.18t
Very small corporate staff—most HR managers and professionals out in businesses	.21*
Rotation Into and Out of the HR Function[1]	.15
People rotate into HR	.15
People rotate out of HR to other functions	.13
Self-Service[1]	**.28****
Some activities that used to be done by HR are now done by line managers	.25**
Some transactional activities that used to be done by HR are done by employees on self-service basis	.22*
Outsourcing[1]	**.16[t]**
Transactional work is outsourced	.19*
Areas of HR expertise are outsourced	.07
HR Teams Provide Service and Support the Business	**.24****
HR Practices Vary Across Business Units	**-.06**
Self-Funding Requirements for HR Services	**.00**
HR Systems and Policies Developed Through Joint Line/HR Task Teams	**.33****
People Rotate Within HR	**.27****

Zero order correlation: [t] $p \leq 0.10$ * $p \leq 0.05$ ** $p \leq 0.01$ *** $p \leq 0.001$
N = 119
[1]Scale score for 2 Items that follow

Table 8.

design. Table 8 shows the relationship between how the human resources function is organized and its rated effectiveness. A number of significant relationships are in the predicted direction. For example, having corporate centers of excellence and the deployment of resources to business units are associated with high levels of effectiveness. Also associated with effectiveness are the rotation of people within HR, self-service, the use of HR teams to provide service and to support the business, and development of HR systems through joint line/HR task forces. The later relationship is particularly strong and highlights the importance of having line management input and ownership.

A key organizational challenge is how to increase the level of activity in the business support areas of organizational design and development and planning without greatly inflating the number of HR professionals in the organization. Clearly, organizational changes such as the creation of shared services and centers of excellence and a reliance on self-service are ways to leverage resources throughout the organization and free up headcount to deliver business support. The effectiveness of this approach depends, however, on having a quality of information system that can efficiently link decentralized business units and employees to centralized systems and service units.

One way to judge the impact of information technology (IT) on the effectiveness of the HR organization is by the relationship between the degree of IT use and HR effectiveness. Table 9 shows the average overall effectiveness rating of organizations with different degrees of HR process automation. It shows a pattern in the direction of more automation leading to greater effectiveness. Additionally, when statistically comparing the components of effectiveness across companies with different levels of IT process capability, the areas of effectiveness that are most enhanced by increasing IT process automation are providing HR services, tailoring practices to fit business needs, and operating shared service units. Thus, it appears that the HR function can indeed be a more effective service deliverer, can leverage service across business units, and can tailor services more easily if there is good process automation. Process automation currently does not, on the other hand, appear to significantly impact the ability of the organization to provide strategic business support in such areas as change consultation, developing business strategies, and being a business partner, presumably because it depends more on responsive support from knowledgeable HR professionals. On the other hand, by automating transactional and some functional services, it may be possible to free time and people for business support activities.

Relationship of HR Process Automation to Effectiveness	**MEAN EFFECTIVENESS RATING**
Completely integrated HR information system	6.6
Most processes are automated but not fully integrated	6.6
Some HR processes are automated	6.0
Little automation present in HR function	6.4
No automation present	5.9

Response scale: 1 = Not meeting needs, 10 = All needs met

Table 9.

Conclusion

Overall, the results show relatively strong relationships between how the HR organization operates and its effectiveness. This study provides considerable support for the argument that HR organizations need to be business partners. It suggests that focusing on strategy, organizational development, and organizational change is a high payoff activity for the HR organization. It also suggests that information technology and changes to HR organizations can lead to a more effective HR organization. For HR to do more than simply talk and think about becoming more of a business partner, it is imperative that it change the way it organizes its resources and its mix of activities. Although there is some progress, it appears that at this point in time most HR organizations have been adding new activities and focuses and that the hard work of eliminating some lower value adding focuses and streamlining others is still a journey in process.

Endnote

1. A complete copy of the questionnaire can be found in Lawler, E.E. and Mohrman, S.A. (2000). *Creating a Strategic Human Resources Organization.* Los Angeles: Center for Effective Organizations.

References

Becker, B.E. and Huselid, M.A. (1998). "High Performance Work Systems and Firm Performance: A Synthesis of Research and Managerial Implications." *Research in Personnel and Human Resource Management,* 16: 53–101.

Becker, B.E. and Huselid, M.A. (1999). "Overview: Strategic Human Resource Management in Five Leading Firms." *Human Resource Management,* 38: 287–302.

BNA. (1994). *Human Resource Activities, Budgets, and Staffs.* Washington, D.C.; BNA.

BNA. (1998). *Human Resource Activities, Budgets, and Staffs.* Washington, D.C.; BNA.

Brockbank, W. (1999). "If HR Were Really Strategically Proactive: Present and Future Directions in HR's Contribution to Competitive Advantage." *Human Resource Management,* 38: 337–352.

Corporate Leadership Council. (1995). *Vision of the Future: Role of Human Resources in the New Corporate Headquarters.* Washington, D.C.: The Advisory Board Company.

Csoka, L.S. (1995). "Rethinking Human Resources." Report Number 1124-95. New York: Conference Board.

Csoka, L.S. and Hackett, B. (1998). *Transforming the HR Function for Global Business Success.* New York: Conference Board.

Eichinger, B. and Ulrich, D. (1995). "Human Resources Challenges: Today and Tomorrow." *The First Annual State-of-the-Art Council Report from The Human Resource Planning Society.* New York: HRPS.

Lawler, E.E. (1995). "Strategic Management: An Idea Whose Time Has Come." In B. Downie and M.L. Coates (eds.), *Managing Human Resources in the 1990s and Beyond: Is the Workplace Being Transformed?* Kingston, Canada: IRC Press: 46–70.

Lawler, E.E., S.G. Cohen, and L. Chang. (1993). "Strategic Human Resources Management." In P. Mirvis (ed.), *Building the Competitive Workforce.* New York: Wiley: 31–59.

Mohrman, A.M., and Lawler, E.E. (1993). "Human Resource Management: Building a Strategic Partnership." In J.R. Galbraith and E.E. Lawler (eds.), *Organizing for the Future: The New Logic for Managing Complex Organizations.* San Francisco: Jossey-Bass.

Mohrman, A.M., Galbraith, J.R., Lawler, E.E., & Associates. (1998). *Tomorrow's Organization: Crafting Winning Capabilities in a Dynamic World.* San Francisco: Jossey-Bass.

Mohrman, S.A., Lawler, E.E., and McMahan, G.C. (1996). *Directions for the Human Resources Organization.* Los Angeles, CA: Center for Effective Organizations.

Smith, L.H. and Riley, C.F. (1994). *Human Resources Alignment Study, Best Practices Report: Achieving Success Through People.* Houston: The American Productivity and Quality Center.

Ulrich, D. (1997). *Human Resource Champions.* Boston, MA: Harvard Business School Press.

Ulrich, D., Losey, M.R., and Lake, G. (eds.). (1997). *Tomorrow's HR Management.* New York: Wiley.

Wright, P.M., Dyer, L. & Takla, M.G. (1999). "What's Next? Key Findings from the 1999 State-of-the-Art & Practice Study." *Human Resource Planning,* 22(4): 12–20.

Walker, J.W. & Reif, W.E. (1999). "Human Resource Leaders: Capability Strengths and Gaps," *Human Resource Planning,* 22(4): 21–30.

Row Henson

Row Henson has been involved in HR and HR Management Systems for the past thirty years. For eight years she held the role of Vice President of HRMS global product strategy at PeopleSoft, Inc. where she was involved in setting the direction for their flagship human resources product line. Before PeopleSoft, she spent fifteen years in the computer software industry with Dun & Bradstreet Software (previously MSA) and Cullinet Software, primarily focused on marketing, sales, support, and development of Human Resource Systems. Voted one of the "Top Ten Women in Technology" by *Computer Currents*, Ms. Henson is the recipient of IHRIM's coveted Summit Award for lifetime achievement in her field. In 2002, Ms. Henson was named the first Visionary of HR Technology at the Annual HR Technology Conference. She is a frequent speaker and has been published in numerous personnel and software periodicals, including *Personnel Journal*, *CFO Magazine*, *Software Magazine*, *IHRIM Journal,* and *Benefits & Compensation Solutions Magazine*. Ms. Henson can be reached at row_henson@peoplesoft.com.

four : **5**

HR in the 21st Century:
Challenges and Opportunities

Challenge is always offset by opportunity. Today's widespread market volatility, coupled with layoffs, talent shortages, and rapid shifts in technology, points to heightened challenges for human resources (HR) organizations. While appropriately leveraging HR has been a key topic of discussion for the past decade, organizations still struggle with how to make this strategic shift as a department.

What will help HR most in running the people side of the business? Over the next decade the HR profession will face a wide range of issues, which can be consolidated into a list of major hurdles. While the hurdles discussed here might not be all encompassing, addressing these predominant issues provides impetus for turning challenges into opportunities. As a starting point, one of the most important challenges for an organization is becoming an employer of choice. This involves creating an environment where people want to come and work, contribute while they are there, and stay long enough to make a difference. HR's success in surmounting its challenges is evidenced by ROI not only in terms of money, but also in efficiencies, effectiveness, and organizational best practice. Undoubtedly, technology plays a pivotal role in addressing any HR challenge by facilitating solutions that optimize success.

All great companies look for the best ways to perform HR-related tasks. However, thinking about HR only as a department obscures HR's enterprise-wide function, which permeates throughout the entire organization. Just as finance touches every area of a business—usually in the form of a budget—human capital is an entity affecting the enterprise in its totality. Therefore, instead of regarding HR as an isolated department, great companies shift their focus toward enterprise-wide people processes, of which HR is an integrated part.

Facing the Primary Challenge: Being the Employer of Choice

Becoming and remaining an employer of choice is the top-ranking HR-related challenge organizations face today. Establishing employer-of-choice status is HR's responsibility, and if HR does this well, all other practices become subordinate to this goal. The most important objective on the people side of the business is establishing a place where individuals want to work and remain working. HR should be concerned with providing potential, current, and even past employees with this environment. Employees need a culture, a place in which to grow and feel good about their surroundings.

Delineating the Corporate Culture

Corporate culture is a dramatic force behind every employer of choice. Unique to each organization, culture has many drivers, such as the organization's leadership or the product or service produced. In cases when mergers or acquisitions are involved, cultural redefinition might be required.

At the very least, HR should be the designated keeper of the corporate culture. At its best, HR can be instrumental in creating or maintaining a culture that is truly great. HR must first clearly identify the kind of culture the company should have, then define that culture for the workplace and support the environment that emerges. An identifiable culture attracts employees, gives them a sense of purpose, and offers a basis for participation in decision-making.

Whether investigating not-for-profit institutions, government employment, a large banking firm, or start-ups, job seekers continuously evaluate whether or not a prospective employer is the employer of choice for them. A suitable culture signifies different things to different people—companies attract those who find their culture desirable. This attraction might mean anything from having a lot of freedom to participating in business decisions to working with a mission to save lives.

A suitable culture signifies different things to different people—companies attract those who find their culture desirable.

What does it mean to be an ideal—or "cool" for some sectors—place to work? While a number of criteria are involved in answering that question, in general the cultural images successful companies portray fully address these categories: work/life balance, sense of purpose, celebration of diversity, active participation in management, and an environment that integrates continuous learning.

Creating a culture where people are treated well, regardless of title, is becoming more and more important today. Whether Baby Boomers or Generation X, almost every 21st century employee at every level wants to be influential in company decision-making. One of the many ways to achieve this is rewarding employees for innovative suggestions no matter where they are in the organization. Such a practice can benefit the company as well. "What is important about the frontline workers' view is that these people capture a fuller picture of what the organization faces and what it can actually do. In most cases, they see more chances for bold action than the executives at the top."[1]

Inevitably, culture changes as a company grows and its mission evolves. It is HR's mandate to capture that culture and assure its alignment with corporate goals and objectives.

Using Branding to Promote Culture

Branding promotes culture. In the past, branding was assigned to public relations or marketing, but it is indeed an HR function because of its power to attract and retain employees. Working together with marketing, HR must develop a compelling brand image for the workforce.

Great companies do not create an external brand for customers and an internal brand to attract employees. Instead, they leverage their external brand for internal recruiting. Southwest Airlines is an excellent example—it advertises around low-fare, no-frills, humorous service, and its employee population loves to have fun with customers. Southwest does an excellent job of branding for its customers and leveraging that same image to draw like-minded employees.

Branding that pervades a company's web content communicates brand image not only to customers but also to prospective employees. Messaging should work to attract both simultaneously. For example, when posting jobs to the site for recruiting, HR must work with site designers to make interesting, creative postings that tie into company branding. Although Internet-driven recruiting is still in its early stages, it can pull together a wide range of elements and help ease the burden on HR while pushing out to prospects the branding and critical data that speeds selection decisions. Today's college graduate looks at every prospective employer's website before applying for a job. In many cases, a website supplies an applicant with his or her very first image of a company.

HR must take a pivotal role in branding during mergers and acquisitions. When AOL-Time Warner merged two strong cultures, HR's task was to take the best of both organizations' messaging and develop a third survivable, sustainable culture that resulted in a new brand.

Most HR organizations today do not consider themselves branders. They think of themselves in the people practice; but before getting to the people practice, HR must first identify necessary actions in terms of building a culture and branding. Such actions result in the attraction and retention of the right kind of employees to support the organiza-tion's goals and mission.

Staying Attuned to Changing Demographics

The workforce has changed and will continue to do so. Employers of choice recognize and understand the dynamics of the "new workforce," where for the first time four distinct groups of workers labor together under one virtual roof. The over-50 Baby Boomers lend themselves to loyalty and sacrifice, those in their 40s believe hard work will take them to the top, 30-somethings seek a balance between work and home, and new workers in their 20s are realists wired for technology. However, today's employees are even now experiencing a metamorphosis. The role of women and other

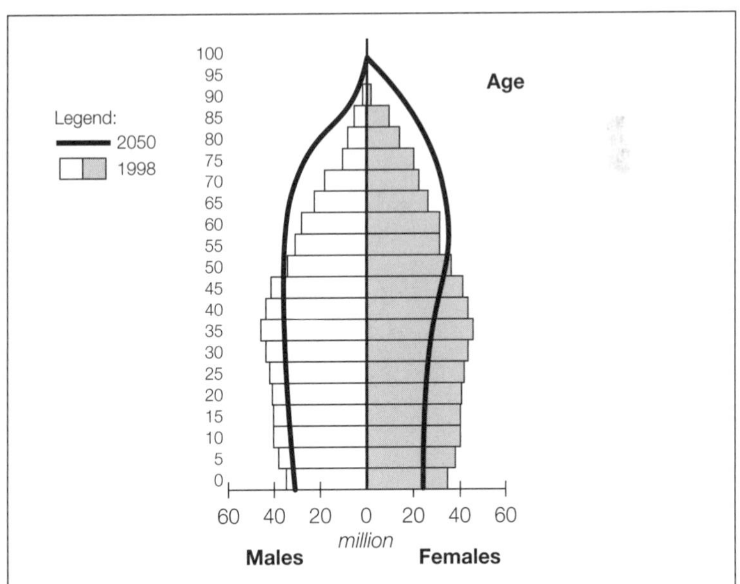

Figure 1. The demographics of working men and women are changing with respect to both numbers and age ranges.

minorities is expanding, median age is increasing, and there is a rise in the contingent workforce.

Organizations are changing as well, creating widespread shifts in work attitudes across age groups. HR's task is to stay attuned with the changing workforce and changing company values and make sure company culture is appropriate to the desired workers. For example, because Ford Motor Company benefits from loyalty—as do most employers of an older workforce—its culture and branding do not support rapid change and high turnover. Likewise, companies based in Silicon Valley are concerned with development and production speed, and turnover is often higher than average. HR's challenge is to strategically match the employee population with that of the organization's culture.

Winning the War for Talent

An employer of choice has already come a long way toward winning the war for talent, which is another significant HR challenge. There is no truce in this war, regardless of economic conditions.

Recruiting and Retaining Over Time

Given suitably competitive offerings with respect to compensation, culture is an organization's number one recruitment and retention tool. In an employer-of-choice environment it is not necessary to pay top dollar if other key factors are in place.

Great companies know not to stop seeking the best talent in a downturn. When the stock market is down, many people are afraid to invest—but that is the best time to do so. The job market is similar.

Top companies always see value in pursuing the best and brightest. Simultaneously, future talent shortages and the expense of recruiting over retention give these employers a consistently keen eye for keeping their top performers. According to Jac Fitz-enz, founder of The Saratoga Institute, "Every six middle managers that a company replaces costs US $1 million in the time and expense it takes to recruit, train and develop replacements to a point where they can be as productive as those who left."[2]

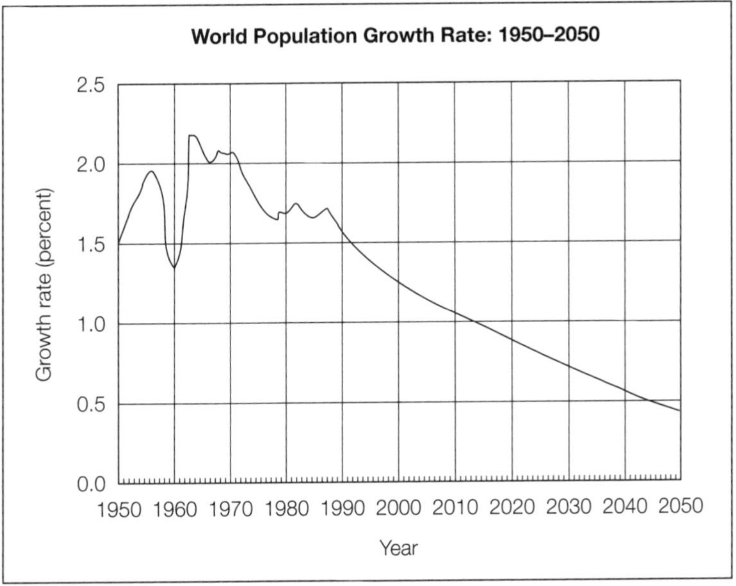

Figure 2. As the size of the workforce decreases, successful companies consistently seek top performers.

Great companies make every employee in the company a recruiter. At a cocktail party, someone who is energized about his company and discusses it in a positive light promotes that company. Cisco is a good example of top-quality referrals. Because Cisco's employee referral program generates 60 percent of all new hires, the company realizes great savings on the high cost of recruiting and simultaneously finds prospects with good personal references.

Customer relationship management (CRM) is a good model for human capital management (HCM). The steps involved in attracting and retaining customers parallel the activities involved in the war for talent. Where millions are spent on the customer relationship, has a similar emphasis been placed on employees?

Understanding the Workforce

Statistics show that the size of the workforce is diminishing—when the economy comes back there will be fewer candidates from which to choose. Although there is an economic slowdown now, in the next ten years demand will outstrip the supply. During a downturn, if companies who are not hiring eliminate their focus on recruitment, they can miss golden opportunities to secure the high performers who might be instrumental in the future.

Winning the war for talent requires knowing the workforce. For example, by 2050 there will be fewer people available to work, and the majority of these will be older than 50. The contingent workforce will also be more critical in the future. Therefore, why not innovate by creating a temporary or part-time environment where the 50-plus population will want to work? What about giving the new mom or dad the opportunity to balance hours at work and at home?

Leveraging an Indispensable Player: Technology

Meeting today's HR challenges would be impossible without technology. Most people want to work for companies that have good technology. For example, college graduates accustomed to using the Internet for their work, research, thesis, and case studies expect the latest technology on the job. Given the widespread availability of technology, a company lacking in this component will not qualify as an employer of choice for the emerging workforce.

Meeting today's HR challenges would be impossible without technology. Most people want to work for companies that have good technology.

Technological development is in every company's best interest. According to Cedar Group, "Organizations continue to report high degrees of success in using technology to meet objectives of business improvement, employee satisfaction and elevation of HR's contribution as a strategic business partner."[3]

Using Technology as a Facilitator

Great companies know how to use technology. Instead of accumulating an excess of technology for technology's sake, they invest in technology specifically as it facilitates accomplishment of their objectives. For example, an employer of choice will leverage the company website to add momentum to branding efforts.

The best companies also wield an educated vision, establishing cutting-edge solutions such as pure-Internet systems that provide longevity and interoperability with future advancements. Preferred for ease of collaboration, pure-internet systems require only a browser—no code on the workstation—and support a number of standards. Web-based solutions are ideal foundations for portals, self-service, and collaboration because they can continually draw from a single repository of enterprise-wide data.

Entering the Portal Gateway

Critical to the employer of choice, portals provide organized, efficient access to the customized content, knowledge, reporting structures, analytics capabilities, and transactions each employee needs. An enterprise portal is the gateway to all company functions and offers personalized, role-based access with respect to who employees are, where they are located, what they do and why they do it. Third-party sources of content such as salary surveys or job boards can also be accessed through a portal.

One of the most compelling aspects of portal technology is that it serves as a primary HR tool for establishing image, culture, and branding. Role-based portal designations allow HR to push out messaging to specific groups, and all recipients see the same information simultaneously. Distributed information can include balanced scorecard data, total reward and incentive status updates, company news and promotions, quotes-of-the-day, and other culture-based messaging. More than any other form of technology, this communication tool helps replace the concept of HR as a department with a true sense of the pervasive, enterprise-wide nature of human capital.

Employees use a portal to seamlessly access workflow, event-driven processing, transactions, analysis, and more. Because portal information is filtered based on role, employees see only the relevant information they need to do their jobs. Where before an individual had to enter a password for each application, portals require only a single sign-on for access to all company functions. This saves time and effort and promotes increased productivity.

Establishing Self-Service and Collaboration

People want to work for and stay at companies that empower them to do their jobs, and self-service and collaboration do exactly that. Employee self-service makes HR and other work-related transactions easily accessible 24/7, granting increased workforce autonomy and lightening the HR administrative load.

Self-service has been gaining momentum. According to Towers Perrin, "Despite recent world events, the economic downturn and actual

Extending HR-Related Collaborative Applications to the Workforce
Savings Realized Using Self-Service

Task	Manual Cost	Self-Service Cost	Savings
Enrolll in benefits	$109.48	$21.79	80%
Enroll in training	$ 17.77	$ 4.87	73%
Change in home address	$ 12.86	$ 3.39	74%
Apply for a job	$ 21.31	$11.85	44%
Change compensation	$ 44.67	$18.26	59%
Approve a promotion	$ 48.64	$14.01	71%
Create a job requisition	$ 36.89	$11.11	70%

Table 1. Studies show rapidly increasing evidence of the benefits of employee self-service.

results to date with self-service, half to more than two-thirds of responding companies polled in November 2001 plan to step up investments across a wide variety of HR applications."[4] According to the Cedar 2001 Human Resources Self Service/Portal Survey, self-service has resulted in a 60 percent average reduction in both cycle times and average costs, a 50 percent increase in employee satisfaction, an up to 70 percent reduction in headcount changes, and a 90 percent drop in service-center inquiries. The Cedar 2001 HR survey reports a 100 percent ROI in less than twenty-two months based on implementing multiple applications.[5] In addition, the Watson Wyatt 2001 study revealed that a significant one standard deviation (1 SD) improvement in focused HR service technologies created a positive 6.5 percent market impact: "Our research shows that if HR groups use new technology for the fundamentals—improving accuracy, service and cost-effectiveness—it pays off in 6.5 percent higher shareholder value."[6]

Web-based collaboration streamlines communication by connecting the disparate systems of all constituents—company-based and third party—for integration with back-office applications and content suppliers. Improved decision-making and effective workflow result from integration of knowledgebase access, transactional information, analytics, team input, and more.

An excellent example of collaboration is the recruiting process, which extends from posting a requisition to communicating with and making an offer to the candidate. Online collaborative processes create documented evidence of what took place, which is helpful in recalling details and evaluating workflow success.

Analyzing All the Data

Analytics statistically measure what is and why, and also provide data as to what should be, what could be, and what will be. By drawing from a central repository of all pertinent internal and external company data, workforce analytics enable organizations to model, simulate, report, compare, and leverage the metrics most important to HR and the entire organization.

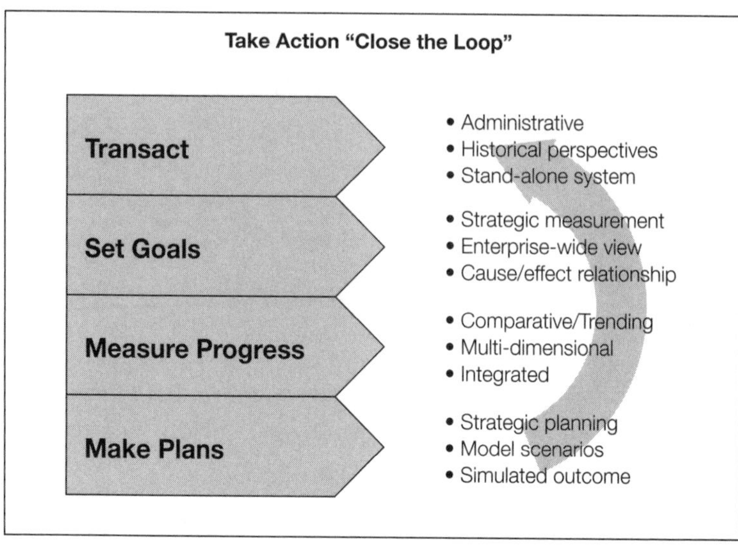

Figure 3. Analytic tools help HR leverage enterprise-wide data developing workforce planning cycles that maximize productivity.

Workforce analytics also help measure HR effectiveness, support processes for addressing gaps in skills and labor, derive metrics for trend and benchmark analyses, assist with talent development, provide compensation and retention planning tools for proactive analysis, and much more. The time is now to leverage analytics. According to Gartner, "Enterprises that want to outperform their industry competitors should understand the implications of corporate performance management and immediately start building their strategy."[7]

Great companies use analytic tools to manage human capital, calculate its value, and align the workforce for maximum productivity.[8] These tools are instrumental in anticipating the impact of inevitable external and internal business trends that precipitate change, and in realizing savings by strategically allocating human capital.

Recognizing the Workforce as a Profit Center

Historically undervalued, human capital is in reality a strategic asset. Watson Wyatt's 1999-2001 Human Capital Index survey of over 750 international companies statistically proved that implementing HCM

The Impact of HCM on Market Value

Practice	Impact on Market Value
Total rewards and accountability	16.5%
Collegial, flexible workplace	9.0%
Recruiting and retention excellence	7.9%
Communications integrity	7.1%
Focused HR service technologies	6.5%

Sample size: 750 companies. Expected change in market value associated with a significant one standard deviation (1 SD) improvement in HCI dimension.

Table 2. The Human Capital Index study provides evidence concerning HR practices that affect shareholders.

best practices is a leading—not lagging—factor in increasing shareholder value. "Effective human capital practices drive business outcomes more than business outcomes lead to good HR practices," stated Bruce Pfau, Ph.D., author of the study.[9]

Accounting for People: A Necessary Expense?

Watson Wyatt provides clear evidence of the success of effective HCM.[10] Yet, if optimized, human capital is powerful enough to drive success; why is it common that the only executive-level mention of human capital is an expense line on the income statement? Such an approach forces inverted behavior. For example, a company might employ the fewest people at the lowest cost simply to enhance the income statement. However, this "enhancement" is a hidden stress on overall performance.

"Oddly enough, while economists and business strategists agree that intellectual capital is the key to success for companies in today's knowledge-driven economy, there is currently no generally accepted means of quantifying these assets and accounting for them on a company's balance sheet," states Dr. Charles E. Grantham, founder, Institute for the Study of Distributed Work.[11]

Quantifying the Intangible: Human Capital

Since the early 1980s, companies' predominant source of market value has shifted from tangible fixed assets to intangible assets. Intangibles include human capital, structural capital, customer capital, and organizational capital, human capital contributing by far the biggest portion. Great companies are using HCM to leverage human capital by tying individual performance to key organizational objectives and are seeing the difference in corporate profits—the workforce is indeed a profit center.

The standard deviation of top- and high-potential performers represents twice the productivity of the average performer. States founder Bill Gates regarding Microsoft, "Take away our 20 most important people, and I tell you we would become an unimportant company."[12] The critical value of key people is all the more reason to invest in human capital, HCM, and supporting technologies.

HR responsibilities include many specific details involving compensation, workforce trends, and so on. However, it is critical that HR can answer questions such as:

- Who are our top performers and how can we retain them?
- Who are our high-potential employees and how can we develop them?
- Who are we at risk of losing and how can we reduce that risk?

Contributing as a Strategic Business Partner

Although there is emphasis today on getting HR out of record keeping and making it more strategic, a lot of HR people are not equipped for this. Often a company wants an HR representative to think like a businessperson but does not give them the respect, time, tools, and other provisions to do so.

HR's role as a strategic business partner comes from both the company and from HR's own initiatives. One factor that supports HR in functioning better in the business world and becoming a key business partner is appropriate use of the right technology. Technology can help HR assess opportunities, manage risks, take action, and communicate with employees.

Measuring performance and tying it to overall business objectives is essential for demonstrable results at the corporate level. Yet an unfortunate number of performance evaluation criteria have nothing to do with overall company objectives. Measuring things like clocking in on time and getting along with coworkers does not provide tangible data that ties employee performance to overall company success. HR needs to evaluate the factors that have direct impact on corporate objectives.

HR takes on significant responsibility during mergers and acquisitions. In the recent acquisition of Compaq by HP, it is unthinkable that HR was not examining culture, benefits, salaries, and employee skill sets to make the acquisition work.

Cultivating Leadership: E-Learning and Development

Today's college graduates are less concerned with starting near the top as they are with being empowered to learn and make company decisions. Most people instinctively want to learn, which is very different from being "trained." Learning is an environment that promotes the ability to gain knowledge, whether via a course, access to expertise in the form of mentors, or participation in innovative projects.

Most people instinctively want to learn, which is very different from being "trained."

Loyalty to a single company is rapidly becoming a thing of the past. While culture attracts a new hire, the reason an employee stays on is because the working environment is challenging and meaningful, engendering growth and development. The number one reason an employee leaves a company is lack of respect of the immediate supervisor. The culprit is the aging workforce, which causes organizations to promote younger individuals before they might be ready to be managers.

Organizations can address this retention issue on both the employee and managerial sides by creating an environment that continuously fosters learning and development. This helps train supervisors to be effective and provides learning that employees eagerly embrace. Instead of secluding a new hire in months of constant training, this environment lets employees learn as they go using supportive tools and technology.

While technology is better today than ever, today's e-learning is only in its infancy. In this new world, people learn what they need to learn on their own time, at their own pace. Right-brain people can have more on-the-job learning, while left-brain thinkers can do more analytical learning online. Usually e-learning is accessed via collaborative self-service that leverages third-party expertise and/or content, which is what many are calling knowledge management today. In the future, e-learning will simply be a way the workforce is developed in an ongoing, as needed basis.

In the new organization of the future, adaptive virtual organizations replace rigid organizational structures, and the organization at any one time consists of the sum total of people and companies involved in successful completion of a project. Individuals recognize that continuous learning and nurturing of skills are vital to productivity and professional satisfaction. People seek opportunities to stretch themselves while employing their unique abilities, choosing jobs and projects that provide them with the best learning experiences and opportunities to excel.[13]

Thinking Globally, Complying Locally

Even small organizations deal increasingly with customers and employees on a global basis. Great companies know how to think globally and comply locally. They act like a global organization, yet an understanding of the local environment permeates every relationship.

Making global differences a part of corporate culture is a valuable endeavor. Indeed, diversity itself is a source of greatness. Organizational headquarters that have the attitude that "corporate knows best" will have a difficult time instilling a viable culture. Education and awareness make all the difference, especially in the following areas.

Legal and regulatory issues. It is important to be familiar with laws and regulations in locations where the organization has a presence. For example, in some countries tracking religion is mandatory, while in others it is illegal.

Data security and data flow. Organizations must not only obey regulations with respect to data, but they must also be aware of how sensitive and important the security of personal data is in most of the world.

Culture. Each country has a differing set of cultural values apart from company culture. For example, some base their attitudes on love/hate polarities, while others use approval/disapproval. It is very important for smooth global operations that HR understands discrepancies between country culture and company culture and implements the appropriate processes.

Culture-based motivation. Incentive programs for people of different cultures should present true incentives by offering valued rewards. While pay for performance motivates US workers, in Germany, title is motivational. In Japan, "the nail that sticks up gets hammered," so individual performance is valued less, while efforts toward achieving group goals receive stronger reinforcement.

To help an organization efficiently leverage the global workforce, HR must acknowledge that one size does not fit all. While legal compliance is critical and can be greatly assisted by a global portal, the main focus is cultural awareness and sensitivity.

Incorporating Flexibility and Adaptability

For years companies have been moving away from hierarchical, structured environments because they are neither effective for organizing nor comfortable for employees. HR needs to mirror this movement by allowing employees—particularly managers—to be flexible, adaptable, and nimble. For example, instead of restricting a creative requisition that strays from an exact, predefined job description and salary range, HR can allow for variances that fit special circumstances.

Guidelines, rules, band benchmarks are important, but flexibility is even more critical, particularly where people are concerned. Collaboration with all constituents requires adaptability. Organizations today are less about physical structure than logical structure supported by technology.

Before doing anything else, HR must create a flexible environment where top prospects seek to be employed. This is a place where employees look forward to coming to work, enjoy working while they're there, feel they play an important role in the company, and want to stay because the company is continuing to develop them and care about them.

In great companies today, HR ties in all the ingredients for success and leverages technology to capitalize on economic and organizational change. Successfully turning HR challenges into opportunities to become an employer of choice creates a dynamic place where people want to work and choose to remain. Efficiency, effectiveness, and monetary return are characteristic of the employer of choice in the 21st century. These lay the groundwork for world-class HCM.

Endnotes

1. Keith H. Hammonds, "5 Habits of Highly Reliable Organizations," *Fast Company*, May 2002, p. 126.
2. Jac Fitz-enz, The Saratoga Institute, June 6, 2002.
3. Cedar 2001, Human Resources Self Service/Portal Survey.
4. "Web Self-Service Technology Begins to Deliver Results...," Towers Perrin e-Track Survey press release, Towers Perrin, January 16, 2002.
5. Cedar 2001, Human Resources Self Service/Portal Survey.
6. "Watson Wyatt's Human Capital Index: Human Capital as a Lead Indicator of Shareholder Value, 2001-2002 Survey Report," Watson Wyatt Worldwide, p. 9.
7. Nigel Rayner, Lee Geishecker, Gartner, Corporate Performance Management: BI Collides with ERP, December 2001.

8. META Group Inc., Workforce Management study, 2001.

9. "Study Identifies Certain HR Practices as Leading Indicators of Financial Success," Watson Wyatt 1999-2001 Human Capital Index Survey press release, Watson Wyatt Worldwide, October 29, 2001.

10. "Watson Wyatt's Human Capital Index: Human Capital as a Lead Indicator of Shareholder Value, 2001-2002 Survey Report," Watson Wyatt Worldwide.

11. "A Framework for the Management of Intellectual Capital in the Health Care Industry," C.E. Grantham, L.D. Nichols and M. Schonberner, *Journal of Health Care Finance*, Vol. 23 no. 3, Summer 1997, page 1-20.

12. "Corporations of the Future," McKinsey & Company, *Month by Month*, August 1997.

13. H. Wayne Hodgins, *Into the Future: A Vision Paper*, Commission on Technology & Adult Learning, February 2000, p. 13.

| CHAPTER FIVE |

Maximizing Human Capital Management's Global Value Proposition

Karen V. Beaman

Karen V. Beaman, Division Vice President, ADP Global Services, is currently responsible for the coordination and delivery of ADP's professional services across the Americas, Europe, and Asia Pacific. She has more than twenty-five years of experience with information systems and human resource management specifically in the development, integration, and management of enterprise-wide HR systems. An internationally recognized speaker and writer, Ms. Beaman has published works in the fields of both Linguistics and HRIS. She is the co-founder and current Editor-in-Chief of the *IHRIM Journal*, and past-Chair of the *IHRIM.link* Magazine Editorial Committee. Her first edited volume, *Boundaryless HR: Human Capital Management in the Global Economy* was released in 2002 and her second, *HR Outsourcing: Strategy, Organization, People, Process, and Technology*, is scheduled for 2004. In 2002, Ms. Beaman received IHRIM's Summit Award, recognizing her outstanding achievement in the HR technology field. Ms. Beaman can be reached at Karen_Beaman@adp.com.

five : **1**

The New Transnational HR Model: Building a Chaordic Organization[1]

> [The] most abundant, the least expensive, the most underutilized and constantly abused capacity in the world is human ingenuity. The source of that abuse is mechanistic, industrial-age organizations, and the management practices they spawn. —*Dee Hock, Founder/ Chairman Emeritus, VISA*

In the age of increased global mobility, falling trade barriers, and explosive growth in international business, global expansion is on the agenda of most large enterprises. The question on every global company's mind is (or should be) how can they best organize themselves for international operations. Can you do business around the world the same way you do business around the corner? Or, are substantially different organizational and management approaches required to meet the challenges of global business? How do we avoid the trap Dee Hock speaks of above and build a "chaordic"[2] organization that is adaptive to changing conditions, controlling at the center while empowering at the periphery, leveraging worldwide learning capabilities, and that transcends geographic and divisional borders? If the company as a whole faces such questions, the HR[3] organization needs to anticipate emergent human capital needs in order to meet the challenges created by the company's globalization goals.

The trillion-dollar question becomes how to implement a global HR business model that is, in the words of Dee Hock, chaordic—an organization that thrives on the border between chaos and order—"chao-ordic." The fundamental paradox that faces most enterprises is how to be simulataneously controlled from the center, responsive locally, and innovative enough to take advantage of new opportunities, while at the same time preserve a common vision, be adaptive to changing conditions, and coordinate activities globally. The global organization of the future must be able to foster both competition and cooperation simultaneously. The goal is to find the right balance between extreme autonomy and competition, which leads to lack of coordination and turf wars, and excessive authoritarianism and micromanagement—which stifles creativity and leads to futile bureaucracy (Hock, 1999). One structure that supports many of Hock's chaordic principles is Bartlett and Ghoshal's (1989) "Transnational" model—an organizational model that seeks to achieve optimal balance between centralized control and decentralized autonomy while maximally leveraging innovation and knowledge sharing across the enterprise.

Borrowing from Hock's chaordic principles, this article presents a model for building a world-class transnational HR/Payroll organization, exploring in detail three critical components: strategic visioning, organizational development, and people orientation, or global mindset. Developing a shared global vision for the organization and aligning the organization's strategic objectives with that vision is clearly the first step. The company's vision of the future, as well as its business culture and administrative heritage, then determine how best to move the enterprise closer to the chaordic, transnational model. Finally, and probably the most critical component of any business model is the people who make up the organization: Their alertness, agility, motivation, and global orientation—in essence, their mindset—that allows them to see, interpret, function, and act chaordically with a culturally relative perspective, identifying and leveraging opportunites for competitive advantage. After defining the new, chaordic transnational HR model, this article also offers some guidelines on how to facilitate change within the organization and build chaordic, transnational competency across the enterprise.

While globalization is clearly a multi-faceted issue, to be successful in today's ever-increasing competitive environment, it is essential that international organizations become masters of the paradox—enabling, rather than stifling—developing a common sense of purpose and a cohesive set of principles by which to govern and to help reconcile apparent paradoxical demands. While many organizations may not yet be prepared to evolve into true "chaords" (in Hock's purest definition of the word), all organizations can benefit by adapting Hock's chaordic concepts and integrating what aspects may be appropriate into their business. To bring the organic benefits of a chaordic entity to the enterprise, there are three critical success factors: the creation of a strong and intensely shared vision including, the development of a trusting, empowering, self-organizing culture; the alignment of the company's organizational model with their corporate history and overall strategic objectives; and the development of globally alert leaders who have the ability to identify and leverage opportunities for competitive advantage.

Transnational HR Model

> All organizations are merely conceptual embodiments of a very old, very basic idea—the idea of community. They can be no more or less than the sum of the beliefs of the people drawn to them; of their character, judgments, acts, and effort. —*Dee Hock*

While organizations are clearly a product of their leaders' vision, beliefs, and values, they are also heavily influenced by their cultural origin and administrative heritage—or corporate history—as well as by the attitudes and orientations of the people who populate them.

The new, chaordic transnational HR business model brings together this corporate heritage, along with the vision and values of the enterprise, the organization's structure, and the global orientation of its associates. Together with a foundation of well-defined, structured business processes and the appropriate supporting technology, the emerging chaordic, Transnational HR Model comprises the following five core components (Figure 1).

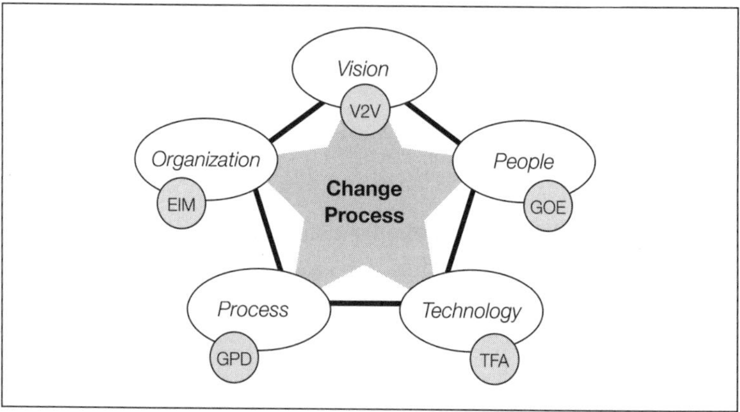

Figure 1. Transnational HR model

- Vision—sets the overarching framework, direction, and values for the organization.
- Organization—defines the organizational structure that the enterprise will function within.
- People—comprises the organization's associates; their skills, competencies, and orientations.
- Process—delineates the processes that individuals in the organization are to follow.
- Technology—provides the underlying infrastructure to support the people and the processes.

The new Transnational HR model must be adaptive and responsive to changing conditions and must at the same time preserve overall cohesion and unity of purpose. The fundamental paradox facing most enterprises today is that healthy, vibrant organizations naturally exhibit a dynamic tension between chaos and order: The chaordic organization must foster as much initiative and competition as possible, while building in mechanisms for cooperation and control. "Neither competition nor cooperation can rise to its highest potential unless both are seamlessly blended.... Either without the other swiftly becomes dangerous and destructive" (Hock, 1991).

To ensure that the new HR business model is a living, breathing process, actively used in the day-to-day operations of the business, there must be a way to measure the organization's progress according to the model—because, in the well-known words of Peter Drucker, "You can't manage what you don't measure." Thus, the new Transnational HR Model includes methods for measuring each of its components.

- The Vision-to-Values (V2V) assessment process aids in defining a global vision and set of values for the organization, placing quantifiable, measurable values—or metrics—on the global enterprise vision and strategic objectives.
- The Efficiency Innovation Model (EIM) assesses where the enterprise is along the path in its global evolution and points to some leading practices to help move the organization further along in its development.
- The Global Orientation Evaluation (GOE) approach assesses the associates in the organization to determine whether they have the appropriate personality characteristics and global mindset for leading a Transnational enterprise.

Due to scope limitations, the remainder of this article will address only the first three components in the Transnational HR Model—vision, organization, and people—the ones that form the underpinnings of the enterprise and hence are critical to success for the global company.

Strategic Visioning

> An organization's success has enormously more to do with clarity of a shared purpose, common principles and strength of belief in them than to assets, expertise, operating ability, or management competence, important as they may be. —*Dee Hock*

Most companies have a vision statement, but does the HR department? Do you know how the company's HR plans, policies, and programs align with the company's overall global vision and strategic direction? How many vision statements have you participated in developing, only to find them stuffed in a drawer and not looked at again for another five years? Why do we continue to participate in such efforts, only to find ourselves repeating the same activities again and again with little or no progress?

Although there are probably many reasons (or perhaps more appropriately, excuses), I surmise that there are two major ones: The vision statement bears no relevance to the day-to-day activities of the people in the organization; and, there is no way to measure progress against the vision to know whether the organization is on the right track or whether they should be steering another course—and quickly!

The vision statement does not present a precise plan for the organization to follow, but rather sets the purpose and a clear sense of direction, defining a common set of values or guiding principles for the organization. Since the introduction of the Internet and with the increase in global mobility, the speed of change has accelerated substantially, rendering the creation of a detailed plan futile—it would be obsolete even before starting. Rather, our time is better spent in defining a clear vision and set of values and tying that vision to the organization's strategic goals and specific objectives, than ensuring that all associates can see the relevance and connection between them. With a concise, well-understood vision, linked to a common and attainable set of objectives, the organization is better prepared to face the surprises the future will inevitably hold.

To help prepare for the future, many organizations use an approach called "Scenario Planning" (De Gues, 1997; Georgantzas, 1995;

Schwartz, 1991; Stambaugh, 1999 and 2003). This process basically consists of thought leaders in the organization envisioning multiple, different scenarios—some likely, some unlikely—of what the future might bring, from war, to economic slowdown, to the emergence of a new competitor, etc., and what the company's reaction to that future might be including layoffs, acquisition, re-training, etc. "Using scenario planning, we can open a window into the future and do much of the identification and assessment before the event itself" (Stambaugh, 2003). While the actual scenario will undoubtedly not happen exactly as it was envisioned, we will be better prepared to react cogently, swiftly, and effectively when some new event does occur, because we have exercised our minds and explored many different possible futures and outcomes. Scenario planning is an excellent way to promote out-of-the-box thinking, to open up new horizons, and to rid ourselves of the old ideas that inhibit truly creative, strategic thinking. Again in the words of Dee Hock, "the problem is never how to get new, innovative thoughts into your mind, but how to get old ones out."

A practical approach to visioning and strategic planning can be found in Scott Bolman's *IHRIM Journal* article, "Developing a Global HR Systems Strategy" (2001). As Bolman says, "simply put, strategy is about choices, or more clearly, the elimination of choices." The goal of the strategic visioning and planning process is to review alternative approaches for the business, eliminating those that are not appropriate and focusing on one strategy at the expense of the others. Bolman defines five steps critical to creating an effective strategic HR business plan.

- Identify key drivers/business goals to create alignment.
- Identify global processes to define the scope.
- Identify current processes and systems to establish a baseline.
- Develop alternatives to define the desired future state.
- Evaluate and decide which alternatives to arrive at the best possible decisions.

At the core of a solid HR business model are the articulation of a clear vision and set of business goals, based on the real activities of real associates in the organization—that is, global processes—and the development of an understandable and achievable strategic plan that is both qualitative and quantitative.

Vision-to-Values Process (V2V). As previously stated, the first step in developing a chaordic, Transnational HR Model is to clearly define the overall vision, goals, and objectives the organization is trying to reach, and tying that vision to specific, quantifiable values—that is, metrics. The Vision-to-Values (V2V) Process is a structured approach that ensures the organization's vision and objectives are clearly defined, that all stakeholders are committed and aligned toward the same goals, and that value metrics are explicitly identified to meet the vision. The output of the V2V process is an explicit framework for the organization to operate within that defines a roadmap for the future. There are four basic steps to the V2V Process:

- SWOT analysis
- Vision definition
- Value metric identification
- Stakeholder mapping

SWOT Analysis. The SWOT Analysis—a process of identifying the organization's strengths, weaknesses, opportunities, and threats—is a well-established approach that many organizations use to assess their current state of affairs vis-à-vis the current market situation and economic environment (Figure 2). The SWOT process consists of a series of brainstorming sessions in which the relevant areas of the organization are assessed and delineated. It is important to ensure appropriate and adequate representation in the SWOT process across the organization, both horizontally and vertically, to make certain different perspectives and approaches are being considered. The output of the SWOT is then used to develop the organization's vision statement.

Strengths These are areas that the organization considers their strong areas—factors that give them a competitive advantage over their competitors.	**Weaknesses** These are areas that the organization feels they do not perform well in or are factors that are a disadvantage with respect to their competitors.
Opportunities These are the areas that the organization should explore to find opportunities to take advantage of their strengths and/or minimize their weaknesses.	**Threats** These are threats to growth, profitability, survival, competitive edge, etc., if the organization does nothing or doesn't take advantage of their opportunities.

Figure 2. SWOT analysis process

Vision Definition. Vision Definition is a statement of what the company expects to achieve in the future; it conveys the goals, objectives, and expectations of the company's executives and key stakeholders. The Vision Definition step answers the question, "What is the organization's raison d'être?" While there are many ways to express a vision statement, the most effective, in my opinion, is one that is concise (consists of one sentence), concrete (contains one or more specific objectives), action-oriented (begins with a verb), and measurable (identifies a quantifiable goal).

Value Metric Identification. The Value Metric Identification process brings a quantifiable dimension to the strategic visioning process by taking the objectives from the Vision Definition and assigning a value—or metric—to each (Figure 3). The Value Indentification step answers the question, "How will the organization achieve its stated vision?" Value Identification starts with the end result, identifying the outcome(s) or objective(s) the organization is trying to reach (e.g.; improve service levels, decrease costs, build global infrastructure). Next, the relevant stakeholders are named, the current process is defined, the required inputs are identified, and the sources of the inputs are documented. Because they are measurable, value metrics put the teeth into the process and are the key drivers in tying the vision to the day-to-day business operations.

Sources	Process	Stakeholders
Establish the sources for the input data required that will enable the desired process (e.g.; HR, IT, finance, managers, industry, other providers)	Document the current process and describe how it will need to change in order to meet the desired outcome (e.g.; if improved service is an outcome, then move to a shared services model may be appropriate; if reduced headcount is an outcome, then move to BPO may be an option)	Define the stakeholders who are interested in and will affect the outcome of this process (e.g.; users, managers, outside providers)
Inputs Identify the input data needed in order to enable the defined process (e.g.; current costs, industry and inhouse benchmarks, management expectations)		**Value** State the desired objective you are trying ot obtain (e.g.; reduce costs, increase service levels, improve synergies across business units)

Figure 3. Value metric identification process

Stakeholder Mapping. Stakeholder Mapping is a well-established approach in the industry for identifying the interested parties who are directly involved in, have an influence on, or are simply interested in any given project, effort, or enterprise (Figure 4). Stakeholders include the organization's associates, executives, board members, investors, stockholders, third party providers, vendors, etc., anyone who is either directly or indirectly concerned with the effort. The Stakeholder Mapping process answers the question, "Who will be involved and influence the effort?" It consists of brainstorming with the relevant individuals and entities and identifying their potential impact on the effort, that is, their level of trust and agreement with the goals of the organization. The goal of this process is to identify those stakeholders who are allies, and hence supporters of the effort, and those who are opponents, adversaries, and/or double agents. The purpose of this effort is to build strategies to leverage the allies and neutralize the others. In the ultimate chaordic organization, once the shared vision and guiding principles are defined, everyone should be aligned toward the

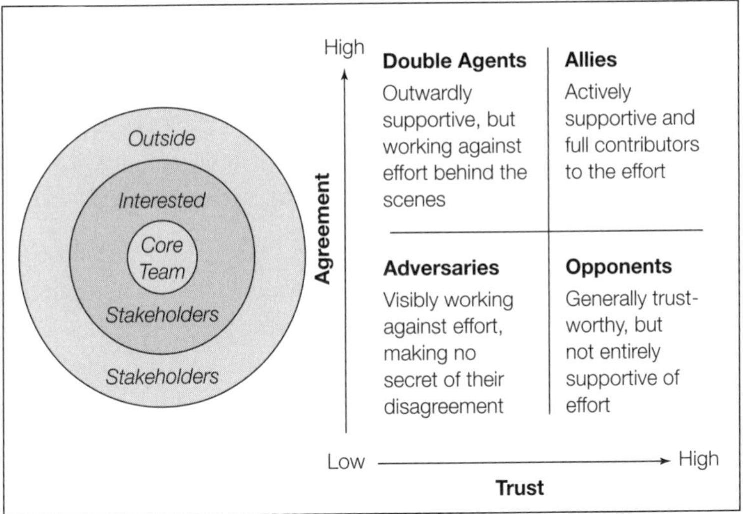

Figure 4. Stakeholder mapping process

common goal, with few adversaries, opponents, and double agents working against the vision.

Organizational Development

> No function should be performed by any part of the whole that could reasonably be done by any more peripheral part and no power should be vested in any part that might reasonably be exercised by any lesser part . . . Authority . . . [must] come from the bottom up, not the top down.
>
> —*Dee Hock*

The second component of the chaordic, Transnational HR Model involves the organizational structure of the enterprise. Hock's theory of the chaordic organization is a synthesis of the theories of Lao Tse, Adam Smith, and Thomas Jefferson: Rather than enforcing cooperation by restricting what associates in the organization can do, individuals are encouraged to compete and innovate as much as possible. In the chaordic model, the organizational structure is transparent, not controlling and delegating, rather guiding and empowering. To build this type of structure requires that responsibility and accountability be distributed to the lowest possible level in the organizational structure. Concepts like delegation, empowerment, and decentralization cannot be treated as the latest management fads dreamed up by over-paid consultants, but must be made real. We must follow Hock's mantra and transform our oppressive and stifling, albeit benign, dictatorships into prospering and highly productive democracies (Hock, 1999).

Bartlett and Ghoshal's (1989) transnational model embodies many of Hock's chaordic principles and provides the foundation for transitioning the global HR organization to meets the challenges of the paradox: It is responsive to local needs, cooperative for global activities, innovative to new ideas, and flexible to change. In their seminal book, *Managing Across Borders: The Transnational Solution*, they define four basic structures or models that organizations manifest in their global development.

- A Multinational organization is one that is highly decentralized, consisting of numerous independent local business units and little control at the center—generally not much more than financial oversight (Figure 5).

- A Global organization is one that is highly centralized and standardized, minimizing the needs of the local business units in favor of one single, uniform operating environment—the "one size fits all" approach (Figure 6).

- An International organization, while still largely centralized, takes a learning and sharing approach by adopting innovations from local business units, integrating them into the global business model and rolling them back out throughout the organization (Figure 7).

- A Transnational organization is a chaordic, networked structure with no centralized controlling unit per se, but with a well-defined set of centralized coordinating and cooperative processes that govern how the organization functions (Figure 8). This type of organization is enabling and self-organizing, exemplifying effectiveness without being controlling and coercive.

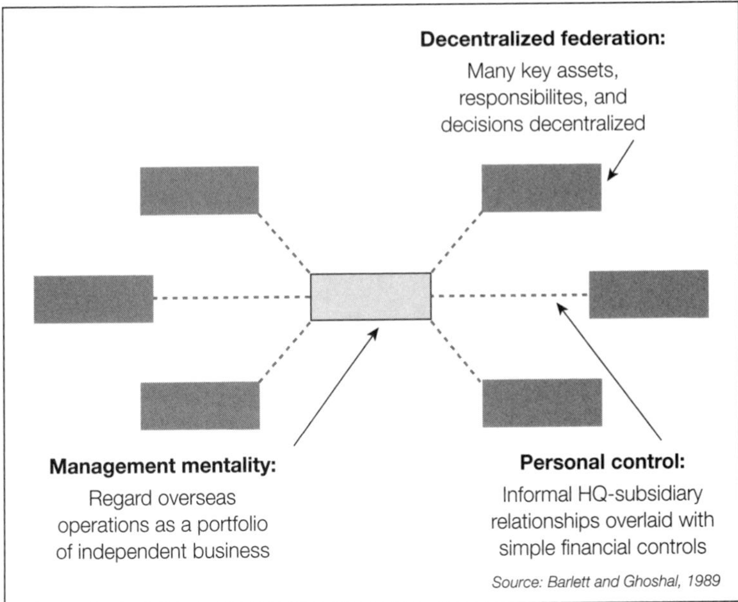

Figure 5. Multinational model

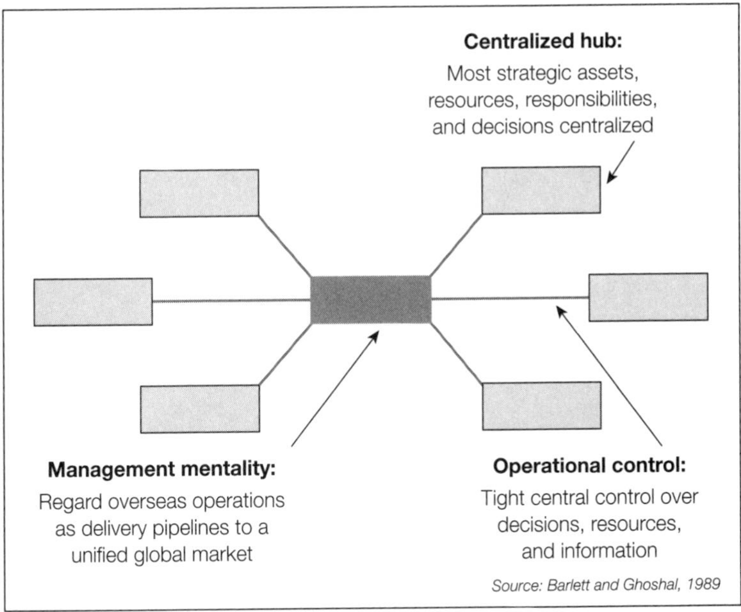

Figure 6. Global model

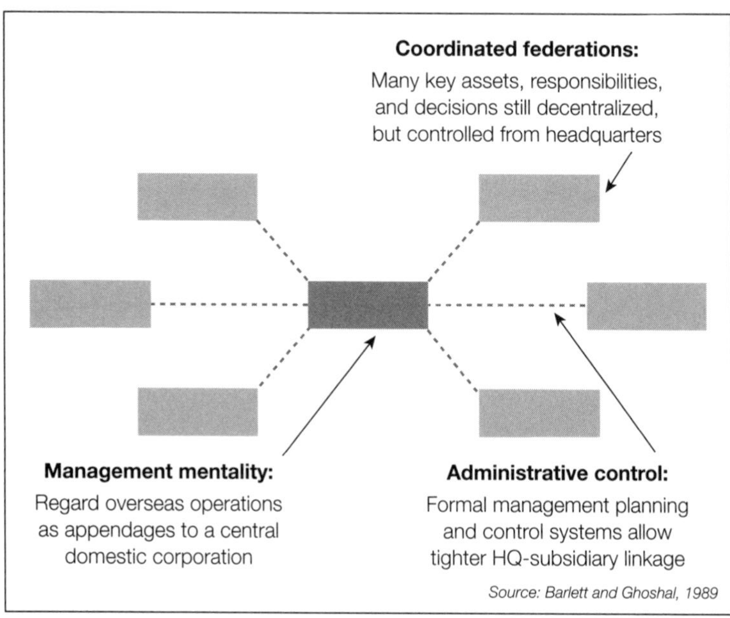

Figure 7. International model

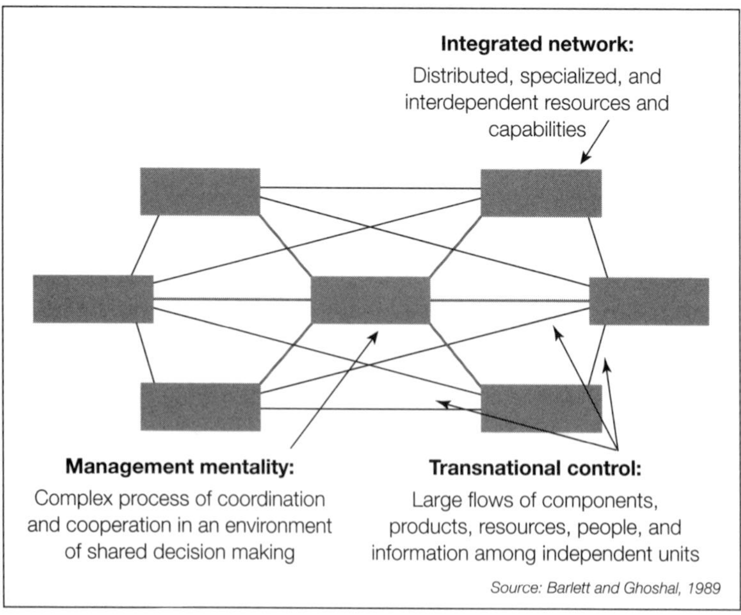

Figure 8. Transnational model

In their global evolutionary development, it has been postulated, that organizations evolve from a purely domestic stage through the Multinational and Global stages, then to the International stages, and ultimately to the Transnational stage (Beaman and Walker, 2000; Beaman and Guy, 2003) (Figure 9). This natural evolutionary development is stimulated by an intrinsic need to seek out best practices that can assist the organization in dealing effectively with the mounting complexity of the global business environment—survival of the fittest! It is important to keep in mind that best practices are relative and can only be understood, appreciated, and implemented in the appropriate setting: What may be good for one company at one point in its development may not be good for another company, or even for the same company at a different point in its development. It is also important to point out that organizations can skip intermediate stages in their development, jumping from one stage to another, in a punctuated equilibrium approach (Stambaugh, personal communication).

Jay Galbraith's (2000) "Multidimensional Multinational" exemplifies a practical approach to building a global organizational model that supports chaordic principles through its multi-structure approach to managing individual business units—and hence managers' objectives—across the corporation (Figure 10). Profit and loss statements

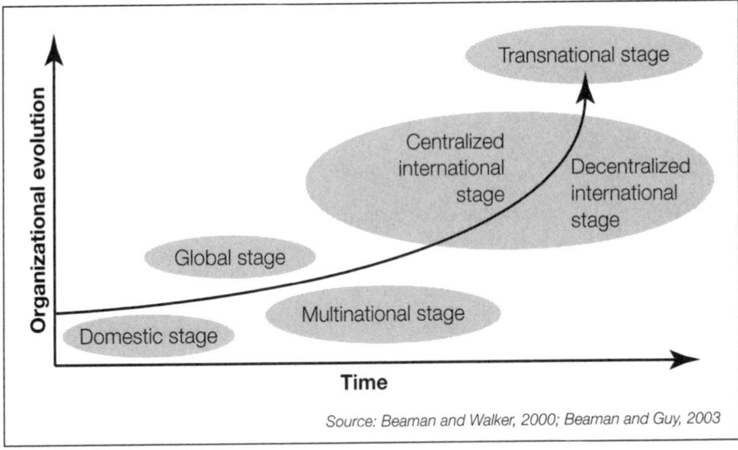

Figure 9. Organizational evolutionary development curve

(P&Ls indicated by gray square boxes in Figure 10) are defined at the lowest possible level (e.g.; for a single product in a single country in a single line of business) and are then linked together for different managers and functions depending on their areas of responsibility. For example, one director may be responsible for all the lines of business in one country (indicated by the outlined and shaded area in Figure 10), whereas another may be responsible for one product across different countries and functions (indicated by the thick black line linking various P&Ls together). Divisions are generally organized into global lines of business (LOBs) indicated by the shaded area in Figure 10. Likewise, customer relationship managers may be responsible for a single customer across multiple countries and product lines (indicated by the thin black line linking various P&Ls). This multidimensional structure allows the organization to dynamically link individual views of the business, slicing and dicing the objectives and financials in various ways depending on the functional need and the type of business.

This multidimensional, transnational model provides an approach for coordinating multiple, different objectives across diverse financial units and business functions in a chaordic manner. Such an approach is essential in any highly matrixed environment that demands different ways to evaluate and measure progress against goals. It is particularly relevant for a global HR business model because HR organizations are inherently matrixed: By their very nature, HR must answer to multiple chiefs and respond across diverse business functions and geographical units. The ability to implement an appropriate organizational structure with worldwide coordination capabilities is a key criterion in building a successful transnational HR business model.

As previously mentioned, in order to effectively understand an organization's current structure is according to Bartlett and Ghoshal's four models, significant consideration must be given to the heritage and corporate culture of the organization. For example, if the company has largely grown through an acquisition strategy, the Multinational model will prevail. If the company has grown primarily through an organic green fields approach, then the Global model will be more prevalent. The challenge is to move the organization in the direction

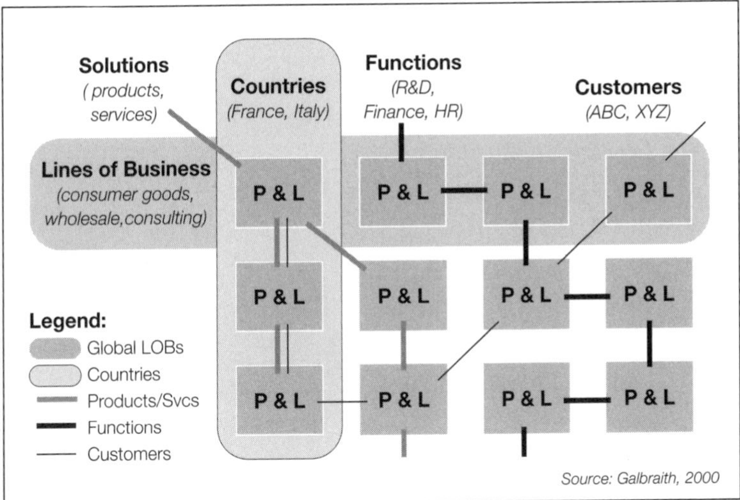

Figure 10. Multidimensional multinational

of the Transnational model along the Evolutionary Development Curve (Figure 9). To affect this change, it is critical to first understand where the company currently is in their development and then to uncover what practices can be employed that can best influence the necessary changes.

Efficiency Innovation Model (EIM) In order to assess where an organization currently is along its evolutionary path in moving toward the Transnational HR Model, Beaman and Guy (2003) propose the Efficiency Innovation Model (EIM) (Figure 11).

The EIM is based on the two dimensions most critical to the transnational organization:

- Efficiency—the degree of centralization/decentralization, with the goal to provide optimal balance between central control and local independence (the horizontal axis in Figure 11), and
- Innovation—the degree of innovation that is supported and leveraged, with the goal to foster innovation and knowledge sharing across the organization (the vertical axis in Figure 11).

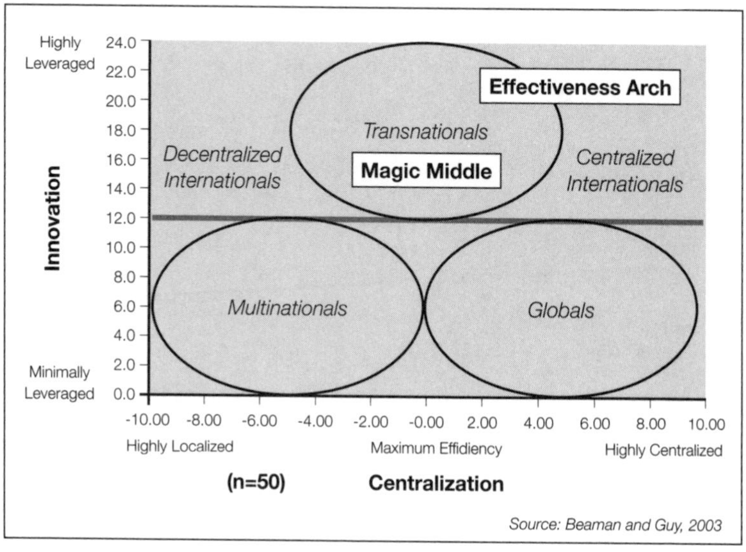

Figure 11. Efficiency innovation model (EIM)

The basic tenet of the EIM is that an effective organization must find the right balance between centralization and decentralization in order to maximize innovation; overly decentralized organizations lack formal mechanisms for disseminating innovations throughout the company, while overly centralized enterprises allow innovations to languish in the field through the arrogance of corporate headquarters—the "not-invented-here" syndrome. The EIM predicts that organizations move along the Effectiveness Arch from either the Multinational or the Global stage, to the International, and ultimately, the Transnational stage, toward the Magic Middle—the point of optimal efficiency and maximum innovation (Beaman and Guy, 2003 for further details). Based on a pilot study of fifty global companies, organizations appear to be well distributed across Bartlett and Ghoshal's four organizational models, with the most effective organizations clustering around the Magic Middle. These organizations are best positioned to take advantage of cost savings and productivity improvements through centralization and most able to leverage innovations and best practices through a high level of responsiveness to local requirements.

Transnational Leading Practices. Beaman and Guy (2003) also identified several industry trends and leading practices among the transnational corporations in their study. One salient finding from their study is the more frequent occurrence of Shared Service Centers in International and Transnational organizations, highlighting these organizations' focus on a high-level of efficiency and leveraging of shared infrastructure. Transnational organizations are also much more likely to have frequent face-to-face global HR meetings, facilitating sharing of ideas and communication across business units. They are also more receptive to new ideas from local and regional business units and to implementing common strategies across the organization—globally, regionally, and locally. Additionally, Transnational organizations also tend to use a single provider and/or technology platform globally for their HR solution, facilitating their ability to coordinate activities across the worldwide organization.

Global Orientation

> Hire and promote first on the basis of integrity; second, motivation; third, capacity; fourth, understanding; fifth, knowledge; and last and least, experience. Without integrity, motivation is dangerous; without motivation, capacity is impotent; without capacity, understanding is limited; without understanding, knowledge is meaningless; without knowledge, experience is blind. Experience is easy to provide and quickly put to good use by people with all the other qualities.
>
> —*Dee Hock*

The third component of the Transnational HR Model that this article considers deals with the people who make up the organization and their global orientation, and hence suitability to work in a chaordic, transnational environment. This aspect is undoubtedly the most critical, as well as the most complicated, component of the entire model. Nothing in business functions without people: People are the thinkers behind the ideas, the doers of the activities, the managers of the processes, the recipients of the services, the leaders of change. In any enterprise—indeed in any human endeavor—people are the fundamental asset that allows the effort to function and prosper. While there are many critical human attributes that interact in the professional environment, we discuss three aspects of this multi-dimensional issue that appear to be most relevant for building the people component of the Transnational HR Model.

- Motivation
- Cultural adaptability
- Global mindset

Motivation. Much research in this area has shown that individual characteristics (including age, gender, language, personality, prior experience, etc.) are inadequate predictors of success in an international setting. Rather, the principle attributes that make a difference are the individual's motivation and receptiveness to different cultures (Baruch, 2002). Motivation appears to be both an inherent personal characteristic as well as a situational attribute heavily influenced by the individual's work environment. Other work suggests that motivation is stimulated by blending values from various cultures and establishing a single global vision and common set of objectives (Begley and Boyd, 2000). Premoli's (2003) polynomial theory of motivation also argues that success is achieved when organizational values and individual objectives are closely aligned, thereby creating a motivating environment.

Consistent with these and many other observations about the connection between motivation and success, in their study of 90 expatriates, Beaman and Guy (unpublished research) also found a strong correlation between motivation and success in an international environment. The more motivated an individual was to learn the language, adapt to the culture, socialize with locals, etc., the more successful, and less frustrated they were. Guy and Beaman (forthcoming) also found a strong correlation between motivation and the expatriate's satisfaction with their assignment: Not surprisingly, successful individuals are more satisfied than dissatisfied ones; and quite naturally, satisfied individuals are more motivated.

Dee Hock's philosophy on hiring (see above quote) also supports the belief that motivation is a key attribute required for success in any endeavor. Of paramount importance in building an effective Transnational HR Model is the selection of highly motivated, alert, and committed associates to seed the organization. Motivated individuals are contagious: They propel others along with them. These are the desirable leaders in the organization—they build expansive and productive social networks that help the organization flourish. From these findings and other studies, it is clear the motivation is a strong determinant for success and an attribute that should be sought after in building a transnational HR organization.

Cultural Adaptability. The new transnational environment requires a plethora of individuals who can work internationally—who are ultimately flexible, accommodating, and adaptable to different cultures and varying ways of doing things. Studies on the success or failure of individuals in an international setting have indicated that American expatriates experience a failure rate of 30 to 40 percent as compared to many Europeans and Japanese, whose failure rate has been estimated as low as 6 percent (Tung, 1988). It appears that some countries or cultures are more effective at producing successful global professionals than other countries.

Moore (2003) argues that there are ten countries that produce the largest number of "good" global managers: Canada, the Netherlands, Switzerland, Belgium, Ireland, Sweden, Denmark, Singapore, Australia, and Finland. According to Moore, what these ten countries have in common is their size. While they are not dominant powers in their geographic regions, they are considered significant players on the international stage. These middle-economy countries face the everyday reality that they are not the most important culture in their region and thus they find themselves constantly negotiating between their own culture and identity and that of surrounding dominant cultures. In order to be successful, individuals growing up in mid-sized countries learn to embrace multiple ways of looking at the world. They grow up with a duality (or plurality) that obliges them to work effectively with their neighbors. It is this ability to be "all things to all people" that helps such individuals to be successful in a global context. "When working on global teams or in other countries, the ability to think outside your own culture and see an issue through the eyes of another is critical to success" (Moore, 2003).

In the field of psychology considerable work has been conducted on people's sensitivity to intercultural issues and their ability to adapt to other cultures and different ways of doing things. Some organizations have moved to personality testing to better ascertain the likelihood of success of individuals working in an international environment. There are many approaches to personality assessment, and a number of assessment instruments are available such as the Myers-Briggs Type Indicator (Keirsey and Bates, 1978), Big Five (Goldberg, 1990), IDI Profile (Hammer and Bennett, 1998), Global Awareness Profile (Corbitt, 1998)).

Edward Hoffman (2002), a clinical psychologist working therapeutically with expatriate workers residing in the United States, noted in the clinical setting that several key personality traits seemed predictive of success for individuals living in a foreign country. The Hoffman's Cultural Adaptability Inventory (HCAI) comprises four subscales assessing intercultural liking (an evaluation of a subject's openness to other cultures), risk-taking, amiability, and extroversion/introversion. An individual's score on this test can serve as a general predictor of suitability for international work experience, and hence likelihood of success as an expatriate.

Global Mindset. Much has been written on the influence of culture and global orientation on business (Hofstede, 1980, Trompenaars, 1998; Henson, 2002), as well as on different mental models, cognitive maps, states of mind, and global mindsets (Perlmutter, 1969; Sullivan, 2001; Guy and Beaman, forthcoming). Peter Senge (1994) defines mindset as those "deeply ingrained assumptions, generalizations, or images that influence how we understand the world and how we take action." In the international environment, Daniel Sullivan (2001) has used global mindset to define how individuals "interpret, analyze, and decide situations in a world of falling boundaries." He describes three basic models (Figure 12).

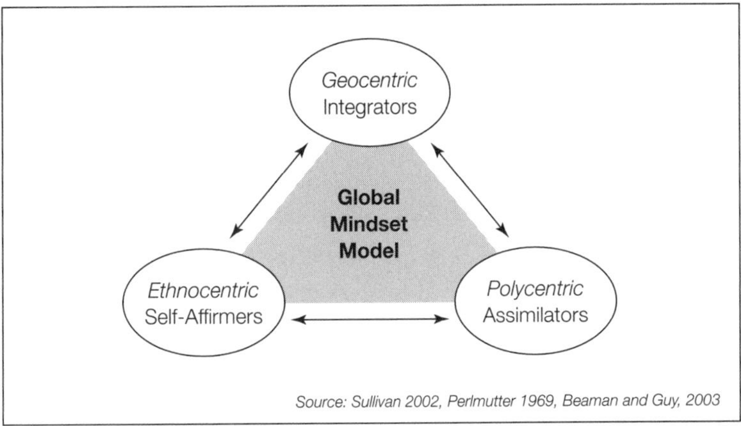

Figure 12. Global mindset model

- An ethnocentric mindset is one that basically holds one's own values, beliefs, and culture are intrinsically superior to those of others. Ethnocentric individuals interpret the world through the eyes of their own culture, not recognizing, even devaluing, cultures that are different from their own. "If it works here, it'll work anywhere," exemplifies the ethnocentric individual. Ethnocentrics can play an important role in preserving standards and uniformity across the global corporation.

- A polycentric mindset is one that adapts and assimilates to the values, attitudes and beliefs of another culture. Because they are highly attuned to the conditions and expectations of other cultures, polycentric individuals can play the role of empathetic advisors, effective at bridging the gap and transferring knowledge between the local environment and corporate. The danger with the polycentric mindset is the tendency to go native, sometimes to the detriment of the organization's objectives.

- A geocentric mindset is one that believes there are certain cultural universals and commonalities in the world and that no culture is superior or inferior to another. "The geocentric mindset accepts the premise that bright people [do] bright things around the world" (Sullivan, 2001). Also called cosmopolitans, these types of individuals focus on "finding commonalities . . . [and] spread[ing] universal ideas and juggl[ing] the requirements of diverse places" (Kanter, 1995).

Sullivan's premise is that there is no one ideal mindset; rather, we need to seek out the right mindset depending on the job to be done. Ethnocentric individuals are appropriate in roles where there is a need to preserve the company's standards and provide a uniform approach. Polycentrics are effective in roles that require a deep understanding of the language and local market conditions in order to be effective. In the transnational organization, a geocentric mindset that transcends cultural boundaries and seeks commonalities in beliefs and practices across the universe is critical.

Along the same lines as Sullivan's global mindsets, Bartlett and Ghoshal (1992) contend that there is no such thing as one single ideal type of global manager; rather, there are four different types of global leaders that are needed in order to build an effective transnational organization.

- Business Managers (ethnocentrics) support a single set of uniform operational standards and oversee the efficient distribution of assets across the organization by coordinating activities and linking capabilities and resources across the globe. They serve as the global strategists, business architects, and coordinators, unifying cross-border interactions and protecting the corporation's global interests. They "have one overriding responsibility: to further the company's global-scale efficiency and competitiveness" (Bartlett and Ghoshal, 1992).
- Country Managers (polycentrics) are focused on the local market situation, ensuring that the organization is sensitive, flexible, and responsive to local country needs, aware of and responding to local and external competitors, and adhering to the demands and regulations of local governments. These managers must have a deep understanding of the local environment and be able to defend the interests of local operations. However, "sometimes a country manager must carry out a strategy that directly con-

flicts with what he or she has lobbied for in vain" (Bartlett and Ghoshal, 1992).

- Functional Managers (geocentrics) are the lynchpins that connect different areas of functional specialization across the globe. As champions of a given function or product, their primary role is one of finding commonalities across diverse business units, connecting resources and capabilities, and transforming piecemeal information into strategic intelligence. "Functional managers must scan for specialized information worldwide, cross-pollinate leading-edge knowledge and best practice, and champion innovations that may offer transnational opportunities and applications" (Bartlett and Ghoshal, 1992).

- Corporate Managers (corporate sponsors) are the company's top executives who manage this complex web of interactions across the global organization and identify and develop talent through effective succession planning, job rotation, on-the-job training, coaching, and the career development processes. "Corporate managers integrate many levels of responsibilities, playing perhaps the most vital role in transnational management" (Bartlett and Ghoshal, 1992).

In the transnational organization, it is vital to maintain a balance among all four types of managers, using expatriate assignments and job rotation practices to ensure that associates have the opportunity to act in multiple, different roles throughout their careers. Gone are the days where local country managers can set up their fiefdoms and control their operations as warlords to the detriment of the rest of the organization. Effective managers today need to develop multiple competencies, able to perform in a variety of roles, and capable of wearing many different hats.

Developmental Model of Intercultural Sensitivity. Milton Bennett's Model of Intercultural Sensitivity provides a useful roadmap for understanding the acquisition and maturity of individual cultural awareness and global orientation. Bennett (1993) postulates a development progression that all individuals go through as they develop into geocentrics or cosmopolitans (Figure 13). As individuals mature globally, they move from the ethnocentric stages of denial, defense, and minimization to the ethnorelative stages of acceptance, adaptation, and integration. Other empirical work has demonstrated that the more international experiences individuals have, the less ethnocentric they become (Guy and Beaman, forthcoming). Hence, associates who have reached the ethnorelative stages of their individual development—those with geocentric mindsets—are vital for the new chaordic, transnational HR organization to function effectively.

ETHNOCENTRIC STAGES	ETHNORELATIVE STAGES
I. Denial A. Isolation B. Separation	**IV. Acceptance** A. Respect for behavioral differences B. Respect for value difference
II. Defense A. Denigration B. Superiority C. Reversal	**V. Adaptation** A. Empathy B. Pluralism
III. Minimization A. Physical universalism B. Transcendent universalism	**VI. Integration** A. Contextual Evaluation B. Constructive marginality

Source: Bennet, 1993

Figure 13. Developmental model of intercultural sensitivity

Global Orientation Evaluation (GOE). Uniting each of these people-related aspects, we can build a global orientation component in our Transnational HR Model to evaluate the suitability of individuals to work in a chaordic, transnational environment (Figure 14). There are four basic parameters to the global orientation component of our Transnational HR model.

- Hoffman's Cultural Adaptability Inventory (HCAI)—a tool for evaluating the basic, intrinsic personality characteristics vital to individuals in an international setting (Hoffman, 2001).

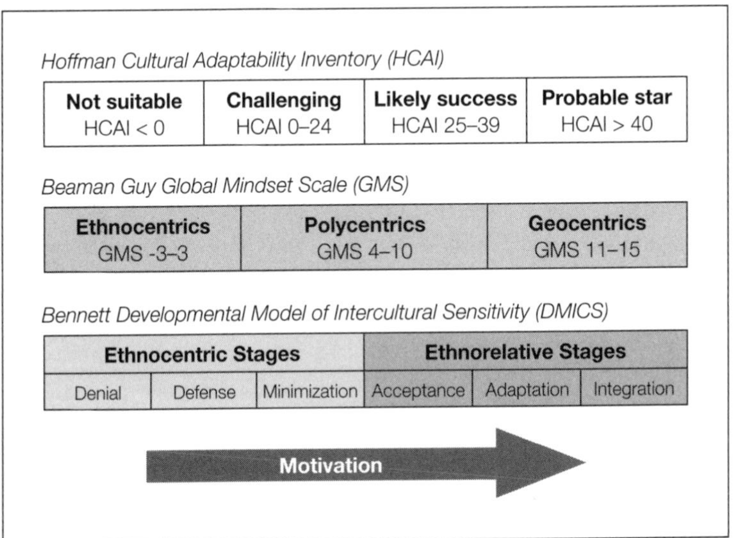

Figure 14. Global orientation evaluation (GOE)

- Beaman Guy Global Mindset Scale (GMS)—a technique for assessing an individual's mindset, from ethnocentric to polycentric to geocentric (Guy and Beaman, forthcoming).
- Bennett's Developmental Model of Intercultural Sensitivity (DMIS)—a method for evaluating an individual's position on the development continuum of intercultural sensitivity (Bennett, 1993).
- Motivation—an elusive personality characteristic that seems to be a major driver of success.

Change Facilitation

> Lead yourself, lead your superiors, lead your peers, and free your people to do the same. All else is trivia. —*Dee Hock*

So once the new transnational enterprise has been defined and built, how do you get people on board with the change? The change process itself is at the core of the Transnational HR Model (Figure 1). Nothing will kill a new initiative faster than failure to facilitate an effective change management process. Bartlett and Ghoshal (1989) present a different approach to affecting change in an organization. Traditionally companies have tried to implement a new initiative by changing the formal organizational structure: Announcements are made, new processes are designed, and updated organization charts are printed and distributed. Then they sit back and wait to see the change in people's attitudes, behaviors, and relationships. A more successful model for change is one that starts with fostering change in people's attitudes and mentalities first (cf. the white space according to Rummier and Brache, 1995); then, naturally, change in relationships and processes follows. It then becomes a purely administrative matter to change the formal structure and reporting relationships to match the new organization (Figure 15).

An important component in facilitating change is to identify the individuals who are supporters and champions of the new initiative and those who are opponents and possible detractors to the effort. Similar to the Stakeholder Mapping process (Figure 4) discussed earlier, Don

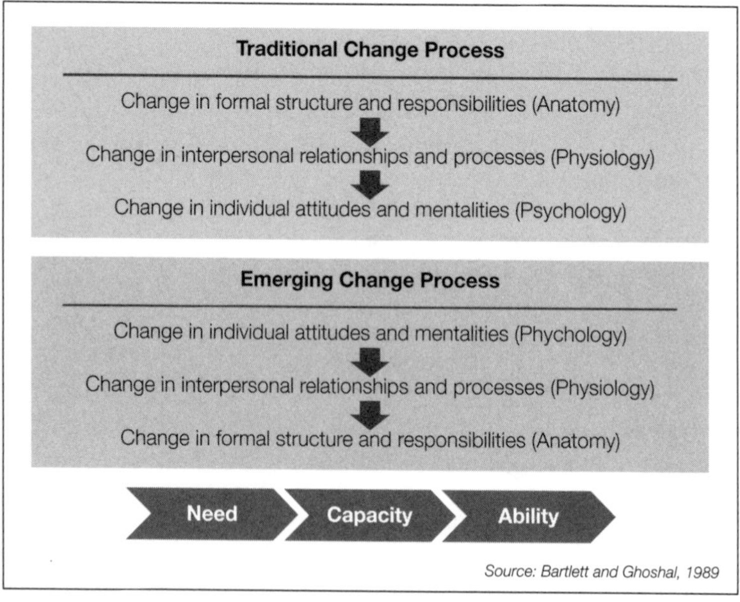

Figure 15. Transnational change process

Tosti's Energy Investment Model (Figure 16) provides a useful tool for identifying and assessing the attitudes and energy levels of individuals in organizations. Those individuals with positive attitudes and high levels of energy are called players—the evangelists, so to speak—those who can help sell the initiative throughout the rest of the organization. Players can be leveraged to go after the cynics and spectators and convert them. Those individuals with low levels of energy and poor attitudes—the walking dead—need to be either moved into more productive, better-fitting roles or transitioned completely out of the organization. Identifying where your supporters/players are and building individual strategies to bring the others along is a vital aspect of the change facilitation process.

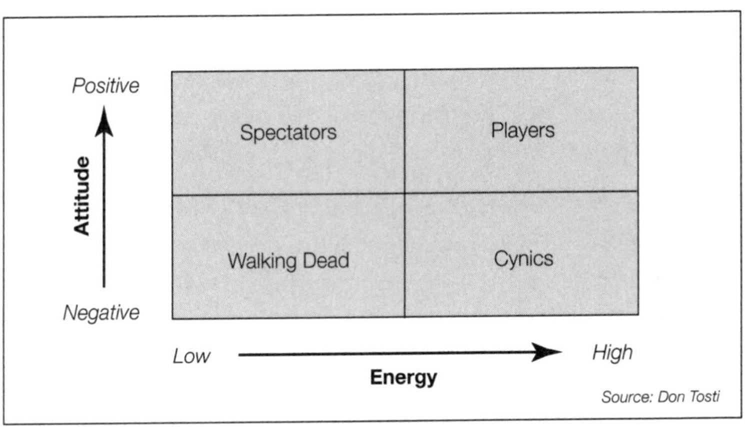

Figure 16. Energy investment model

Identifying where your supporters/players are and building individual strategies to bring the others along is a vital aspect of the change facilitation process.

The well-known family psychologist, Virginia Satir (1991), provides a useful model for understanding the change process as it happens within individuals. Satir's model encompasses five stages that individuals go through as they change (Figure 17).

- Status Quo—This is the current environment before a change emerges. This steady states gives people a sense of security, they know what to expect and how to react. Then a foreign element is introduced, impacting current business processes, disrupting people's day-to-day lives, and threatening existing power structures and relationships.
- Resistance—When first presented with a change, most people will, at first, deny its existence and actively resist the new idea/process/element, trying to protect the status quo. In this initial phase, people generally do not understand the change or admit the need for the change, so there is generally considerable active and loud resistance to the proposed new effort.
- Chaos—There is always a period when chaos reigns as people begin to explore the change and try to make sense of the new idea/process. For a while performance plummets as the people seek to integrate the change into their day-to-day lives. Finally people begin to understand "what's-in-it-for-them" and so start to let go of the old ways and explore new ways.
- Integration—Finally, a transforming idea emerges that shows individuals the way to integrate the change into their lives and take advantage of the opportunity it presents. At this stage people begin to take ownership for the change and become committed to carrying out the new mission. Here the strongest resisters can be become the most fervent evangelists!
- New Status Quo—Once the idea has been fully integrated, people enter a new status quo. Because they have been successful at integrating the change into their environment, this new state is generally at a significantly higher level of performance than the previous state, and the cycle begins again.

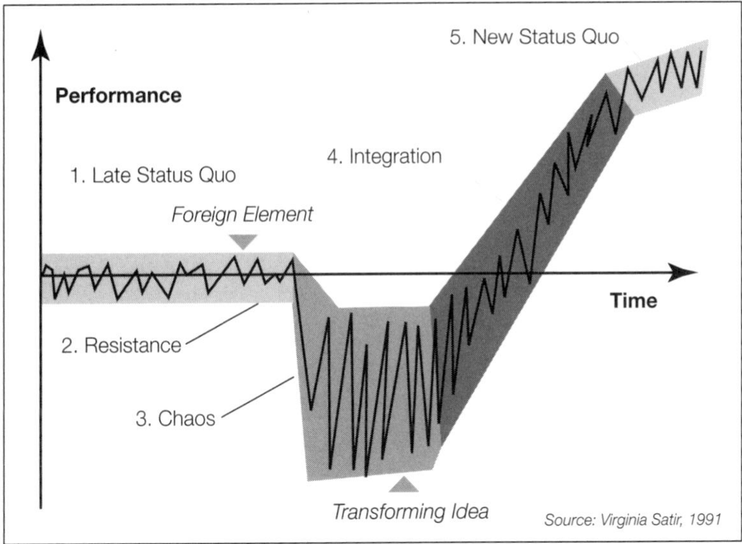

Figure 17. Satir change model

It's important to note that all people go through these same steps when confronted with change. Although some may move faster through the cycle than others, it's not possible to skip steps along the way. The challenge for HR leadership is to minimize the depth of the performance dive and to speed the integration of the change throughout the organization by working with individuals to help them develop the skills needed to be successful in the new environment. Figure 18 provides some guidelines to help move people effectively through the stages of the change process.

The challenge for HR leadership is to minimize the depth of the performance dive and to speed the integration of the change throughout the organization.

Stage	Description	How to Help
1	Old Status Quo	Encourage people to seek improvement information and concepts from outside the group.
2	Resistance	Help people to open up, become aware, and overcome the reaction to deny, avoid, or blame.
3	Chaos	Build a safe environment that enables people to focus on their feelings, acknowledge their fear, and use their support systems; help management avoid attempts to short circuit this stage with magical solutions.
4	Integration	Offer reasurrance and help finding new methods for coping with difficulties.
5	New Status Quo	Help people feel safe so they can practice.

Source: Virginia Satir, 1991

Figure 18. Facilitating the change process

Transnational Competency

> Given the right chaordic conditions, from no more than dreams, determination, and the liberty to try, quite ordinary people consistently do extraordinary things. —*Dee Hock*

This brings us to the question of how do you build chaordic-like transnational competency in your organization. This section will highlight four basic strategies that are critical to advancing transnational competency across the enterprise.

- Establish a clear vision
- Foster a transnational outlook
- Transform the organization
- Communicate actively

Without a clear vision and specific, measurable goals and objectives, the organization will flounder.

Establish a Clear Vision

Of overarching importance is the ability to establish a clear vision through the Vision-to-Values Assessment process. Without a clear vision and specific, measurable goals and objectives, the organization will flounder. Some specific guidelines to help you with this process are:

- Ensure that the vision depicts a compelling need for change and that all associates are involved in the solution and keenly aware of how the change will improve the current situation.
- Ensure that the change plan clearly demonstrates the WIIFM principle—what's in it for me?—so that associates can relate the results of the change to their day-to-day lives.
- Involve multiple, diverse stakeholders in the process from various lines of business and multiple levels in the organization to ensure buy-in throughout the enterprise.
- Gain commitment from all stakeholders—those both directly and indirectly involved in the success of the effort—and neutralize the opponents and cynics.
- Establish priorities openly and logically—remember, "we can do anything, but we can't do everything".
- Create objectives/metrics that are easily quantifiable and measurable and that can be influenced by those concerned.
- Set up processes to regularly and publicly report on the status of the objectives, encouraging friendly competition among business units to beat the numbers.

- Build an environment that fosters honesty, openness, and freedom of expression to encourage the free flow and exchange of ideas.

Foster a Transnational Outlook

Transnational competency entails fostering a new outlook—a new way of thinking and acting that continually looks to leverage new ideas and opportunities wherever they appear. Moving to a transnational culture requires cultivating a shift in attitude throughout the organization—from one of controlling a hierarchy to one of managing a network of interconnected parts and activities. Emphasis must be placed on the process of socializing individuals into the transnational business culture and building an outlook—a mentality—that appreciates the need for multiple strategic capabilities, analyzes problems and opportunities from the global, regional, and local perspectives, and interacts with others across the organization with openness, alertness, and agility.

Continually look to leverage new ideas and opportunities wherever they appear.

Following are some basic guidelines to consider when fostering a transnational outlook and transforming the global mindsets of international associates.

- Encourage multiple overseas assignments for all key associates in order to broaden their experiences and to build an awareness of the impact of culture on business success.

- Consider the type of international assignment and match the global mindset of the associate with the skills required to meet the objectives of the position.

- Develop strategies to seek out motivated, engaged, alert, and committed individuals to lead the new organization.

- Ensure explicit performance measures are in place to reward those responding positively to the change and to alienate—transition out—those who are not.
- Recognize that people go through different stages of the change process in different ways and at different speeds and provide the needed individualized support and flexibility.
- Transform corporate thinking from the traditional control-oriented and hierarchical management style to a flexible and delegating leadership style.
- Put emphasis on learning, sharing, self-development, socialization, and acculturation to this new way of thinking.

Transform the Organization

To build the enabling organization that Dee Hock espouses requires commitment to egalitarianism and eradication of authoritarianism. The organization must support a peer-to-peer communication structure that facilitates collaboration across space and time. Following are some general guidelines to help in building the chaordic, Transnational HR organization.

- Identify appropriate transnational practices to implement in your organization based on the organization's culture and corporate history.
- Build a matrix in associates' mind, creating an understanding of the need to support multiple objectives simultaneously.
- Define roles and responsibilities clearly, being careful to set visible lines of authority and avoid overlapping responsibilities.
- Foster multiple levels of decision-making, pushing accountability to the lowest level possible in the organization.
- Ensure that the change process has active senior management sponsorship and visible support; without support from the top, the change will fizzle and die.

- Craft strategies to effectively coordinate activities and facilitate knowledge sharing across the transnational network.
- Encourage competition, cooperation, and sharing among business units, banning the "not-invented-here" syndrome.

Communicate Actively

To build a Transnational HR model, a solid communication network must be put in place that facilitates coordination, encourages sharing, and enables cooperative work among individuals and business units in far-flung places. With the ubiquity of the Internet, the growth of social networks and communities of practice, and the ever-increasing compatibility of global software and service providers, online real-time collaboration across the globe is becoming a reality.

As with any new initiative, proactive, frequent, and widespread communication is of paramount importance. It is essential to set up a detailed global communication plan that includes methods, media, frequencies, audiences, and messages to be conveyed. Some formal processes and tools need to be developed and put in place across the organization to ensure that information is getting to the right people at the right time. Some communication and collaboration approaches to consider are the following:

- Build a comprehensive communication plan that explicitly details the who, what, where, when, and why of the message to be communicated.
- Hold annual company conferences, physically bringing people together across the organization to discuss and work issues.
- Set up regular strategic theme meetings targeted to specific topics and audiences and empower ad hoc development committees to keep people involved.
- Make extensive use of new technologies for tele-, video-, and web-conferencing to hold monthly and quarterly meetings.

- Implement or expand company or HR newsletters to incorporate updates on the strategic vision, organization change, and people orientation initiatives underway.
- Foster communities of practices and build knowledge bases to facilitate effective collaboration across space and time.

As with any new initiative, proactive, frequent, and widespread communication is of paramount importance.

Conclusion

> Substance is enduring, form is ephemeral. Failure to distinguish clearly between the two is ruinous. Success follows those adept at preserving the substance of the past by clothing it in the forms of the future.
>
> —*Dee Hock*

As Hock illuminates, the ability to understand, preserve, and leverage the past (i.e.; the cultural heritage of the organization) in order to build the future (i.e., the new chaordic, Transnational HR Model) is key to finding the right structure and gaining wide-reaching acceptance throughout the organization. Bartlett abd Ghoshal's transnational model provides an important transitional stage that can help organizations move from their structured, regimented past to the chaordic entity of the future. Of course, no such change can happen over night—organizational evolution is a journey that must be nurtured and managed over time through the establishment of a clear vision for the organization and the transformation of the mindsets of the associates. The fundamental message in this article is that no organization can succeed today with a relatively uni-dimensional strategy, emphasizing mainly efficiency or focusing primarily on local needs or leveraging merely the mother company's capabilities. To be competitive, we have to become masters of the paradox and be all three things simultaneously: globally efficient, sensitive to the needs of local business units, and, at the same time, with the facility to leverage innovation and worldwide learning across the enterprise. To function effectively in the new chaordic organization, we have to develop globally alert associates who are motivated to succeed and are committed to the company's strategic vision and objectives. It is only by embracing these chaordic, transnational principles that we will be successful in the increasingly complex and ever-changing world. In closing, I leave you with one final quote from Dee Hock:

> If one is to properly understand events and to influence the future, it is essential to master four ways of looking at things: as they were, as they are, as they might become, and [most importantly] as they ought to be.

References

Baruch, Yehuda. 2002. "No Such Thing as a Global Manager." *Business Horizons.* University of Delaware Library. Vol. 34, No. 1. January-February 2002. 36–41.

Bartlett, Christopher and Sumantra Ghoshal. 1992. "What is a Global Manager?" *Harvard Business Review.* September-October. 124–132.

Bartlett, Christopher and Sumantra Ghoshal. 1989. *Managing Across Borders: The Transnational Solution.* Boston: Harvard University Press.

Beaman, Karen V., Charles Fay, Gregory R. Guy, and Alfred J. Walker. In Progress. "Best Practices in Global HR Technology." A collaborative work project with ADP, Towers Perrin, Rutgers University, and New York University.

Beaman, Karen V. and Gregory R. Guy. 2003. "Transnational Development: The Efficiency Innovation Model." *IHRIM Journal.* Vol. VII, No. 6. November 2003.

Beaman, Karen (Ed.). 2002. *Boundaryless HR: Human Capital Management in the Global Economy.* Austin, TX: IHRIM Press.

Beaman, Karen V. and Alfred J. Walker. 2000. "Globalizing HRIS: The New Transnational Model." *IHRIM Journal.* Vol. IV, No. 4, October-December 2000.

Begley, T. M., and D. P. Boyd. 2000. "Articulating Corporate Values through Human Resource Policies. *Business Horizons.* July-August 2000. pp. 8–12.

Bennett, Milton J. 1993. "Towards Ethnorelativism: A Developmental Model of Intercultural Sensitivity." In R. M. Paige (ed.). *Education for the Intercultural Experience* (2nd edition). Yarmouth, ME: Intercultural Press. pp. 21–71.

Bolman, Scott A. 2001. "Developing a Global HR Systems Strategy." *IHRIM Journal.* Vol. V., No 6. November 2001.

Brinkmann, Ursula and Oscar van Weerdenburg. 2003. "A New Approach to Intercultural Management Training: Building Intercultural Competence." *IHRIM Journal.* September 2003. Vol. VII, No. 5.

Corbitt, J. Nathan. "Global Awareness Profile." Yarmouth, ME: Intercultural Press.

De Geus, Arie. 1997. *The Living Company.* Boston: Harvard Business School Press.

Drucker, Peter. 1993. *Managing for Results.* New York: HarperBusiness.

Galbraith, Jay. 2001. "Organizing Around the Global Customer." *IHRIM Journal.* Vol. V, No. 4. November 2001.

Galbraith, Jay. 2000. *Designing the Global Corporation.* San Francisco: Jossey-Bass.

Georgantzas, Nicholas C. and William Acar. 1995. *Scenario-Driven Planning: Learning to Manage Strategic Uncertainty.* Quorum.

Guy, Gregory R. and Karen V. Beaman. Forthcoming. "Global Orientation and Sociolinguistic Accommodation as Factors in Cultural Assimilation."

Hammer, Mitchell R, and Milton J. Bennett. 1998. *Intercultural Development Inventory Manual.* Portland, OR: The Intercultural Communication Institute.

Handy, Charles. 1994. *The Age of Paradox.* Boston: Harvard Business School Press.

Henson, Row. 1999. "The Globalization of Human Resources." *IHRIM Journal.* Vol. III, No. 3. September 1999.

Hock, Dee. 2001. "Conversation with Dee Hock. " *IHRIM Journal.* Vol. V, No. 1. January 2001.

Hock, Dee. 1999. Birth of the Chaordic Age. San Francisco: Berrett-Koehler.

Hoffman, Edward and Marcella Bakur Weiner. 2003. "The Big 12 Personality Traits: What Every HR Professional Needs to Know." *IHRIM Journal.* September 2003. Vol. VII, No. 5.

Hoffman, Edward. 2001. Psychological Testing at Work: How to Use, Interpret and Get the Most Out of the Newest Tests in Personality, Learning Styles, Aptitudes, Interests, and More. McGraw-Hill Trade.

Hofstede, Gerte. 1980. Culture's *Consequences: International Differences in Work-Related Values.* Beverly Hills: Sage Publications.

Jeannet, Jean-Pierre. 2000. *Managing with a Global Mindset.* London: Pearson Education Limited.

Kanter, Rosabeth Moss. 1995. *World Class: Thriving Locally in the Global Economy.* New York: Simon and Schuster.

Keirsey, David and Marilyn Bates. 1978. *Please Understand Me: Character and Temperament Types.* Prometheus Nemesis Book Company.

Moore, Karl. 2003. "Great Global Managers." *Across the Board.* New York: The Conference Board. May/June. Vol. 2, No. 24.

Pedersen, John L., Margaret Wheatley, and Myron Kellner-Rogers. 1998. "The Year 2000: Social Chaos or Social Transformation?" *IHRIM Journal.* Vol. II, No. 3. September 1998.

Perlmutter, H. 1969. "The Tortuous Evolution of the Multinational Corporation." *Columbia Journal of World Business.* January/February 1969. 9-18.

Premoli, Miguel. 2003. "Motivation: The Polynomial Theory." HR.com. www.hr.com. June 2003.

Rummier, Geary A. and Alan P. Brache. 1995. *Improving Performance: How to Manage the White Space in the Organization Chart.* San Francisco: Jossey Bass.

Satir, Virginia M, John Banmen, Marie Gomori, and Jane Gerber. 1991. *The Satir Model: Family, Therapy and Beyond.* Palo Alto: Science and Behavior Books.

Schwartz, Peter. 1991. *The Art of the Long View.* New York: Doubleday/Currency.

Senge, Peter. 1994. *The Fifth Discipline: The Art and Practice of the Learning Organization.* New York: Currency/Doubleday.

Stambaugh, Robert H. 2003. "HRIS: Human Resource Intangible Systems." *IHRIM Journal.* Vol. VII, No. 5. September 2003.

Stambaugh, Robert H. 1999. "Post-Modern HR Systems (Part 4)." *IHRIM Journal.* Vol. III, No. 4. December 1999.

Stambaugh, Robert H. 1998. "Early Learnings—Lessons From The Future." *IHRIM Journal.* Vol. II, No. 1. March 1998.

Sullivan, Daniel. 2001. "Managers, Mindsets, and Globalization." *IHRIM Journal.* Vol. V, No. 6. November 2001.

Trompenaars, Fons and Charles Hampden-Turner. 1998. *Riding the Waves of Culture: Understanding Cultural Diversity in Global Business.* New York: McGraw-Hill.

Tung, Rosalie Lam. 1998. "American Expatriates Abroad: From Neophytes to Cosmopolitans." Journal of World Business. Vol. 33, No. 2. Summer. pp. 124–144.

Tung, Rosalie Lam. 1988. *The New Expatriates: Managing Human Resources Abroad.* New York: Harper & Row.

Wheatley, Margaret. 2001. *Leadership and the New Science: Discovering Order in a Chaotic World.* Berrett-Koehler.

Endnotes

1. Several of the models presented in this article have been developed in collaboration with Dr. Gregory Guy of New York University, to whom I am indebted for lending his analytical abilities, editorial attention, and collegial advice to my efforts. I would also like to acknowledge Charles Fay, Row Henson, Bob Stambaugh, and Al Walker for their partnership and inspiration over the years in helping to craft many of the ideas in this paper. Likewise, I am appreciative of the support of ADP and their 500,000 clients who have made much of this work possible. Of course, any deficiencies or inaccuracies are entirely my own and should not be attributed to any other individual or organization.
2. Dee Hock, Founder and Chairman Emeritus of Visa Corporation, coined the word "chaordic" from "chaos" and "order." Based on the concepts of chaos the-

ory, the chaordic organization is one that thrives on the edge of chaos: too much chaos leads to confusion, turmoil, and lack of clarity and shared purpose; too much order leads to hierarchical, inflexible, regimented organizations unable to learn and innovate.

3. In this article, use of the term "HR" comprises all areas of human resources, human capital management, benefits management, and payroll processing.

Jenni Lehman

Jenni Lehman, Vice President of Global Human Capital Management (HCM) Product Strategy at PeopleSoft, Inc., is responsible for leading the strategic direction for the entire HCM product division. Prior to joining PeopleSoft, Inc., Ms. Lehman served as Vice President and Research Area Director at Gartner Inc., a leading strategic consulting services firm based in Stamford, Connecticut. While at Gartner, Lehman was responsible for the ERPII business applications area. She managed a team of analysts covering enterprise resource planning (ERP) systems, and corporate financial and HR applications. Ms. Lehman was also previously employed at Cyborg Systems, where she played a lead role in defining global product strategies for advanced technology products. Ms. Lehman can be reached at jenni_lehman@peoplesoft.

five : 2

Getting the Best of All Worlds: Strategies for Successful Global HRMS Projects

On the same day, the vice president of human resources for an international toy manufacturer receives two requests: one from the company's CEO and another from the Hong Kong field office. The CEO wants to know how many administrative assistants the company employs worldwide, and the Hong Kong offices needs help assembling an international project team to optimize the company's product distribution process. Both requests require that the vice president access data about his global workforce. Unfortunately, the information resides in multiple systems across the globe, over twenty different job function codes appear to exist for administrative assistants, and skills information is disparate and not aligned. Without a consolidated view of the worldwide workforce, the VP of HR becomes a bearer of bad news—he can't help his boss or the Hong Kong office.

For companies operating on a global scale, global HRMS implementations are no longer an option; they're a necessity. As advances in communications technologies erase boundaries and collapse distances, businesses are stretching into new territories to remain competitive. While expanding into global markets often promises lucrative benefits, companies that fail to prepare for the operational impacts of globalization may face a rude awakening when they begin to integrate each new country's operations. For a human resources department, aligning employees and best practices from disparate cultures, languages, and priorities with corporate objectives can seem daunting. Any benefits an HR department may reap from worldwide operations—reducing costs, increasing efficiencies, optimizing the global workforce, ensuring global alignment to corporate objectives, reducing IT errors, and simplifying maintenance—may be overshadowed by the monumental task of managing simple HR functions across a fractured organization.

Operations in different countries can quickly become islands unto themselves. Your French HR headquarters may have no visibility into your operations in Malaysia or Brazil, for example. Standardization of technology and best practices can seem impossible, as each country has business practices unique to its culture, not to mention disparate regulations, languages, and currencies. With hundreds of systems in as many countries, you may not be able to consolidate your data—such as employee profiles, workforce skills, turnover rates, and compensation information—making it difficult to manage human resources from a global perspective. Many companies are beginning to implement global Human Resource Management Systems (HRMS) to combine local functionality with a global architecture that provides collaborative business processes and a consolidated view of the worldwide workforce. Yet while global HRMS projects can prevent some of the challenges inherent in running a global enterprise and offer tremendous benefits such as cutting costs, optimizing global business processes, and increasing productivity, they require careful planning to be most successful.

> "After the merger, our organization was much larger, and we needed an effective way to communicate and collaborate—to give ourselves a platform for collaboration between the two employee bases," said Scott

Ramsey, Supervisor of HR and Corporate Administrative Systems at Anadarko Petroleum Corporation. "We have operations in the Congo, Gabon, Georgia in the former Soviet Union, Canada, and Guatemala. Basically, we realized that if we were going to keep growing internationally, we needed a platform through which to communicate."

The ABCs of Successful Global HRMS Projects

A few words of advice on how to reap maximum benefits from your global HRMS implementation: First, in order for your global initiative to be successful, it is important to secure ground-up support from managers in each locale. With careful planning, a global HRMS project will enable each country to maintain specialized operations while also gaining access to a greater depth of resources and information—such as surveys and data from throughout the company, analytic applications that provide insight into trends and practices, HR policies and procedures, and financials—that can only come from a single, centralized system.

Second, an HRMS project should match HR and IT requirements with the right technology. Planning jointly with the IT department, you must define the objectives most important to the company.

- Does your company plan to continue expanding into new countries?
- Are mergers and acquisitions occurring regularly?
- Do employees need anytime, anywhere access to their personal information?
- Does your HR department need to analyze data across the entire enterprise?
- Do you require better visibility into the worldwide competencies available?
- Is your HR department trying to automate or push down tasks to managers and employees, regardless of their location?

By carefully answering questions such as these, you can provide the IT department with a blueprint for technology functionality that will facilitate the joint process of choosing the right vendor. For example, if it is important to you that your HRMS solution supports the country rules and regulations of satellite offices, you would choose a vendor with a flexible product that can easily be localized.

Finally, it is tantamount that you have a sound strategy for implementing a successful global HRMS project. Different goals will drive different strategies. There are three basic approaches to HRMS projects: IT-centric, process-centric, and workforce-centric. Considering one or more of these strategies can help you set your organization's parameters and priorities for implementation, while defining the metrics by which your project's success may be judged.

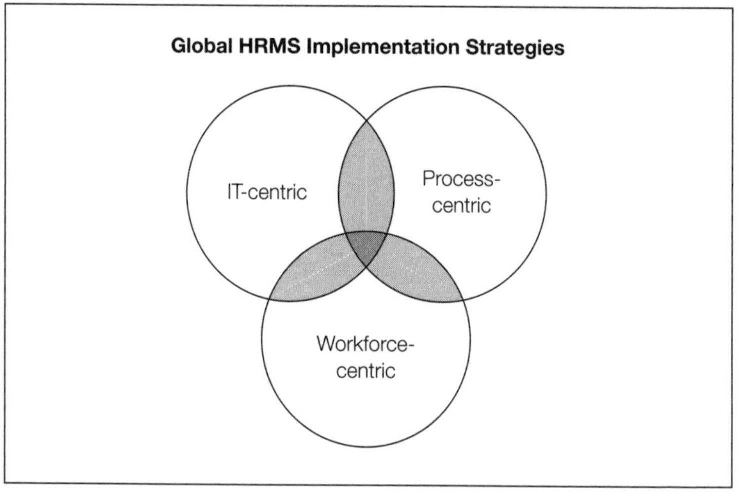

Figure 1.

An IT-Centric Strategy

An IT-centric approach recognizes the strain global expansion has on the IT function, and focuses on reducing IT costs and complexity. Using a single HRMS application worldwide, the IT department implements the same system in multiple locations, consolidating global HR information into one database. By using the internet, an

HRMS can facilitate browser-based access of multiple users regardless of their location, dramatically reducing IT maintenance and upgrade costs. This approach recognizes the value of a single platform: It provides repeatable IT practices for maintenance and upgrades, economies of scale through shared services, and easy knowledge transfer. An IT-centric strategy may make architecture flexibility a main priority, opting for a technology solution with one alterable code line rather than a hard-coded solution, or a single rules-based engine with country extensions rather than multiple country-specific engines.

While an IT-centric strategy focuses on using technology to cut costs, it also poses some risks. One potential risk is that it may be harder to support HRMS practices in smaller locations, putting a dent in your objective to consolidate business processes worldwide. Another is that your HR department can be cut out of decisions that ultimately impact operations. For example, if each country is allowed to choose its own vendors without considering the needs of the global organization, the HRMS implementation may ultimately fail to produce the expected cost benefits across the organization. On the other hand, if a global solution is selected without proper consultation with all of the impacted regions, it may prove difficult to get user acceptance and could fall equally short of reaching its goals. To minimize these risks, it is important to carefully assess the organizational goals for the HRMS implementation at all levels and for all regions and determine whether an IT-centric strategy captures all of your objectives. For example, if one of your organizational goals is to better leverage your workforce skills throughout the enterprise, you may choose to augment your IT-centric approach with the workforce-centric approach outlined below.

While an IT-centric strategy focuses on using technology to cut costs, it also poses some risks.

A Process-Centric Strategy

Rather than looking at saving costs by focusing on technology economies of scale, the process-centric approach focuses on maximizing efficiencies by improving business processes and standardizing best practices. With the process-centric strategy, the HRMS is ultimately a tool for imposing best practices and business rule compliance through application implementation. For many HR professionals, the process-centric approach may offer particular appeal, since it is designed to delegate administrative functions and enable corporate HR to be more strategic.

With elaborate self-service functionality, the HRMS entrusts employees and managers with using the system to conduct online tasks that were once paper based and routed through the HR department. An organization adopting a process-centric strategy may choose a technology solution based on an architecture that fully leverages the internet. Web-based self-service applications provided through a comprehensive portal would allow employees to collaborate and manage their own benefits, procurement, and travel. Rather than making requests for training through HR, employees would access their personal profile via the internet and sign up for company or third-party training online. Research from the Cedar Group shows tremendous savings: Self-service, internet-enabled applications reduce cycle times and error rates by 60 percent and headcounts by up to 70 percent. The same study also demonstrated that savings for base HR processes such as approving a promotion or benefits enrollment can be as high as 80 percent.[1] In addition to these substantial savings, corporate HR resources are no longer drained with basic administration; instead, they're reserved for strategic initiatives that can help the company maintain a competitive edge.

Like all strategies, the process-centric approach introduces its own risks. Those adopting this approach may fail to consider the variety of needs within an organization in an effort to standardize practices. Changing processes within a large organization can be slow, costly, and painful. For example, offices accustomed to using their own job codes may resist a move to consolidate job codes company-wide. The process-centric approach may not be the answer if your organization has many different lines of businesses, each with its own particular processes, embedded many layers deep. Careful due diligence can help you determine whether the process-centric approach is right for your organization. Achieving success with this approach requires the cooperation of managers and employees throughout the global enterprise, so it is important that you rally worldwide support for the changes you advocate.

A Workforce-Centric Strategy

Human capital is typically the most important and costly asset of any business. How well you manage global human capital can tip the scales of success or failure. The workforce-centric approach to HRMS projects aims to obtain a global view of the workforce to support your business objectives. By analyzing performance indicators, simulating scenarios to determine the impact of change, and managing the allocation of human resources, you can leverage human capital to its full potential.

How well you manage global human capital can tip the scales of success or failure.

With a workforce-centric strategy, the HR department identifies which HRMS data is relevant to support business decision-making. For example, the ability to view granular details about human capital all over the globe would enable you to efficiently disperse skills throughout the enterprise. If a project manager in the Japan office needed to speak with an engineer specializing in wireless network components, you could simply search the central data repository to find employees around the world with that particular skill-set. The workforce-centric approach recognizes the value of focusing at a global level on human resource management, and constantly realigns the workforce investment with business objectives.

Without setting up proper metrics to measure outcomes, however, the workforce-centric approach can fail to articulate a compelling business case for the HRMS project. This strategy will appeal to knowledge-intensive organizations more than to companies dependent mostly on manual labor. To minimize the risks inherent in the workforce-centric strategy and ensure that the strategy works for you, it is important to consider how you can show the impact of improved workforce management on the bottom line.

A Hybrid Strategy

Quite likely, you will combine the elements and perspectives of each approach outlined above to arrive at a hybrid strategy uniquely yours. Because HRMS projects have the potential to impact so many facets of corporate operations, it is important to prioritize your objectives and carefully consider the benefits and risks of each strategy prior to choosing an approach for your global HRMS implementation.

A hybrid strategy combining elements from the IT-centric and the process-centric approaches may appeal to many organizations. In this case, a company's objectives may be twofold: to streamline operations around the world by implementing a single technology platform and to create standard business processes and best practices that will improve efficiencies. For example, a global shipping corporation that has just acquired ten smaller companies around the world wants to align the practices of each newly acquired operation with those of the corporate office, while at the same time standardizing on a single HRMS application. With a hybrid approach to its HRMS project, the shipping company uses elements from both the IT-centric and process-centric strategies to achieve the implementation's dual objectives.

For other organizations, managing human capital effectively and improving business processes on a global scale may take precedence. These organizations may choose to combine a process-centric strategy with a workforce-centric approach. For example, a global pharmaceutical company dependant on its intellectual capital wants to improve the way it assigns employees to R&D projects and streamline its best practices across offices in five countries. Combining process-centric and workforce-centric strategies ensures that the pharmaceutical company's HRMS project will focus on both issues.

Because every company has its own special needs, your company may not fit neatly into one strategy. Therefore, it is important that you carefully consider which combination of strategies will best help you achieve the benefits a global HRMS implementation offers.

Benefits of the Three Global HRMS Implementation Strategies

IT-Centric Strategy

- Reduces costs by using a single HRMS application worldwide
- Ensures repeatable IT practices for maintenance and upgrades
- Captures economies of scale through shared services
- Eases knowledge transfer

Process-Centric Strategy

- Increases process efficiency and reduces process costs
- Standardizes best practices and business rule compliance
- Improves data integrity and quality
- Decreases redundancy

Workforce-Centric Strategy

- Provides global view of the workforce to support business initiatives
- Integrates global workforce information with business processes
- Aligns workforce investment with business investment
- Enables strategic deployment of workforce on project basis

HP Adopts a Hybrid Approach for Implementing Its Global HRMS

Hewlett-Packard Company (HP) wanted to standardize its HR technology, cut operational costs, and give employees instant access to the global HR information they needed to make strategic decisions. The company decided on a pure internet HRMS that would streamline HR processes in eight languages for over 90,000 employees in over 120 countries.

Despite the IT-centric advantages, Steve Rice, Director of HR Global Enterprise Programs and Technology at HP, reveals that his company also adopted a workforce-centric approach. "This implementation isn't just about software. It's about changing the way we deliver HR services across our enterprise." He continues, "We wanted to push information out to employees and managers and put them at the center of what we call the HP ecosystem."

HP's HRMS project allowed it to transition from four geographic instances of HR software to one; save $3 million annually in hardware, software, databases, and maintenance costs; and drop from twenty-five servers to ten. As for taking advantage of the workforce management benefits? "I've already re-deployed forty developers from our organization," said Rice.

Assessing Risks

Global businesses are complex, as they encompass a multiplicity of languages, regulations, and cultures and operate on an immense scale with diverse regional policies. Regardless of the implementation strategy you select, you may face challenges that fall into three main risk areas: those associated with an inadequate business case, a lack of project momentum, or an overspent budget. Avoiding these risks should help you stay within budget, receive continuing support from executives, and realize the full benefits of your HRMS project.

Inadequate Business Case

Many HR organizations lack experience in justifying large-scale technology projects. Even for the savvy HR manager, building a feasible business case to defend a significant HRMS investment is not easy. However, a compelling business case—one that quantifies the benefits of a global human capital management strategy—should help secure full corporate commitment to your global HRMS project.

To build a strong business case, first assess how the global HRMS project will impact your company. For example, an HRMS with a solid self-service component would allow HR officers to recruit online and would reduce the calls that managers make to the HR department. Second, calculate the savings in time, money, and human capital resulting from these changes. It is important to emphasize these quantitative benefits in your business case.

It is also helpful to include less tangible benefits, such as improved employee satisfaction and increased quality of business processes, to bolster your business case. While time-consuming to build, a strong business case can help you receive the financial and operational support you need to implement an HRMS project on a global scale.

Lack of Project Momentum

Global HRMS implementations are long-term projects with many phases. For some companies, maintaining momentum can be a challenge. The project may exceed its projected budget or implementation deadline, tempting the company to rush through the deployment or cut it short. However, if a project is prematurely concluded, it may not produce all of the expected benefits. It is important to remember that for most companies, HRMS projects aim to impact multiple aspects of the business—including critical changes to existing processes. Implementing the technology is just the first step.

For example, a multinational retailer implements a global HRMS project to standardize on a single system, streamline administration, provide better training, and conduct recruitment over the Web. After completing the technology implementation, the retailer loses momentum. In this case, the company has met only one of its four objectives—standardizing on a single system. Without further effort, the retailer is unlikely to improve its administration, training, and recruitment processes. Thus, it is important to remember throughout the long implementation process that an HRMS project is not a simple technology fix but rather a vehicle that can positively impact the way your entire organization does business.

Overspent Budget

Staying within budget is never easy. With a global implementation, the sheer scope of the project can make it difficult to rein in costs. However, the total cost of ownership for the HRMS must be carefully monitored and controlled, since it has a direct relationship to the system's expected return on investment (ROI). During the implementation and production stages, it is important to set realistic cost assumptions that correlate accurately to the envisioned benefits. If a one-year project becomes a two-year project, the ROI is delayed. The most severe impact to ROI results from a change in the "I", or the cost of investment. If you decide midproject that you need local interfaces for an additional twenty countries, the cost of your investment skyrockets and upsets the ROI equation.

To maintain control of your budget, it is important to clearly define your needs before you embark on the HRMS project. A global bank avoided altering its project scope midstream by sending project teams to each country before it began implementation. After conducting workshops for a week, the team defined the project scope and cost for each country. By carefully planning and soliciting local support, the project team eliminated the chance that the countries would request changes in the project during construction. With careful planning, you too can ensure that your global HRMS project stays on track and on budget.

A Sample Implementation Methodology

After considering various strategies for implementing your global HRMS projects and assessing the potential risks, you may want to spend time considering a methodology for undertaking the implementation. Global implementations can be complex, with the success or failure of one phase potentially influencing the next. Therefore, it is essential that an implementation methodology target the entire project lifecycle. A successful implementation methodology recognizes the following phases:

- Strategy
- Planning
- Structure
- Construction
- Transition
- Deployment

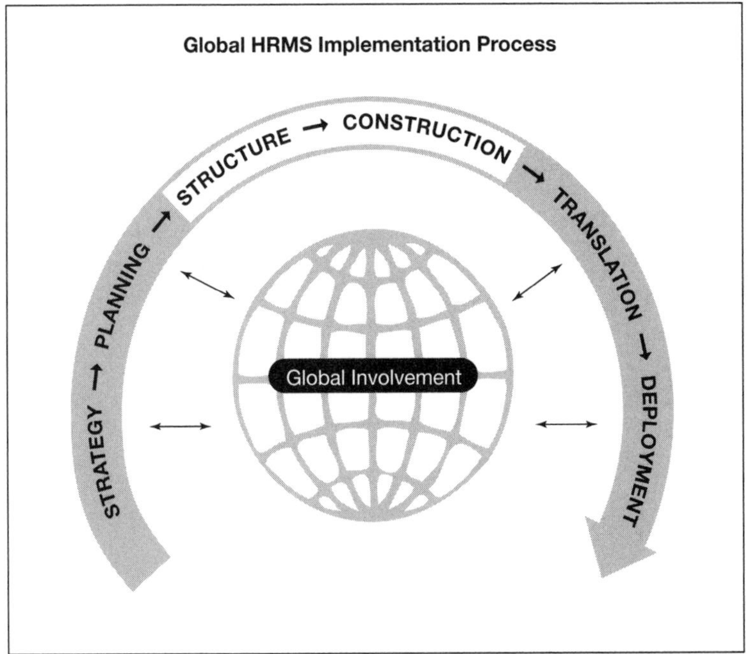

Figure 2. During global HRMS implementations, it is particularly important to secure participation of regional and local offices during the beginning (strategy and planning) and final (transition and deployment) phases.

Strategy

As discussed above, the choice of strategy is an important component of a successful global HRMS project. During this phase, a company determines the appropriate strategy for the project—IT-centric, process-centric, workforce-centric, or some hybrid of these—considering factors such as global corporate objectives and expected ROI. The strategy phase becomes the foundation for the project and involves executives who will ultimately champion the project within the organization.

Planning

In the planning phase, a company conducts a technical feasibility analysis, defines project member roles, and sets realistic timelines and budgets. This is the phase during which all practical issues are considered. For global implementations, this may mean determining how and when different countries will get involved in the project. Fastidious attention to detail and scope in the planning phase should allow you to anticipate and address potential challenges before they occur. To keep the entire organization aligned behind the same objectives, it is important to communicate project goals and phases to the appropriate executives. This phase also acts as another checkpoint for ensuring that the plan supports your organization's overall business objectives.

To keep the entire organization aligned behind the same objectives, it is important to communicate project goals and phases to the appropriate executives.

Structure

A solid implementation approach pays particular attention to the structure phase of the process. Essentially administrative in nature, the structure phase builds the skeleton for your global HRMS project. You assemble project teams, define roles and responsibilities, and build structures for conducting quality assurance, communicating effectively, providing consistent feedback, and comparing business needs with the project's progress. Many companies choose to form an international project team or steering committee to oversee the human capital management and project implementation at a global level. The goal of the structure phase is to ensure that the project will actually deliver the business solution promised. While scope changes in this stage are acceptable, surprises down the road are not.

Construction

In the construction phase, all of your diligent strategizing and planning begins to pay off. The actual construction of the global HRMS project is under way. Monitoring progress is a key element of this phase. Throughout construction, maintaining open communication with project teams ensures that the process moves smoothly—on budget and on time. To ease the transition to the final phases of the implementation process, you may also choose to concentrate on future-oriented activities, such as building disaster recovery plans, during this phase.

Transition

Once your HRMS is in place, it is time to start involving different categories of users. In the transition stage, a company will employ various users with disparate job functions and expertise to test the system. By watching users interact with the new system, you can set up specialized training for all employees who will access it throughout the global organization. In this way, the HRMS will meet the requirements of all countries, cementing support for the system on a local level. Countries that have invested personnel and provided input to the process will be more likely to encourage employees to take full advantage of the HRMS.

Deployment

Finally, the payoff. In the final stage, the HRMS project is deployed across the entire enterprise. Often companies adopt a phased-deployment approach defined by geography. For example, the company may train users, cut over to the new system, install quality assurance, and conduct project reviews in Europe before it tackles the United States. By deploying the system at regular intervals, a relatively small team can perform user training and handle the actual changeover. A stepped-deployment approach renders the deployment process more manageable and helps companies avoid risks associated with simultaneous global deployments. However, it also delays the benefits offered by the HRMS system.

Conclusion

Implementing an HRMS offers tremendous benefits to global companies: It cuts costs through economies of scale, optimizes global business processes and streamlines best practices; empowers employees by giving them universal access to important information; enables managers to assemble talent for projects from all over the enterprise; and allows each country to meet unique regulations and still integrate operations and data across the global corporation. Undertaking a successful global HRMS project requires the cooperation of your entire organization. Thus, it is important that you plan carefully, considering which blend of implementation strategies—IT-centric, process-centric, or workforce-centric—will help you meet your corporate objectives. With assiduous planning, you can address sensitive areas that may undercut a project, such as building a strong business case, maintaining momentum throughout the life of the project, and staying within budget. If you understand the implementation methodology from the beginning, you can monitor progress with each phase, from strategy to deployment, ensuring that you meet all of the project goals. With an HRMS in place, you will have the tools you need to effectively manage your global HR operation while delivering remarkable benefits that impact all departments of the organization.

Endnote

1. The Cedar Group, Human Resources Self Service Survey, 2001.

Mark Lange

Mark Lange, Vice President of Global Product Marketing for the Human Capital Management (HCM) division at PeopleSoft, Inc., is currently responsible for overseeing the development and deployment of global marketing strategy for this industry-leading suite of solutions. Mr. Lange has more than nineteen years of experience in workforce policy and technology business development. Prior to joining PeopleSoft, Inc., he was a founding member of the executive team at BrassRing, a Waltham, MA-based provider of enterprise recruiting solutions. Mr. Lange worked at the White House as Speechwriter to the President from 1988 through 1991, where he crafted the State of the Union address and numerous oval office statements during the first Gulf War. Prior to that, as Chief Speechwriter to two United States Secretaries of Labor, he defined and positioned US policy in the 1980s on workforce and competitiveness challenges—particularly the impact of the skills gap and technical employee shortages on corporate productivity. Mr. Lange can be reached at mark_lange@peoplesoft.com.

five : **3**

Human Capital Management:
Strategies and Technology for Competitive Advantage

Most managers intuitively grasp the importance of people. Any company's website will suggest that their people are their most important asset.

Very few organizations, however, understand how to create meaningful connections between the people they attract to their cause; their development, retention, and performance; and the firm's operating and financial results.

You'll soon be hearing more about companies that do—and you'll see it reflected in their stock price.

For the rest of this decade, the defining characteristic of competitive success will be the way a firm identifies, recruits, engages, develops, retains, and deploys human capital—in all of its forms, and at every stage of the business cycle.

At the intersection between people, technology, data, and process management, the discipline of human capital management (HCM) is gaining momentum. It is being honed and refined by HR and IT leaders who are using technology to link formerly disconnected domains, enable collaboration, and drive enterprise-wide visibility into the ultimate source of an organization's success.

The goal of this chapter is to challenge the way you think about people, business processes, and competitive success—to give you ways to bring those words on your website to life—and to make sure those well-intentioned managers are following more than their instincts.

Why Human Capital Is Strategic

In most minds, the value of human capital tends to be framed in terms of direct costs and opportunity costs—the lost productivity of open positions or skill shortages. And on the basis of direct costs alone, the story is staggering.

Consider turnover. In 2002 there were 112.7 million full-time employees and nearly 24 million part-time employees in the US.[1] The voluntary turnover rates were 23.8 percent for full-time employees and 45.9 percent for part-timers.[2] Based on median salaries from The Bureau of Labor Statistics (BLS)[3] and with direct recruiting and replacement costs conservatively estimated at three months' salary for both groups, the direct cost of turnover is $239 billion for the US alone. That's about 2.3 percent of the gross domestic product (GDP).[4]

Consider the potential hard-dollar impact of a workforce that lacks the right skills and training. In a typical manufacturing plant with 300 full-time production workers, the cost of workdays missed to injury each year is $4,514.83. And that figure doesn't take into account the reduced productivity of workers who didn't miss days but who had their work activities restricted by injury.[5]

What about the cost of a workforce that's not even prepared to be a workforce, let alone master complex skills? It's been estimated that the seven million British adults who lack basic literacy and numeracy skills cost the UK economy about £10 billion per year. The annual cost to a typical company with fifty employees is £165,000.[6]

Even companies that hire the best talent haven't won the battle. Putting workers in jobs that don't match their abilities and interests can lead to disengagement, a significant problem for American companies. Gallup Organization conservatively estimates that actively disengaged employees—workers who are uncommitted, unmotivated, and have negative attitudes—cost American companies $254 to $363 billion per year.[7]

Putting workers in jobs that don't match their abilities and interests can lead to disengagement.

Not to mention compensation. Rewards and accountability are considered by Watson Wyatt and others to be the area of HCM in which companies can achieve the greatest increase in shareholder value. Companies that make a significant improvement in each the sixteen factors that fall under this heading can expect their market value to increase by 16.5 percent—but offering above-average pay is just one of the keys to success.[8]

Executives understand costs. But the cost focus, particularly in HCM, misses the larger point.

Human capital is strategic.

In fact, it is the only factor that ensures every other form of capital investment—in products, infrastructure, systems, technology, and hard assets—pays off.

Behind the tremendous productivity improvements enabled by information technology are the people who do all of the knowing, building, planning, collaborating, executing, supporting, and competing.

How well should an organization deploy and manage the one asset that ensures that every other investment pays off? As well as it can—and most could do far better than they are. Making that case in the executive suite has been a critical factor in the growing relevance of HR functions in world-class organizations.

It's a path to a more meaningful seat at the boardroom table, and to a more substantial role in corporate governance.

Why Almost Nobody Does Enough About It

Sounds like an easy sell: Identify high performers, help them be more effective, and watch all of your investments pay off at a faster rate. So why doesn't HR drive this agenda more aggressively?

The obvious answer is that keeping the administrative trains running on time consumes every available resource. The average HR department operates on 0.5 to 1 percent of revenue, and is under increasing pressure to do more with less. HR headcounts shrunk by as much as 50 percent over the course of the 1990s.[9]

But there's a deeper reason that many in HR haven't been able to make human capital a strategic priority. There's a tendency in the executive suite to regard people as another inventory to be managed (and in a recession, blown out the door at a loss). The short-term unemployment rate—6.1 percent in the US as of this writing[10]—tends to whipsaw perception and muddy thinking about talent. In a contraction it's too easy to think, "The economy is cooling off. At least we won't have so much trouble recruiting."

Stay tuned. Recruiting is just one of the four main challenges HR professionals face as they seek to refocus their organizations on the value of human capital.

The Leading Challenges in Managing Human Capital

1. Recruiting expense and turnover
2. Education and training
3. Workforce deployment and engagement
4. Compensation

1. Recruiting Expense and Turnover

The recent economic slow-down has taken some of the heat off recruiters—in some sectors more than others—but it's only an opportunity to change the wheels on the car at 35 miles per hour before they spin back up to 75 again.

Three-quarters of corporate officers surveyed by McKinsey & Co. say their companies are "chronically talent-short across the board," or suffer from "insufficient talent sometimes."[11]

And it's now common knowledge that even demographics are plotting against employers to keep the market on the job seeker's side.

Job creation, spurred largely by technology across business sectors, is outpacing workforce growth. We all see the train coming: baby boomers (born 1946 to 1964) begin to retire in 2011, creating a net decline in the number of employed Americans. The BLS reminds us:

- From now until 2020, workforce growth will decline each year.
- By 2008, we'll face a shortage of 10 million workers.
- US companies will need to fill 55 million jobs over the next decade, but only 29 million potential employees will be available to take those jobs.[12]

The picture[13] is clear.

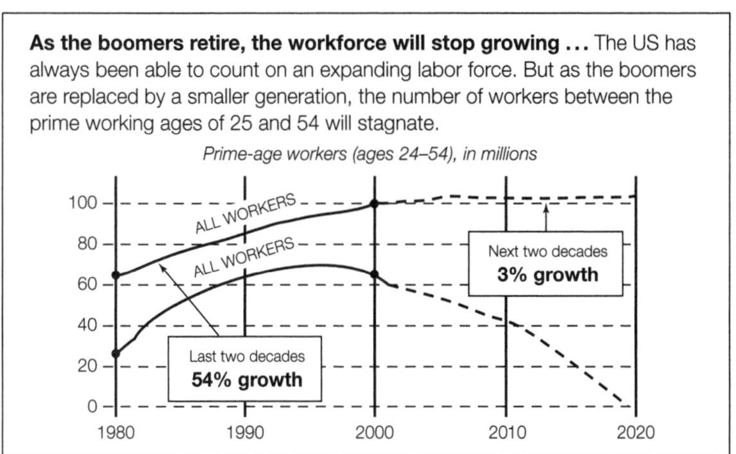

As the boomers retire, the workforce will stop growing ... The US has always been able to count on an expanding labor force. But as the boomers are replaced by a smaller generation, the number of workers between the prime working ages of 25 and 54 will stagnate.
Prime-age workers (ages 24–54), in millions
100
80
60
40
20
0
ALL WORKERS
ALL WORKERS
Next two decades
3% growth
Last two decades
54% growth
1980
1990
2000
2010
2020

Figure 1.

Compounding the difficulty of filling this gap are real process inefficiences. Even world-class organizations still procure full-time employees (FTEs) and contract talent in silos. HR owns the FTE process, and procurement or IT owns contractors and the vendor management systems used to clear transactions with contract staffing firms. Very rarely does the organization have a clear, integrated view of all the talent that can be available when the doors open at 8:00 A.M. tomorrow morning—never mind eight months or eight years from now. Winning organizations will.

2. Education and Training

But the bigger issue isn't quantity of talent, it's quality—a situation compounded by a growing and increasingly critical skills gap. A more complex economy is generating demand for more sophisticated talent at all levels:

- Our friends at BLS predict that through 2006, jobs requiring advanced degrees will grow at double the rate for all employment.
- One study states that by 2005, "there will be around three million new jobs involving tasks that do not even exist at the moment."[14]
- Between 2000 and 2002, US companies only filled 50 percent of their IT openings, due to a lack of qualified applicants.[15] This during the most pronounced slowdown in tech activity in the last ten years.
- Traditional blue-collar and lower-skilled service jobs are requiring increasing levels of skill and comfort with information systems, cybernetic controls, and use of technology.

The skills gap is growing.[16]

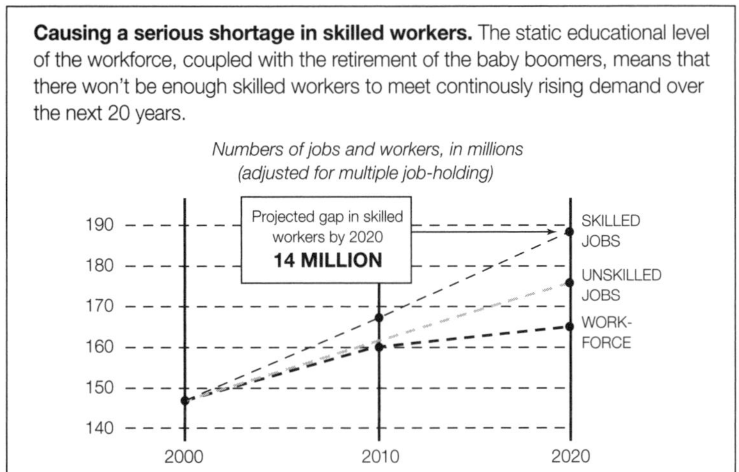

Figure 2.

Desperate for skilled workers in high-technology operations, many American companies continue to hire temporary employees through the H-1B visa program, despite the costs and delays involved.[17]

Other organizations may soon be forced to teach people the basics of being an employee. In a 2001 study by the National Association of Manufacturers, companies reported that their main reason for rejecting applicants for hourly positions was a lack of basic employability skills such as attendance, timeliness, and work ethic.

According to Walker Information, just 45 percent of employees believe that their companies care about developing people for long-term careers, while 31 percent believe they don't.[18]

Intuitively, that sounds like fertile ground for retention issues. Fortunately, we're moving beyond intuition. Through HCM and Financials software combined with data warehouse and scorecard technology, organizations are now able to tie investments in training to employee performance at the individual and worker type level—and the associated impact on individual and group attainment of quota, manufacturing throughput, same-store retail sales performance, or virtually any operating or financial metric that matters to a CFO.

Who, in turn, is in a better position to fund those investments in training programs.

3. Workforce Deployment and Engagement

Poorly-deployed employees squander opportunities to provide services, deepen relationships, cross-sell products, drive efficiencies. Your CFO feels the hurt on your top and bottom line. Organizations in every industry began focusing on customer retention after the publication of a groundbreaking 1990 *Harvard Business Review* study:

- Companies that retain just 5 percent more of their customers can increase their profits by almost 100 percent.
- Companies with long-time customers can often get away with charging more.
- Reducing customer defections by 50 percent will more than double a company's growth rate.[19]

Consider the loss of profits that can result from not putting the right people in the right jobs at the right time.

- A services organization that lacks a complete view of its talent and project pipeline—and is forced to operate in reactionary mode, either scrambling (and possibly overpaying) for talent or laying off valuable people to cut costs. Knowing the availability and skills of its consultants would enable the organization to deploy them in ways that maximize their billable hours.

  But without consistent measurements of its costs per project, the organization cannot identify its most profitable relationships and must use extra resources to appease overly demanding customers who yield only a thin profit margin. Ironically, the low-maintenance, high-profit customers are the ones who then must suffer.

- A high-speed internet provider that lacks a user-friendly talent inventory struggles to assign the right technician to each customer problem. With an array of ISP options available at ever-

> decreasing prices, frustrated customers have little incentive to stay with a company that cannot provide reliable internet access.
>
> Realizing that it is losing the battle on the customer service front, the company reinvents itself as the low-price leader and cuts into an already shrinking profit margin to win back customers. But to protect profits, the company must lay off additional employees, further hampering its ability to provide good service.

As you read this book, chances are good that about two-thirds of your employees are only moderately engaged.[20] These people are the undecided voters of the workforce. With the right (or wrong) motivation, they can become highly productive stars—or jaded underachievers who drag their team down.

4. Compensation

In the quarter before this writing, the cost of employment in the US increased by 3.7 percent. Yet while salaries and wages notched their smallest percentage increase in 22 years of data at 2.7 percent, given the persistence of a "jobless recovery," the cost of benefits increased by 6.3 percent.[21] Year-over-year increases in benefits have been in double digits for the last three years.

Two issues arise here. First, considering the aging of the baby boomers, companies ignore the increasing costs of benefits at their own peril. Second, companies may be weathering an economic slowdown by freezing pay or at least controlling its increase.

A 2003 Towers Perrin study determined:

- One-third of respondents had significantly reduced their investments in workforce reward programs.
- Greater cost pressures have caused companies to reduce their focus on rewarding top performers.
- Weakening a pay-for-performance program leads to lower morale among top performers over time.

- Companies that are under the greatest cost pressure are less likely to move to a variable pay program that can actually help them manage costs—while better rewarding performance—during an uncertain economy.
- High-performing companies are building rewards programs that reinforce the employee behaviors and actions that drive business performance.[22]

It's not encouraging that many companies still haven't embraced the concept of paying for performance. And employees are taking notice. According to Walker Information, only 37 percent of American workers believe that excellent performance gets rewarded in their workplace. And only 51 percent think pay is fair.[23]

It's not encouraging that many companies still haven't embraced the concept of paying for performance.

A tunnel-vision, keep payroll low approach to managing compensation is the equivalent of selling your soul for short-term financial gain. The silver lining is that in the long run, you won't have to pay your top performers' salaries anymore. They'll be working for a competitor.

Human Capital Management: An Operating Discipline

So what's the answer to these challenges? While there's no silver bullet solution, the best approach is to build an intelligent combination of business processes, information, and technology to drive workforce performance.

HCM isn't a department the way, say, HR is—it's a discipline that extends to everyone in the organization. Just as CRM turned a disparate array of functions, processes and tools into a coherent customer-facing discipline, HCM makes the identification and development of talent an actionable, enterprise-wide priority.

Because talent touches every aspect of operating performance, it is all the more complex—and all the more critical to get it right. HCM means developing people as a strategic asset through every phase of the employment lifecycle:

- Before people become candidates
- While they're being recruited
- After they've been hired
- When they're considering their next move within the company (and before they're at risk of leaving)
- When they're corporate alumni who might refer or help close a key hire
- Always
- All the time

The first step in HCM is streamlining your HR systems to increase the efficiency of your HR operations. Then, building on that effective transactional foundation, the second step is to deploy self-service to employees and managers—reducing transaction costs and giving employees and managers direct access to data and business processes in real time. The third and ultimate step is to align your workforce with corporate goals to drive operating performance.

Pre-flight Checklists for HCM

Putting these efforts into practice involves specific, pragmatic steps:

1. Put systems and tools in place to recruit the right talent at the right time.
2. Develop employees in alignment with organizational objectives.

3. Harness your employees' self-interest to drive business results.
4. Reward good performance—and let your employees know what you're doing.

1. Put the Systems and Tools in Place to Recruit the Right Talent at the Right Time

Concerned about turnover? You have two options. Bravely deal with it when it becomes a problem, or start preventing it during the recruitment process.

From your very first contact with an employee—before he is even an employee—don't focus on what your company wants. Focus on what you can offer. And differentiate your company from the competition. This isn't as hard as it might sound. You can differentiate anything—as long as you offer customers (meaning, candidates) more than they think they need or have learned to expect.

. . . don't focus on what your company wants. Focus on what you can offer.

The easiest way to do this—obvious but rarely used—is to spend time reading your competitors' messaging, job descriptions, and postings on mass-market boards. The vast majority present no clear value proposition to the candidate, fail to differentiate the offer, and instead deliver a very uncompelling recitation of job requirements layered with a few glowing generalities about growth and culture.

Simply reorienting your pitch away from job qualifications and toward the candidate or employee's interests, affinities, and priorities (it is, after all, about fit, which is never a one-way street) can make a tremendous difference.

Which specific skills will help your company achieve its goals? What job profiles can you create from these needed skills? What is your best source for finding these skills? Could contractors do the work more cost-effectively than full-time employees? Could current employees do the job if given the right training?

To answer questions like these, you need an enterprise-wide view of your talent and organizational needs. Using today's integrated recruiting technology, you can:

- Give everyone who's involved in your recruitment process visibility into the pipeline and relevant metrics in real time.
- Base systems for attracting both full-time and contractor candidates on a common skills and competencies database—so managers can make rational decisions about the cost/value trade-offs.
- Use web tools to get to the right applicants more quickly. From there you can invest the more expensive and personal attention of recruiters to build relationships with them by phone, IM, e-mail, or the medium of their choice. Think CRM for talent.
- Onboard new hires quickly by linking your recruiting systems to core HR, payroll, performance management, and compensation planning systems.
- Establish employee referral programs. Employees hired through employee referral programs are typically better qualified and stay longer.
- Enable your managers to take corrective action before small recruitment problems turn into larger ones. Monitoring the following metrics on an ongoing basis is a good start:

    Recruiting effectiveness

    Separation rates

    Workforce composition

    Compensation analysis

    Absence costs

2. Develop Employees in Alignment with Organizational Objectives

Any workforce development program must begin with an accurate assessment of who makes up the workforce. With the help of good software, you can model what your workforce's skill set would look like under different development scenarios.

You'll need to offer a wide variety of learning programs for the many types of employees under your roof:

1. Determine the level of workforce performance that will enable your organization to meet its objectives.

2. Identify the key competencies that are essential to reaching this level.

3. Define job profiles and roles based on these competencies.

4. Assess the competencies of your current workforce, and see which employees match these profiles and roles.

5. Identify major skill gaps.

6. Develop personalized learning programs that help employees develop the missing skills and behaviors.

7. Deliver these programs in the most convenient format for each employee.

8. Deploy self-service learning tools to your employees. Let them register for courses, chart their progress, and control their professional destiny. There's no better way to tell employees that their learning is important.

9. Test and evaluate your employees' progress. This step is about more than attendance and completion. It's about measuring how learning affects your bottom line.

10. Then—most important—*refine* those competencies by tracking their association with subsequent performance in role.

Bringing Analytics to Life

Even the best-designed development programs can't deliver value unless they're looped in with meaningful feedback and performance management tools.

Analytics are not the endgame, of course—they're simply a means of enabling better, faster decisions that result in greater workforce performance. They're the best way to determine whether your programs are on target, and the spend is delivering results.

With good analytics:

- A manufacturing shop floor can set a goal of reducing the types of injury that typically result in multiple days off work. It can hold safety seminars designed to prevent these injuries, and then monitor the decrease in injury reports. It can then weigh the cost of the seminars (including man-hours spent attending the sessions) against the savings achieved by preventing injury days.
- A retail organization that delivers training on kiosks in store breakrooms can track which employees have completed the course. It can monitor their subsequent individual performance, monitor the performance of all employees of that type worldwide who have completed the training, and determine the financial impact of the training in terms of increased revenue per store.
- A service organization can match its people and skills with its opportunities for profit. It can see the true cost of each project—including development costs—and in turn can measure the profit earned on each billable hour. From there, the organization can identify its most profitable customer relationships and devote more resources to strengthening them.
- A healthcare organization can chart its recruiting spend against its ability to keep hard-to-hire medical talent on staff. It can connect its ability to deploy people intelligently to its success in covering shifts. It can monitor its compliance with accreditation

organizations such as JCAHO, to preserve Medicaid and other funding sources and reduce litigation exposure.

3. Support Your Employees' Self-Interest to Drive Business Results

Employees are more effective when they feel they're doing their jobs for themselves and for a company they care about—not just for an above-market-value paycheck, and certainly not to advance some manager's agenda. They must believe that by pursuing their own career goals—certifications, promotions, increased responsibilities, more stock options—they're building a path for themselves that leads to real growth.

Fighting a Common Paradox

In most organizations, however, there's a paradox at work. On one hand, employees want to drive their own career development and advancement. On the other hand, too many managers act as if it's in their best interest to keep those employees contributing right where they are—productive, static, and ultimately unhappy.

One solution is to make a talent development objective an explicit part of the goals managers are compensated on. Rewarding managers based on the number of people grown and promoted out from under them might sound heretical—but it helps.

Another way to unglue this paradox is to create transparent, visible business rules through HCM systems that encourage early and better communication between managers. When managers can search for needed skills within the employee base quickly, see a list of current employees who have those skills, and directly contact another manager, they eliminate the secrecy and territoriality that typically plague workforce deployment.

Enlightening some managers in this area may not sound easy. But much as the fax machine helped drive *glasnost* in the Soviet Union and the democratic impulse in China, web-based HCM systems enable an open market for talent within an organization—creating a context for business rules, communication, processes, transparency, and trust.

Working Toward Changing Objectives

The best way to keep your employees working toward organizational objectives is to establish individual and departmental goals that cascade directly down from these objectives—even when the objectives change. That means moving beyond the ritualistic routine that makes performance management a static, once-a-year process.

As you fine-tune your performance management programs:

- Make sure that employees and managers are involved in the goal-setting process.
- During the performance period, encourage two-way feedback—whether it's formal or informal—and record it securely. Your managers will be surprised by the things their employees notice, overlook, take pride in, worry about, or laugh about.
- Enable employees to track their own progress towards goals.
- Stress to all stakeholders that performance management shouldn't just be a means of justifying rewards decisions. When performed regularly in the form of coaching and collaboration, it's a valuable method of developing outstanding performance.

Helping Employees See the Bigger Picture

But what about the actively disengaged? How do employment relationships go south, and how can they be recovered?

After completing its largest ever study on the attitudes and behaviors of successful workforces, Gallup concluded that "full engagement is a product not only of the way employees think but also of how they feel." Gallup identified twelve conditions that must be present for maximum employee engagement. Among them, you must:

- Let your employees know what is expected of them.
- Give employees the opportunity to do what they do best, every day.
- Offer praise and recognition for good work.
- Encourage development.
- Make employees feel that their opinions count.
- Talk to employees about their progress.[24]

Employees need clear, consistent communication to help them see the connection between their work and larger company objectives—the so what of what they do every day. The degree to which your people understand what drives customer and market value—and have a clear and compelling thread in their minds between what they do and financial results—is a critical driver of alignment, engagement, and performance.

This communication must continue throughout the employee lifecycle. Employee loyalty is not about preserving the status quo—it's about the way the employment relationship, like any relationship, must evolve over time to remain vital.

4. Reward Good Performance—and Let Your Employees Know What You're Doing

META Group has found that top-performing organizations (in terms of revenue) give merit raises tied to performance to more than 87 percent of their employees, versus only 23 percent of employees in bottom-performing organizations.

There's plenty of evidence that incentive pay programs get results. They're the perfect strategy for motivating employees, while linking employment expense to company performance.

But where do you begin implementing these programs?

1. Collect as much external market survey data as you can.

2. Tailor this information to your job codes and calculate market rates using weighted averages.
3. Compare your current pay levels and structures to the market.
4. Assign existing jobs to pay ranges.
5. Tweak this new pay structure until it supports your compensation strategy.
6. Combine existing workforce data with projections about your organization's workforce growth and reduction, so that you can make projections.
7. Based on this information, create scenarios that analyze the cost and ROI of your proposed compensation plans. Does each plan support organizational objectives at a reasonable cost?

Communicating Compensation to Employees

Regardless of what you're offering, you must communicate to employees the full value of their compensation packages. If employees don't believe pay is fair, then it's not fair.

Include regular pay, overtime pay, pay premiums, commissions, performance-related bonuses, benefits, and profit sharing in your communications. Make this information available online in real time, so that employees can have an instant reminder of the monetary advantages of staying with your company.

Managers typically need guidance in tying meaningful (and not just monetary) rewards to outstanding employee performance. Make sure your managers understand:

- What employees value at different stages of their careers.
- What your company can offer beyond pay and benefits.
- How these things appeal to different segments of your employee and candidate population—particularly the high performers you want to keep.

But avoid a blanket, retention at all costs strategy. Universal retention without regard to performance or potential is neither possible nor desirable—and tends to demoralize stronger employees. A better approach uses highly targeted efforts aimed at particular individuals—including creative compensation, job customization, and strengthening employees' social ties to teammates.[25]

Universal retention without regard to performance or potential is neither possible nor desirable…

Warning: If You're Restructuring or Downsizing, HCM Is *More* Critical, Not Less

Another myth borne of the outdated inventory view of talent is that HCM doesn't matter in a downturn. In fact, the opposite is true.

Announcements of mass layoffs aren't simply devastating to the affected employees. They seriously compromise the confidence of those who remain—not to mention all that has been invested, in practice and in brand, to develop and support the company's reputation as an employer of choice. And the research shows that widespread layoffs rarely generate the cost savings expected in the short run—and almost always compromise competitiveness.[26] Across-the-board cuts, early retirement, and departure packages have taken a heavy toll on company strength and long-term performance.[27]

HCM provides an important opportunity for companies to do a better job managing the inevitable swings, restructurings, and the need to accommodate the business cycle that will never quite go away.

By creating meaningful links and feedback loops between recruiting, assessment, performance management, deployment and compensation systems, HCM technology provides an opportunity for more surgical, strategic changes that strengthen an organization, using performance as a guide.

Fully 73 percent of companies continue to hire talented employees in the midst of downsizing, and nearly half have created targeted programs to retain top performers.[28] HCM provides a solution to these cycles—to hire more selectively, develop more actively, cultivate the employment relationship more deliberately, and make hard decisions based on individual performance data.

Large scale, mass layoffs are the human equivalent of blowing out inventory below cost—except the "inventory" walks out with the institutional and process knowledge, customer relationships, skills, and experience that help the company compete. An organization that practices HCM knows better.

HCM Drives Higher Shareholder Returns

Companies are reporting twelve and eighteen month payback on investments in HR self-service technology as a result of reduced transaction costs and cycle time. Leading-edge HCM solutions are enabling Fortune 500 firms to save tens of millions of dollars in recurring direct costs.

But as we saw earlier, making the case based on cost savings is only part of the story. There's a much bigger point to be made.

If you're still wondering whether HCM will resonate in the executive suite, consider The Gallup Organization's study of three million employees and 200,000 managers. Gallup measured the attitudes and behaviors of the most successful employees and departments and identified twelve conditions that drive their success.

Among the findings, business units that measured in the top half on employee engagement had:

- A 56 percent higher success rate in customer loyalty.
- A 44 percent higher success rate in controlling turnover.
- A 50 percent higher success rate in productivity.

- A 33 percent higher success rate in profitability.[29]

Other research supports the connection between human capital and financial performance. "Superior human capital practices are not only correlated with financial returns, they are, in fact, a leading indicator of increased shareholder value.... Superior HR practices are a key to attraction, retention, and, more and more, business outcomes."[30]

While there's a reasonable link (correlation .19, according to Watson Wyatt's studies) between companies' positive financial results and better human capital practices (which is logical enough—wealthier companies fund better programs) there's much stronger correlation (.41) between better human capital practices and financial return.

In other words: In Watson Wyatt's view, good human capital management practices aren't simply associated with good business outcomes—*they create them.*[31]

In a seminal book published in 2000, Jac Fitz-enz of Saratoga Institute argues that "the focus on the interaction between human capital and financial outcomes is a leading rather than a coincidental reason for their long-term financial success."

"The belief in people at a financial level is extremely rare," he writes. "I struggle for words of sufficient power to cause you to stop and contemplate this. No matter what the public relations department puts out about people being important, on a daily basis in the executive aerie, people are considered to be an expense... beyond the sales function [where an incremental sales head can drive incremental revenue], executives don't have the slightest inkling of how to tie human effort directly to financial results."[32]

HCM provides a framework, a process, and information technology to do precisely that.

Summing Up HCM

This chart sums up the differences between traditional HR and the evolutionary step forward represented by HCM.

Traditional HR	Human Capital Management
Reactive	Proactive
Administrative	Strategic
Confined to HR staff	Everyone's responsibility
Transactional	Collaborative
Just-in-time	All-the-time
Promises soft-dollar benefits	Delivers hard-dollar benefits
Adds paperwork	Adds value
Counts heads	Heads counts
Downplays its drag on the bottom line	Adds to the bottom line

Table 1.

In the classic hierarchy of the modern corporation, investors come first . . . then customers . . . then employees. Perhaps in the post-Enron era, those three elements will warrant something approaching equal attention, and will be considered as interdependent as they truly are.

In the meantime, managing talent effectively in the current market is less an argument from the standpoint of ethics, social equity, or redistributive integrity than it is a matter of sheer competitive self-interest.

We competed on quality in the 1970s, time in the 1980s, and information systems in the 1990s. In this decade we will take on the last critical dimension of competitive advantage: We will learn to compete through talent. Not just for talent—through talent.

We will start working harder to make every employee a competitive asset. All of the people in an organization—who do all of the knowing, building, selling, collaborating, and competing—represent the final frontier in business optimization. They are the ultimate lever for operating performance—turning ideas into products, quotas into quarterly results, potential into profits.

Talent is the last, most difficult, and most indispensable element of competitive advantage. It is the only problem—and the one opportunity—that won't go away.

Endotes

1. US Department of Labor, Bureau of Labor Statistics, Current Population Survey, 2002.
2. Employment Policy Foundation, *HR Benchmarks*, December 3, 2002.
3. Bureau of Labor Statistics, Household Data Annual Averages, 2002. Median salary of $31,668 for full-time employees and $9,776 for part-time employees.
4. Based on 2002 GDP of $10.45 trillion (Bureau of Economic Analysis, US Department of Commerce).
5. According to the Bureau of Labor Statistics, for every 100 full-time manufacturing production workers in 2001, there were 1.8 injuries that required days away from work. Median time missed was seven days. Average wage was $14.93 per hour.
6. Trades Union Congress and Confederation of British Industry, *Brushing Up the Basics*, November 2002.
7. Curt Coffman and Gabriel Gonzalez-Molina, *Follow This Path: How the World's Greatest Organizations Drive Growth by Unleashing Human Potential.* Warner Books, 2002.
8. Watson Wyatt's Human Capital Index 2001/2002 Survey Report.
9. Gartner/Dataquest.
10. The most recent BLS figures available as of this writing put the US seasonally adjusted unemployment rate at 6.1 percent. Source: Bureau of Labor Statistics, US Department of Labor, bulletin dated September 5, 2003.
11. McKinsey & Co., *The War for Talent.*
12. The Towers Perrin Talent Report 2001; US Bureau of Labor Statistics.
13. *Business 2.0.*
14. Trades Union Congress and Confederation of British Industry, Brushing Up the Basics, November 2002.
15. *Bouncing Back: Jobs, Skills, and the Continuing Demand for IT Workers*, Information Technology Association of America, May 2002.
16. *Business 2.0.*
17. General Accounting Office, *H-1B Foreign Workers: Better Tracking Needed to Help Determine H-1B Program's Effects on US Workforce*, October 2, 2003.
18. Walker Information, *The Walker Loyalty Report: Loyalty and Ethics in the Workplace*, September 2003.
19. Frederick F. Reichheld and W. Earl Sasser, Jr., "Zero Defections: Quality Comes to Services," *Harvard Business Review*, Fall 1990.
20. Towers Perrin, *Working Today: Understanding What Drives Employee Engagement*, 2003.
21. US Department of Labor, Bureau of Labor Statistics, Employment Cost Index, Q2 2003.

22. Towers Perrin, TP Track: Managing Performance and Rewards in a Challenging Business Environment, August 2003.

23. Walker Information, *The Walker Loyalty Report: Loyalty and Ethics in the Workplace*, September 2003.

24. Curt Coffman and Gabriel Gonzalez-Molina, *Follow This Path: How the World's Greatest Organizations Drive Growth by Unleashing Human Potential.* Warner Books, 2002.

25. "A Market-Driven Approach to Retaining Talent," Peter Capelli, *Harvard Business Review.*

26. *Wall Street Journal.*

27. Towers Perrin.

28. Ibid.

29. Curt Coffman and Gabriel Gonzalez-Molina, *Follow This Path: How the World's Greatest Organizations Drive Growth by Unleashing Human Potential.* Warner Books, 2002.

30. Watson Wyatt: *Human Capital as a Leading Indicator of Shareholder Value*, 2001/2002 Survey Report.

31. Ibid., Watson Wyatt.

32. Fitz-enz, Jac, *The ROI of Human Capital: Measuring the Economic Value of Employee Performance*, American Management Association, 2000.

| APPENDIX |

Grateful acknowledgement to publishers and authors below for permission to reprint the following in this anthology:

"Why Human Resources Needs Systems Thinking: Avoiding Bad Decisions and Bad Measures" by Jeffrey Pfeffer PhD. Copyright © 2003 by Jeffrey Pfeffer PhD. All rights reserved. Reprinted with permission from author.

"Three Dimensional Human Resource Strategy" by Lynda Gratton PhD and Catherine Truss PhD. Copyright © 2003 by Lynda Gratton PhD and Catherine Truss PhD. All rights reserved. Reprinted with permission from authors. Special thanks from authors to colleagues Professor Veronica Hope-Hailey, Dr. Philip Stiles, and Dr. Joanna Zaleska.

"Human Capital Branding: The New Organizational Effectiveness Model" by Jac Fitz-enz PhD. Copyright © 2003 by Jac Fitz-enz PhD. All rights reserved. Reprinted with permission from author.

"Building Intangible Value from the Outside In" by Dave Ulrich PhD and Norm Smallwood. First appeared in *Leader to Leader*, Spring 2003, No. 28. Copyright © 2003 by *Leader to Leader* and John Wiley & Sons, Inc. All rights reserved. This material is used by permission of John Wiley & Sons, Inc. and authors.

"Tapping the Full Potential of HRIS: Shifting the HR Paradigm from Service Delivery to a Talent Decision Science" by John Boudreau PhD and Peter Ramstad. Copyright © 2003 by John Boudreau PhD and Peter Ramstad. All rights reserved. Reprinted with permission from authors.

"Structuring HR for Maximum Value" by Harry Osle and John Cooper. First appeared in *IHRIM.link*, June/July 2003. Copyright © 2003 by *IHRIM.link*. All rights reserved. Reprinted with permission from *IHRIM.link* and authors.

"Hard Systems, Soft Systems: New Challenges for Twenty-First Century HR Systems, Stakeholders, and Vendors" by Bob Stambaugh. Copyright © 2003 by Bob Stambaugh. All rights reserved. A version of this article appeared in *IHRIM Journal*, Volume VII, Number 5, September/October 2003. Reprinted with permission from author.

"Be Prepared When Your CEO Ask 'Why Don't We Outsource HR?'" by Naomi Lee Bloom. Copyright © 2003 by Naomi Lee Bloom. All rights reserved. Reprinted with permission from author.

"Justifying Workforce Technologies: ROI, JOI, HCM TCO Portfolio Analysis, and Post Implementation Audits" by Alexia (Lexy) Martin. Copyright © 2003 by Alexia (Lexy) Martin. All rights reserved. Reprinted with permission from author.

"The Role of Personalized Knowledge to Support Employee Self-Service Transactions" by Tod Loofbourrow. Copyright © 2003 by Tod Loofbourrow. All rights reserved. Reprinted with permission from author.

"Building a High-Performance Culture—Timeless Lessons from the World's Greatest Entrepreneurs" by Joseph H. Boyett PhD and Jimmie T. Boyett. Copyright © 2003 by Joseph H. Boyett PhD and Jimmie T. Boyett. All rights reserved. Reprinted with permission of authors.

"HR's Role in Driving a High-Performance Culture" by Libby Sartain. Copyright © 2003 by Libby Sartain. All rights reserved. Reprinted with permission from author.

"Forgive and Remember" by Robert Sutton PhD. Copyright © 2003 by Robert Sutton PhD. All rights reserved. A version of this article appeared in *CIO Insight*, June 2003. Reprinted with permission from author.

"Beyond the Vision: What Makes HR Effective?" by Edward E. Lawler PhD and Susan A. Mohrman PhD. First appeared in *Human Resource Planning Journal*, Volume 23, No. 4. Copyright © 2000 by Human Resource Planning Society, 37 Madison Avenue, Suite 1509, New York, NY 10017, Phone: (212) 490-6387, Fax: (212) 682-6851. All rights reserved. Reprinted with permission from publication and authors.

"HR in the 21st Century: Challenges and Opportunities" by Row Henson. First appeared in IHRIM Journal, November 2002. Copyright © 2002 by *IHRIM Journal*. All rights reserved. Reprinted with permission from publisher and author.

"The New Transnational HR Model: Building a Chaordic Organization" by Karen V. Beaman. Copyright © 2003 by Karen V. Beaman. All rights reserved. Reprinted with permission from author.

"Getting the Best of All Worlds: Strategies for Successful Global HRMS Projects" by Jenni Lehman. Copyright © 2002 by Jenni Lehman. All rights reserved. A version of this article appeared in Karen Beaman 2002 (ed.),

Boundaryless HR: Human Capital Management in the Global Economy, IHRIM Press Publishers. Reprinted with permission from author.

"Human Capital Management: Strategies and Technology for Competitive Advantage" by Mark Lange. Reprinted with permission from author.